Social Administration
in Lancashire
1830–1860

For Matthew

E C Midwinter

Social Administration in Lancashire 1830-1860

Poor Law, Public Health and Police

Manchester University Press

Published by
Manchester University Press
316-324 Oxford Road
Manchester 13

GB SBN 7190   0369 5

Printed in Great Britain
by Butler and Tanner Ltd
Frome and London

Contents

Tables

Maps

Footnotes

Footnotes have been kept to the minimum to save the text from undue interruption. The text normally indicates sources, and a select bibliography is included for those anxious to trace material of a more precise nature.

Acknowledgements

Many individuals have helped me during the writing of this book. Initially my interest in administrative history was stimulated by Professor Oliver MacDonagh, now of the University of Adelaide, from whose shrewd and penetrating guidance I benefitted while a student at St. Catharine's College, Cambridge. I am particularly grateful to Dr. W. J. Rowe, Reader in Modern History of the University of Liverpool, who acted as my tutor during the two years I pursued my research at the University of Liverpool, and helped considerably in the structure and organisation of the project. For a further two years I continued my research at the University of York where I was fortunate to be the student of Professor G. A. Williams. I am indebted to him for his thorough and critical analysis of my work and for the unbounded enthusiasm of his encouragement. My thanks are also due to Dr. Eric Sigsworth, of York University, and to Professor Asa Briggs, Vice Chancellor of the University of Sussex, for their aid and advice. I would like to thank Dr. W. H. Chaloner of the University of Manchester for his help, especially in arranging for me to see J. R. Wood's thesis on the Manchester Poor Law; D. Foster, M.A. for information about the early years of the Bolton Police Force; and ex-Deputy Chief Constable J. Platt of Salford for information about the Salford Police Force. Many librarians and archivists throughout Lancashire and at the Public Record Office have given me considerable help. I would particularly like to mention the staff of the Lancashire Record Office, Preston, the Manchester Local History Library (the Central Reference Library, Manchester) and the Liverpool Local History Library (the Picton Library, Liverpool), and the Chief Librarians of Ashton-under-Lyne, Blackburn, Clitheroe, Darwen, Lancaster, Oldham, Warrington and Wigan Libraries. I am indebted to Mr. and Mrs. K. J. Pulham and to Miss M. Byrne for help with the compilation of the Index.

My wife, Margaret, matched her constant encouragement and affectionate forbearance with her cheerful and competent undertaking of the massive secretarial task involved. To her, finally, my manifold thanks.

E. C. Midwinter

I. Introduction

In a typical passage Engels, in 1845, described 'Little Ireland'—the area to the South-West of Oxford Road, Manchester—in the following terms:

It lies in a fairly deep depression on a bend of the river and is completely surrounded by tall factories or high banks and embankments covered with buildings. Here lie two groups of about two hundred cottages, most of which are built on the back-to-back principle. Some four thousand people, mostly Irish, inhabit this slum. The cottages are very small, old and dirty, while the streets are uneven, partly unpaved, not properly drained and full of ruts. Heaps of refuse, offal and sickening filth are everywhere interspersed with pools of stagnant liquid. The atmosphere is polluted by the stench and is darkened by the thick smoke of a dozen factory chimneys. A horde of ragged women and children swarm about the streets and they are just as dirty as the pigs which wallow happily on the heaps of garbage and in the pools of filth. In short, this horrid little slum affords as hateful and repulsive a spectacle as the worst courts to be found on the banks of the Irk. The inhabitants live in dilapidated cottages, the windows of which are broken and patched with oilskin. The doors and the door posts are broken and rotten. The creatures who inhabit these dwellings and even their dark, wet cellars, and who live confined amidst all this filth and foul air—which cannot be dissipated because of the surrounding lofty buildings—must surely have sunk to the lowest level of humanity . . . an average of twenty people live in each of these little houses, which at the moment consist of two rooms, an attic and a cellar. One privy—and that usually inaccessible—is shared by about one hundred and twenty people . . . a number of cellars were filled with earth, and they were gradually emptied again and had now been reoccupied by the Irish. One particular cellar which lay below the level of the river was continually flooded with water which gushed in through a hole which had been stuffed full of clay.[1]

Although not as accurate as he might have been, Engels certainly

[1] F. Engels, *The Condition of the Working Class in England* (1845), Trans. W. O. Henderson and W. H. Chaloner (1958), p. 71.

pointed to the grave social dislocation of working-class life in the
first half of the nineteenth-century. The demographic explosion,
the advances in industrial organisation and production and the
extension of urbanisation wrought a great change in the social
fabric. In one sense, it was more fundamental than the economic
and political change. The commercial economy and the nation-
state, with Parliament the fount of sovereignty, were well-
established; increased mechanisation and electoral reform were
modifications within an existing frame. But the social character
of the industrial era was new indeed. Population is perhaps the
most startling instance of this. The population of Lancashire
sprang from 673,486 in 1801 to 1,335,600 in 1830. It had doubled,
whereas the population of the United Kingdom had risen by less
than 50 per cent, from nine to thirteen millions. In 1700, Lancashire
had had only some 166,000 inhabitants—a mere one-fortieth of the
country's population. In 1830 the county housed one-tenth of the
national total. More significantly, eleven areas contributed 66 per
cent of the increase between 1801 and 1831. These were Liverpool,
Manchester and Salford, Preston, Bury, Burnley, Oldham, Blackburn, Ashton-under-Lyne, Bolton, Rochdale and Wigan. The
first two alone showed an increase of 282,000—45·5 per cent of the
total increase. Not only was population rising, but urban development was accelerating at a mammoth rate. By 1851 Lancashire was,
after London, the nation's most crowded area, with 1,003 people
per square mile. Middlesex, with 546, was the next most densely
peopled county.

This major social re-orientation created a new context for age-
old problems. The problems of clothing, shelter, work, food,
family and so on are constant. So are social ills. Three of the
major ones have ever been poverty, disease and crime, and there
was nothing novel about their existence in Victorian Lancashire.
What was new was the different incidence of the three problems
in terms of the change in social pressures. These stresses were
many and varied, but 'congregation', as Herman Finer observed,
was the chief factor. It was 'congregation' which 'gave rise to new
problems of public health administration and poor relief and the
prevention and punishment of crime'.[1] In brief, compact masses of
people, geared to an industrial economy, meant an intensification
of the three major ills. A vivid illustration of 'congregation' was

[1] H. Finer, *The Theory and Practice of Modern Government* (New York,
1950), pp. 44–45.

the lodging-house, the bane of the social administrator's life. These tightly-packed dens, to be found not only in the large towns but in places like Ormskirk and Bacup, were haunts for thieves and prostitutes, centres for vagrants and paupers and foci for contagious diseases. They were the delinquency of industrial society in microcosm.

This book investigates the first faltering response of society to the dreadful questions which confronted it in early Victorian Lancashire. It would be an underestimate of Lancashire to label it a sample. With one-tenth of the country's population, a fifth of its largest towns and with its early and thriving industrialisation, it foreshadowed the future. It was, of course, of great import then; it also gave warning of the type of society that would shortly embrace much of the United Kingdom. The economic progress of Lancashire has been well documented; its administrative provision less so. Here, possibly, there is a mirror-image of London. Social administration there has had full coverage. Countless tales have been told of horror and misery in London's seamier environs and the steps taken—the Metropolitan Police, the Metropolitan Water Board—to meet such conditions. Conversely, the industrial role of London, in banking, engineering and the like, has been underplayed. This is a modest effort to redress one side of the balance, by inspecting the impact of social legislation, at field-level, in Lancashire. Lancashire existed as an administrative entity, and the county has been surveyed as such. To have cut out the industrialised sectors for investigation would have been most difficult, for so many statistics were calculated in terms of the whole county. This, then, is a study of a political area, within whose ambit there was considerable industrial activity. It also provides some opportunity for comparisons of urban and rural conditions, and of the variations in treatment between town and country.

The period from approximately 1830 to 1860 has been chosen for several reasons. Economically, the industrial system had consolidated itself fairly thoroughly, and, before the eighteen-sixties, was not to be menaced critically by overseas competition. Politically, the period bridges the first two reform Acts, stretching from the last great Whig government to the threshold of Liberalism. Locally, it covers the time of Lancashire's early commercial triumphs, ending, as they did, in the tragedy of the Cotton Famine, when social ills were again given a new and disastrous twist. It is,

however, the administrative aspect which has most meaning. The
period falls within Dicey's 'era of utilitarian reform', when, by his
interpretation, Benthamism and Individualism replaced the
Legislative Quiescence of Old Toryism and presaged the epoch of
Collectivism.[1] Dicey's neat divisions have been attacked recently
by several authors, and a full scale debate on the issues of *laissez-
faire* and state intervention is under way.[2] Many studies must be
completed before the picture is clear; certainly one project should
be a more detailed analysis of national administration at a local
level. This might help us to assess the position of local government
in the conflict between Benthamite orthodoxy and 'administrative
momentum'. It might also make it possible to judge the effect of
national legislation on the everyday life of the ordinary person.
This book is such an attempt.

   The period sees the first serious efforts to alleviate the difficulties
of each of the three spheres at a national level. The Poor Law
Amendment Act of 1834 created the New Poor Law System; the
1848 Public Health Act established the Local Boards of Health;
and clauses in the Municipal Incorporation Act of 1835 and the
County Constabulary Act of 1839 created the first provincial police
forces. Lancashire was divided into thirty Poor Law Unions; it
had, by 1856, eleven Borough Police Forces as well as the County
Constabulary; and, by 1858, it had twenty-six Local Boards of
Health. The obligatory Police Act of 1856 and the Local Government Act of 1858, which led to an overhaul of the public health
administration, serve as chronological limits to the investigation in
those two fields. Most of the Poor Law Unions were formed in the

   [1] A. V. Dicey, *Law and Public Opinion in England*, 2nd Edition (1934),
pp. 62–69.
   [2] D. Roberts, *Victorian Origins of the British Welfare State* (New York,
1960), K. Polanyi, *Origins of our Time. The Great Transformation* (1945);
J. Bartlett Brebner, 'Laissez-faire and State Intervention in Nineteenth
Century Britain.' *Journal of Econ. His.* (Supplement 8, 1948); O. Mac-
Donagh, *A Pattern of Government Growth* (1961); 'The Nineteenth
Century Revolution in Government', *Hist. Journ.* (1958, Vol. I. No. 4); and
'Delegated Legislation and Administrative Devolutions in the Eighteen-
fifties', *Victorian Studies* (Vol. II, 1955); R. J. Lambert, *Sir John Simon*
(1964), and 'A Victorian National Health Service; State Vaccination',
Hist. Jour. (1962); H. Parris, 'Nineteenth Century Revolution in Govern-
ment', *Hist. Jour.* (Vol. III, 1960); R. M. Gutchen; 'Local Improve-
ments and Centralisation in Nineteenth Century England,' *Hist. Jour.*
(Vol. IV, 1961); J. Hart, 'Nineteenth Century Social Reform; A Tory
Interpretation of History', *Past and Present* (No. 31, 1965).

eighteen-thirties, and, by the Cotton Famine, they had practically all been operational for a number of years. Thus Lancashire offers ample scope. There were, of course, several Local Acts, especially in connection with public health, but although they will not be neglected, the main emphasis will be on the effect of general national legislation on Lancashire. In each case, the survey will include an examination of the establishment of the relevant set of authorities and an analysis of their activities.

Map 1.

The County of Lancaster showing the administrative areas of the Poor Law Unions formed under the Poor Law Amendment Act, 1834 (1836–1869).

II. The New Poor Law

i. Introduction of the New Poor Law

General propositions

The Poor Law Amendment Act which came into force on 21 August 1834, was of immense significance both in the lengthy history of English Poor Relief and, more generally, in the social and administrative development of nineteenth- and twentieth-century society. Its one hundred and ten sections failed to include—such, perhaps, was the astuteness of its draughtmanship—either 'explicit plan of reform' or 'scheme for the relief of destitution'.[1] None the less, it was to be later described as 'the first piece of genuine radical legislation',[2] for it created, with far-ranging powers, the Poor Law Commission, which was to reorganise the country's only major social service. Any investigation of the New Poor Law in a given area must necessarily begin with the impact of the Poor Law Commission in that area, and it would seem difficult to do this adequately without outlining, however broadly, the principles on which it proceeded.

In the year of their appointment the Poor Law Commissioners published a fourpenny pamphlet, drawing the public's attention to the faults of the Old Poor Law, as demonstrated by the report of the recent Commission on the problems of pauperism[3] and the plans for the correction of these faults.

In the first place, the pamphlet illustrates the Commission's attachment to the prevailing economic beliefs of the Philosophic Radicals by attacking 'the strenuous demand for continual subsistence' and 'the admitted claim of wages without labour'. An annual expenditure of £6,000,000 and more on poor relief, much

[1] S. and B. Webb, *English Local Government* (1929), VIII, p. 100.
[2] M. Hovell, *The Chartist Movement* (Manchester, 1918), p. 79.
[3] Parlty. Papers, *The Report from His Majesty's Commissioners for inquiring into the state of the Poor Laws in England and Wales.* 1834 (44) XXVII–XXXIX.

of it by way of allowance to able-bodied adults, was anathema
to those who believed in a self-regulating market, for, in the words
of James Mill, such poor laws 'legalise and sanction the condition
of beggary'. The Allowance system, most typically expressed by
the Speenhamland scheme of 1795, was, in the opinion of the
Webbs, 'the decisive element' in making pauperism intolerable to
the English in the opening decades of the last century.[1] By sub-
sidising idleness it placed an obstacle in the path of the free play
and mobility of the labour force, and it was to freedom of activity
in all economic spheres that the middle class of the day paid
allegiance. A modern writer has shown how the self-regulatory
processes of the market economy did, in fact, exert themselves, so
that, with the artificial condition of the allowance system, 'the
productivity of labour began to sink to that of pauper labour' to
'create an economic vortex'.[2] In his *Principles of Population* in 1798,
the melancholy Malthus would have nothing less than 'the total
abolition of all the present parish laws'. Faced with a problem of
such extensiveness, total and abrupt abolition was obviously
impractical, but a solution could possibly be found in forcing the
pauper back on the labour market. Under the influence of Edwin
Chadwick, the principle of less-eligibility was written into the Poor
Law. By making the Workhouse 'an uninviting place of wholesale
restraint', it was hoped that the pauper's situation would always
be less eligible than that of the lowest independent labourer.
This was the cardinal theme of the reform, and 'the rest', according
to Finer, 'was administrative apparatus'.[3] It was a classic Benthamite manœuvre to ensure the requirements of the Classical Economists. Bentham himself had suggested that 'maintenance at the
expense of others should not be made more desirable than self-
maintenance', and this especial operation of the pleasure principle
was employed in a fashion that made the New Poor Law 'entitled
to a place in the "Free Trade Movement" '.[4]

In the second place, the Commission was anxious to create an
administrative system that would implement their schemes more
competently than the then existing 'upwards of fifteen thousand
unskilled and (practically) irresponsible authorities'. In their four-

---

[1] Webb, p. 14.

[2] K. Polanyi, *Origins of our Time; The Great Transformation* (1945),
pp. 80–107.

[3] S. E. Finer, *The Life and Times of Sir Edwin Chadwick* (1951), pp. 44–76.

[4] H. L. Beales, 'The New Poor Law', *History* (Jan. 1931), p. 311.

penny pamphlet they spoke of a central board which would fulfil the need for 'a sufficiently cogent responsibility', which would incorporate parishes 'for the purpose of maintaining a common workhouse, and which would generally avoid the "chance of discretion" and abusive practices' of parochial rule. In praising the administrative techniques envisaged by the Commission, S. E. Finer has neatly summarised them as 'central supervision, central inspection, central audit, a professional local government service controlled by local elected bodies, and the adjustment of areas to administrative exigencies'. Chadwick thus 'injected into the conception of the *laissez-faire* state his maxim of the tutelle' in an attempt to keep the ring clear for unshackled competition by direct governmental intervention.[1]

In the third place, there can be little doubt that, behind the theorising of the political economists and the administrative reformers, the question was largely a financial one. The Commission's pamphlet scoffed at those, sympathetic to the pauper, who were 'apt to forget the rights of hundreds and thousands of poor and industrious rate-payers', and it promised to place 'some steady and enduring check' on the management of the poor. Down would go the rates with a stringent agency operating a severe code—Carlyle observed coolly that 'it is a secret known to all ratcatchers'. The two intractable factors of social distress and local inefficiency made reform imperative, and, so long as less dangerous numbers of paupers could be treated for at lower prices, the rate-payers seemed ready to accept the novelties of such reform quite readily. The respective lights of less-eligibility and centralisation were unimportant besides a drop in the per capita poor rate from 9s. 9d. in 1833 to 5s. 10d. in 1847. In an age when destitution was frowned upon, and to be religious was to be soberly thrifty, it was little wonder that the amended poor law's attraction was its appeal to economies in public spending.

These, then, appear to be the three main features of the New Poor Law—an ever-present demand for reduced rates, answered by an attempt to lower, by artificial means, the number of paupers, geared to a move towards improved efficiency.

The Commission began its work in the South. In November of 1836 a letter from T. Frankland Lewis, one of the three Poor Law Commissioners, appeared in the *Liverpool Mercury* of 18 November 1836. It replied to queries raised in that newspaper by T. A. S.

[1] Finer. pp. 26 and 88.

B

Dowling of West Derby, Liverpool. Towards the end of his letter, Lewis warned that 'the Assistant Poor Law Commissioner will shortly proceed into Lancashire'. By the end of the following year much of Lancashire had been divided into Unions.

The Old Poor Law

For this appraisal to be adequate, it is essential to measure the actual workings of the New Poor Law against the theoretical criteria of its proposals. It is equally necessary to assess the variation between the old and the new, to observe where and where not the new system brought radical alterations in practical Poor Law administration. The first task is to depict some main features of Poor Law business about 1830. With over four hundred differing examples available, this is not simple. The sources are inexhaustible, for Parochial Records abound, containing overseers' accounts, workhouse papers, vestry minutes, rate books and the like. It would seem reasonable, however, to use extracts from the Poor Law Commission's Report. Twenty-six Assistant Commissioners visited or collected information from 3,000 Parishes and Townships. Many of them were Benthamites, and there appears to have been some stress on their obtaining material for 'a convincing indictment'. Sets of printed queries were either sent to Parochial authorities or carried there by Chadwick's henchmen, each one of whom had then 'to use his own discretion as to the places which appear to be most deserving of investigation'. Moreover, they had to 'arrange the times and places of meeting at which the replies already given, or to be given, are to be explained'.[1]

It is evident that Gilbert Henderson, the Assistant Commissioner responsible for Lancashire, did not obey these instructions rigidly. As 'the condition of the towns is more important than the condition of the rural districts; and, indeed, the country districts, in the greater portion of the county, are more affected by agricultural vicissitudes' he confined his report to observations on only ten towns. Pressure of time, apart from his conviction, may well have forced Henderson to this resource, but it does mean that a majority of the answers to the Commissions' queries were completed without his interference. Henderson did not follow the pattern of instructions which demanded investigation under heads of enquiry. He simply described given situations in given

[1] *Poor Law Report*, op. cit., Vols. XXVII–XXXVI and XXXVIII, and *Instructions to Assistant Commissioners, 1833.*

towns and was by no means critical of the poor law in Lancashire. He appeared to regard it sympathetically, even where it departed from Chadwick's known precepts. Of all the reports by the Assistant Commissioners, Henderson's appears to be one of the most detached and—in terms of formula—it is certainly one of the most independent. One is persuaded that much of the information proffered is more accurate, in this case, than most commentators would allow. Furthermore, as many of the questions asked were answered without consultation and, doubtless, without a real knowledge of what the aims of the reformers were, it is probable that they are not wholly inaccurate. It seems to be forgotten that, in any case, any astute replies might be attempts to shore up the existing system—perhaps the compromise of offensive investigator and defensive investigated produced something nearer the truth than is normally imagined. The overall impression given by the Lancashire answers is of earnest, not very bright Overseers and Churchwardens trying desperately to complete the universally difficult task of completing a governmental form. Sometimes they do not answer at all; sometimes their answers are nonsensical; sometimes they may be covering up deficiencies. It could not be pretended that the report plus the answers offer the full story of Lancashire's Old Poor Law. Nonetheless, it provides a very substantial indication of its character. These sets of printed queries were of two types. The rural set was answered by nineteen, and the urban set by seventeen townships. The former represented an aggregate population of 51,198 and the latter of 556,299, including over 300,000 in Liverpool and Manchester. The grand total came to 607,497 or practically a half of Lancashire's 1,336,854 inhabitants at this time. These questionnaires thus provide no mean sample of the county.

In the preamble to his report, Henderson said that the expenditure in Lancashire 'will bear a satisfactory comparison with other parts of the country', with the figure for the year ending 31 March 1831 £293,226 at 4s. 4½d. per head—'being smaller than in any other county in England or Wales'. He regarded this as 'the best test of the extent of pauperism'. There were, however, wide variations, and Henderson noted the 10½d. rate in West Derby as compared with a 6s. rate in Padiham. Expenditure per head varied in the rural areas from 2s. 1d. in Walton-on-Hill Parish, Liverpool to 17s. 2d. in Ulverstone Town and Hamlet. More significantly, in seven of the towns, the actual amount spent on the poor had dropped from the 1821 figures, despite a 50 per cent increase in population. As Henderson explained, the rural areas felt the pinch of the decline of hand-loom weaving more than the towns, where there was often alternative employment, and where power-looms 'by giving employment to their children, alleviate, in a great degree, the evils they had occasioned'. Thus, as in the South of England, although for a slightly differing reason, the agricultural districts fared the worse. Henderson considered that the depression of wages 'had led to a general practice in the weaving districts of making an allowance to able-bodied weavers with more than two children under ten years of age'. He did, however, go on to suggest an important difference between agrarian and weaving wage supplements. As weaving wages were calculated by the piece and as the manufacturers, unlike some farmers, had not combined to drive the wages below their natural level, the 'spur to exertion' had not been lost. The incentive to work remained, and the bounty, normally of 1s. 6d. or 2s. per child, was all but in the nature of a modern Child Allowance. Indeed, in terms of evidence, the point missed by the Poor Law Commission was being made, that there was a distinction between manufacturing and agrarian paupers.

It would appear that the Allowance System was not widespread, nor did it operate with the same mechanics as the Speenhamland System. There was rarely a fixed scale of such relief, and its usage was restricted to pockets of destitute hand-loom weavers. And Henderson suggested that the cure lay in abandoning hand-loom weaving 'with all possible despatch'.

The Commission's *pro formas* offer some interesting information on the Workhouse System in Lancashire. Seven rural districts had their own accommodation; seven shared accommodation with other parishes, three had no such amenity, and two failed to reply in this instance. In the towns the figures were more impressive, for all but Everton and Garstang had Workhouse accommodation. Many of these workhouses organised tasks for their clientele, and three had schools. Six actually made a profit, in the case of Wigan and Bolton amounting to well over £100 per year. Eleven classified and separated the inmates, some of them with a completeness that would have satisfied Chadwick. The Workhouses of Lancashire, especially in the towns, appear to have shouldered some of the burden of pauperism in a reasonably competent fashion. At the same time, out-relief was a major and constant factor in poor relief.

The rural responses are suspiciously reticent about their out-relief, but the towns all allowed it.

Turning to the government of the poor law, Henderson spoke of 202 Select Vestries among the 446 units in Lancashire. 'In many of the large towns', he reported, 'Select Vestries have produced a more intelligent and vigilant administration of the Poor Laws', although 'those best qualified are often unwilling to undertake the office of vestrymen'. 228 Assistant Overseers were employed throughout the county, and where Select Vestries were not in evidence, it was the custom for eight or ten rate-payers to 'manage the parochial business' and 'this system of management has long been extensively established in the county with good effect'. Henderson concluded that 'the magistrates interfere little with questions of relief in Lancashire and usually decline to order relief at home, when the Overseers offer admission to the Work-house'. Although Overseers were 'occasionally thwarted in correct plans of management' by the magistrates' 'mistaken kindness, these worthies never in any place sanctioned a fixed scale of relief, or attempted to control the parish authorities in the free exercise of their judgement, in the first instance, as to the amount to be granted'. Only three country districts felt that improvements in parish accountancy were feasible, and, in most of the towns, the auditing and publishing of accounts were most circumspect.

Liverpool and Manchester were congratulated on their effective managing of Poor Relief activities. Henderson praised the thirteen Overseers of Manchester who 'willingly serve these useful, though troublesome offices' and 'the great perfection' of their schemes for visiting and testing applicants. The Workhouse, although in fact a Poorhouse, was 'in admirable order'. The Over-seers' Minutes illustrate the conscientious and regular orderliness of the Poor Law in Manchester.[1] Liverpool afforded Gilbert

[1] J. R. Wood. The Transition from the Old to the New Poor Law in Manchester 1833–42. Unpublished thesis presented to the Victoria University of Manchester, May 1938; especially pp. 32 ff Redford acknowledged his debt to this thesis in the chapter on the New Poor Law in his work on Local Government in Manchester. The Manchester Poor Law papers were destroyed by enemy action; Redford has since died, and Wood himself was killed in the last war. This thesis has thus become of some import, for it is probably the only guide to the official papers of the Manchester Union. I would like to express my gratitude to Dr. W. H. Chaloner of Manchester University for kindly arranging for me to read and annotate this useful document.

Henderson 'a striking example of the operation of a Select Vestry' with its quite amazing show of reductions in expenditure by dint of 'a thorough examination of all the cases'. Liverpool had five boards subjecting applicants and especially the numerous Irish applicants, to a severe interview. It had the largest and one of the best run Workhouses in the nation. It provided an excellent example of less-eligibility. Oakum-picking 'thinned the house very much', but when oakum was scarce 'paupers flocked in. . . . A load of junk at the door would deter them for a long time'. Despite some tremendous extravagances in the twenties, the Liverpool Select Vestry came to be noted for its 'purity and economy in the conduct of public business' and 'few Townships of that day could point to a more blameless History', with its 'lively spirit of enterprise' and 'enlightened sense of public duty'.[1]

The Old Poor Law in Lancashire was neither ramshackle nor disorganised. It was reasonably successful. Even allowing for obvious exaggerations or sins of omission in the Urban and Rural Queries, there was much that was, administratively speaking, satisfactory. Moreover, there was much that the Poor Law Commission was about to recommend. There were, on a fairly substantial scale, elected boards governing sturdily, with the assistance of salaried officials, well-regulated workhouses, and relatively sound fiscal management. Probably with the rate-payers acting as a self-regulator on expenditure, there had been recent and considerable reductions in expense, and the magistracy had little or no authority. Save in the case of the unfortunate Hand-loom Weavers, the Allowance System was rarely practised although, of course, Out-relief was an important feature of the service. In short, the Old Poor Law in Lancashire was a more vivid advertisement of what the Poor Law Commissioners planned to do, than of the faults they so sternly denounced. Alfred Power wrote to Chadwick in October 1837: 'The high rate of wages and a superior spirit of independence have preserved the mass from all contact with pauperism during the ordinary circumstances of trade . . . in my present district (more especially in Lancashire) the proportion of well-governed townships is far greater than would be found in other parts of England, previous to the formation of Unions.' Probably the Poor Law Commissioners never fully realised a main reason for their quandary in Lancashire. The strict logic of

[1] W. L. Blease, 'The Poor Law in Liverpool 1681–1834', *Lancs. & Ches. Hist. Soc.* (1909), pp. 97–184.

uniformity drove them to meddle with administrations too like their model. They had only one narrow answer, only one rigid instrument, for a many-sided problem. Unionisation meant tidiness but not necessarily an improved Poor Law. Perhaps the Commissioners would have been better employed evolving specific techniques for special cases.

It is interesting to set this analysis of Henderson's evidence against Mark Blaug's general criticism of the Poor Law Report. He claims that the untabulated returns appended to the Report, on which 'no historian has ever reported', were not properly scrutinised. He suggests that the Speenhamland System of wage subvention had all but disappeared by 1832, and that, by confusing the answers relating to wage subsidies and child allowance, the Commissioners permitted the wrong picture to emerge. In his view the high level of relief in the so-called Speenhamland counties was due not to the snowball effect of the Old Poor Law, but to chronic unemployment and naturally low wages. Henderson's unorthodox report certainly suggested that Lancashire was an exception to the norm as indicated by Chadwick and his colleagues. It now seems possible that the 'wildly unstatistical' Poor Law report should, in all honesty, have described the general situation as being nearer the Lancashire position, with low wages leading to outdoor relief, rather than vice versa.[1]

Formation of the Unions

In Lancashire, as in England and Wales at large, poor relief was organised at the discretion of the parish or township authorities. Lancashire's population of 1,336,854 was divided among 466 such authorities. They mirrored the profusion of varieties of parish and township then to be found in England. They ranged from quaint, sparsely inhabited hamlets like Henheads and Yealand Conyers to teeming cities like Liverpool; from the bleak expanse of Over Wyresdale to the cramped confines of Salford. They each controlled their own destiny with regard to poor relief, mainly through the Open Vestry of their parish, or, as 202 of them boasted, through Select or elected Vestry. Manchester had its own local Act, passed in 1790 while, in the north of the county, an 'incorporation' of parishes existed around Caton, based on Gilbert's Act of 1782. Many parishes operated under local acts or under a general act of

[1] M. Blaug, 'The Poor Law Report Re-examined', *Jour. of Econ. Hist.* (June, 1964), pp. 229–43.

1819 normally associated with Sturges Bourne, and Lancashire showed a greater tendency than elsewhere to elective boards. The North had also taken more advantage than the rest of the country of an Act passed in 1662 permitting the partition of parishes. Lancashire had been divided into 69 parishes, but partition had produced a conglomeration of nearly 500 separate units.

The Poor Law Commission, faced with this confusion, was naturally anxious to construct a uniform system. They felt that a series of larger and more equitably distributed units would be more efficacious in the dispensation of relief, and that a central authority would find it more convenient to apply its zealous pressures on such bodies. The *modus operandi* of the Commission has been succinctly described by the Webbs in terms of 'grouping together two of three dozen parishes within a ten-mile radius, geographically centring round the market town'.[1] This realignment of poor law boundaries was the primary work of the group of Assistant Commissioners employed by the Poor Law Commission. G. M. Young describes 'Chadwick's young crusaders, the Assistant Commissioners, scouring the countryside . . . their wallets stuffed with the Tabular Data so dear to Philosophic Radicals, to draft their Sovereign's decrees declaring the Unions, and starting his austere administration'.[2]

The 'young crusader' in Lancashire and the West Riding was Alfred Power, a man trained in the law and a particular friend of Chadwick. One can only marvel at the rapid manner in which he carved his allotted areas into Unions, despite often frantic opposition and the difficulties of transport in the eighteen-thirties. His normal method was 'a preliminary meeting' of consultation with the magistrates, churchwardens and overseers within the area around each market town. Having sized up the geopolitics of each situation in this rough and ready fashion, he rather arbitrarily rationed out parishes and townships to Unions. These worthies were summoned, often at short notice, to, for instance, the Town Hall in Wigan, or, more pleasingly, to the Wellington Inn at Rochdale. In the January of 1837 alone, Bolton, Wigan, Rochdale, Ormskirk and nine others had been 'unionised', and, by the end of February, he was able to report that 368 Lancashire parishes had been united into some twenty-one unions.

In actual fact, the first Union to be formed in Lancashire proper

[1] Webb, p. 43.
[2] G. M. Young, *Victorian England: Portrait of an Age* (1936), pp. 40–41.

had been Ulverstone. The Furness portion of Lancashire, so curiously separated from the remainder of the county, had been included in the brief of W. J. Voules, Assistant Commissioner for Westmorland and Cumberland, and, in the summer of 1836, the entire region came under one heading for poor law purposes. Power's clean sweep of Lancashire in the winter of 1837 left only Manchester, Liverpool, Salford, Lancaster and the Lunesdale district for his attention. In July 1838 the four townships of Salford were assembled together, and in 1840 the Lancaster Union was created. It is probable that the latter Union was left so late, because the Commissioners were hoping to resolve the problems of the Gilbert Incorporations. These caused much inconvenience, and the Poor Law Commission claimed that, without their dissolution, the completion of the New Poor Law system would prove impossible. The Caton Incorporation forced the Lancaster Union into a strange pattern, with a long, wriggling strip of the West Lancashire coast from the Kent Estuary to Cockerham opening out onto a bulge eastward to the Yorkshire border. It was not until 1869 that the seventeen parishes of the Caton Incorporation were taken under the wing of the Poor Law Board as the Lunesdale Union. An act of 1868 brought the last of the Gilbert Incorporations into line; in short, the Poor Law Amendment Act took nearly forty years to take complete effect. Apart from Caton and a few parochial districts, there remained the question of Lancashire's two great cities, Liverpool and Manchester. With regard to Manchester, the Poor Law Commission 'saw no reason for haste', probably because the existing poor law was relatively efficient. The Commission finally moved in 1840, perhaps because of opposition of the new Borough Council, incorporated in 1838, to the Churchwardens and Overseers. By January 1841, Guardians had been chosen, and the work of the Manchester Union began. It consisted of twelve townships, but, by mutual agreement and because of the size of population involved, the eleven outlying townships later formed the Prestwich Union with some 28,000 inhabitants. This left the Parish, Borough and Poor Law Union of Manchester as much the same unit.

The Liverpool Union had a brief and dramatic life. Despite strenuous objection, the Parish of Liverpool was converted, without addition, to a Poor Law Union in 1841. On 4 November 1841 a Special General Vestry resolved that 'it is the decided opinion of this Vestry . . . that the system is more cumbersome

and expensive and is not so efficient or satisfactory either to the
rich or poor as the Select Vestry system'.

The Vestry applied for a local act, and supported it with a
report that was vigorously attacked by Charles Mott, who had by
this time replaced Alfred Power.[1] By this time, Edwin Chadwick
had left the Commission's employ, and it had lost much of its early
doctrinaire vigour. It was allowed that Liverpool, the largest Union
in England and Wales, was a special case. It was a single parish of
223,000 souls, with the peculiar problems of a thriving seaport and
yet with a reputation for parochial affairs 'vigilantly and economically managed'. On 28 July 1842 a Special General Vestry again met
to elect twenty-one members to a reconvened Vestry under a local
act of 1842. The Board of Guardians lasted only sixteen months,
but some contact between the central agency and Liverpool
obviously remained, and the statistics for the city continued to be
included in the blue books. Two other units were later formed by
separation from larger Unions. In 1849 the Barton-upon-Irwell
Union was formed, constituting three townships from the Chorlton
Union and the only two 'non-unionised' parishes in South Lancashire. Finally, by an order dated 13 May 1857, the Township of
Toxteth Park was separated from the West Derby Union. This
Liverpool suburb had become an intensely populated area, and it
was the West Derby Guardians who recommended the alteration
and organised a sub-committee to ensure a smooth transfer.
Although it retained the title of Township in all documents, it
enjoyed the independence and rights of a normal Union.

Lancashire's 466 townships were thus divided into thirty Unions
for Poor Law purposes (see Table I). Although some historians
have seen the Union system as a source of important developments
in local government, little time need be spent on searching for
significance within the bounds of each of these units. Except that,
for ease of arbitration and convenience of administrative practice,
they followed Parochial boundaries, the Assistant Commissioners
thought rarely in terms of organic growth or historical tradition and
apparently shared the rationalising, bureaucratic temper of their
chief, Edwin Chadwick. The speed with which the Unions were
thrown together meant short shift for any elaborate recommendations or attempts to promote natural movements towards unifica-

[1] H. Peet (ed.), *Liverpool Vestry Books* (Liverpool, 1915), p. 364 and
Parlty. Papers, *Grounds of Exemption for Liverpool from the Poor Law
Amendment Act*, 1842 (232), XXV.

Table I: **A List of Lancashire Unions 1836–1869**[1]

Union	No. of Townships and Parishes	Population 1831	Date of Formation
Ulverstone	27	22,563	1836
Ashton-under-Lyne	13*	72,516	1837
Blackburn	24	60,594	,,
Bolton	26	83,369	,,
Burnley	26	48,017	,,
Bury	12	62,599	,,
Chorley	25	33,575	,,
Chorlton	12	46,465	,,
Clitheroe	24*	23,168	,,
The Fylde	24	15,930	,,
Garstang	23	11,918	,,
Haslingden	10	35,304	,,
Leigh	8	24,960	,,
Oldham	8	61,038	,,
Ormskirk	21	30,568	,,
Prescot	2	34,160	,,
Preston	29	59,355	,,
Rochdale	6	52,387	,,
Todmorden	6*	23,397	,,
Warrington	15	27,757	,,
West Derby	23	53,058	,,
Wigan	20	58,402	,,
Salford	4	52,366	1838
Lancaster	19	25,006	1840
Manchester	12	164,130	1841
Liverpool	1	165,175	,,
Barton-upon-Irwell	5	26,316 (1841)	1849
Prestwich	11	28,202 (1841)	1850
Toxteth Park	1	40,235 (1841)	1857
Lunesdale	17	9,044 (1841)	1869

* Nine of the thirteen Townships in Ashton-under-Lyne were in Cheshire; twenty of the twenty-eight in Clitheroe were in the West Riding; and five of the six Townships in Todmorden were in the West Riding.

tion. Save for the obvious cases of the Furness district or the cities of Liverpool and Manchester, geographical considerations, either physical or economic, were also far from the minds of the Assistant Commissioners. Often there seems to be no rhyme or reason for these artificially built *ad hoc* entities. Acreage varies from the extensive Unions of Ormskirk, Preston or Garstang to much

[1] This table is mainly composed of information extracted from the *Annual Reports* of the Poor Law Commission and the Poor Law Board 1836–1869.

smaller ones like Warrington or Leigh without any relationship to population or number of Townships. Even excepting the two major cities, the population densities ranged from 11,000 in Garstang to 83,000 in Bolton, while the number of Townships incorporated varied from four in the case of Salford to twenty-nine in the case of Preston. Attention has been drawn to the misfortune of the Commission in planning their Unions just before the railways transformed 'the popular lines of conveyance', but, even so, the Unions show, as might be expected, signs of a hasty and over-eager approach. Although there were hopes that the Poor Law Unions might be used for other administrative purposes and although the Unions dragged their austere story into the twentieth century, no Lancashire Union is today the unit of any governmental function. They have been completely superseded by the more carefully thought-out and more spontaneously developed County Council and County Borough pattern. The Chadwickian believed that areas should be adapted to suit governmental exigencies, and would presumably rejoice that the Unions did not linger on after their purpose ended. Nonetheless, Chadwick entertained high hopes of his Union areas, and they were, of course, used initially to implement the Registration of Births, Deaths and Marriages. He would scarcely have enjoyed the prospect of the county and parochial boundaries he so contemptuously dismissed remaining fairly constant to the present time.

A flat description of Unionisation in Lancashire might suggest a smooth and simple passage. Needless to say, opposition was always evident and sometimes dramatic, and some discussion of its manifestation is necessary to judge aright the atmosphere in which the New Poor Law was promulgated in Lancashire. Chadwick was not blind to the weaknesses of his schemes. He wished to establish his Unions in the North before opposition had time to gather strength and while times were prosperous, or, failing that to form isolated Unions in suitable parts. The other Commissioners and he were quick to blame 'a high degree of popular excitement and prejudice' for their difficulties in the manufacturing districts, and they complimented themselves on their progress 'in the face of considerable resistance'. In their reports of 1837 and 1838 they were equally keen to bemoan the 'continuance of the interruption to manufacturing industry' and the 'continued and severe distress amongst the manufacturing population'. The rigours of the New Poor Law were certainly diluted in the North when the Commissioners found themselves beset with such difficulties. There were many who were ready to criticise the New Poor Law, from the indolent, denied easy doles, to those clergy who were horrified at the idea of civic registration of marriage. Three main planks, however, formed the basis of opposition, each one the converse, in a sense, of the triple proposals of the reformed Poor Law examined above. Many commentators have indicated how the Commission's economic diagnosis was invalid because a free market in labour already existed in the North, thus making the remedy of less eligibility irrelevant. The Webbs also concluded that pauperism, and not the destitution that caused it, was inspected by the Poor Commission. They claimed that the problem was too much assumed to be one merely concerning the able-bodied, whereas many paupers were infirm, aged or juvenile. Moreover the Workhouse Test acted 'not as a dam but as a sieve'. The genuinely destitute continued to be subjected to the strain of the very examination they had been deemed to pass, for the severity of the Workhouse was both test and treatment. In brief, because of the ramifications of a capitalist economy, there were often periods of distress in spite of a free mart in labour, and not because of its absence. It has been suggested by Blaug that this was also true of agricultural areas, and that the Old Poor Law, far from reducing the efficiency of the agricultural worker, was a proper device for dealing with distress in the rural sector of the economy.[1] Certainly in Lancashire the 'all or nothing' principle was neither practical nor logical, and the out-and-out individualists of the Manchester school were contemptuous of Chadwick's meddling plans. Threatened with a brutal and stark system, the labouring population were often sullen and angry—although they rarely pondered the delicacies of obtuse economic theorising, they could spot the possibilities of suffering implicit in the New Poor Law, and, often with justification, the prospect appalled them. Both on academic and pragmatic grounds, therefore, stout objections were raised at the Commission's economic thinking and action.

Secondly, as might be expected, strong exception was taken to the administrative devices of the New Poor Law. To the *laissez-faire* purist, the organisational technique was but a symptom of

[1] M. Blaug, 'The Myth of the Old Poor Law and the Making of the New', *Jour. of Econ. Hist.* (June 1963), pp. 151–84.

the economic malpractice. For their part, the workers cried 'No
Bastilles', and feared the arrival of 'continental' management, with
the 'blue-bottle' police ever ready to pounce. Here the Tories,
with their long anti-state tradition, took up the offensive. Their
grave suspicion of state intervention matched the growing local
pride of the North Western 'shopocrats'. 'We are at length', wrote
the *Manchester Courier* dolefully in 1841, 'fairly under the mighty
triumvirate of Somerset House.'

Thirdly, there was the widespread belief that the New Poor
Law would not and did not reduce the rates. This opinion was
well supported in Lancashire, for the poor rate per head in 1837
was still only 2s. 9d., at a time when the Poor Law Commission
was boasting of a national reduction to 5s. 10d. from 9s. 1d. in
1834. Typical of these protagonists was Thomas Smith, who
served West Derby both as Overseer and Guardian. He condemned the central administration of the Poor Laws most forth-
rightly from 1837 onward. He condemned it before he had even
read the Act, on the culinary grounds that one did not have to
know the ingredients to taste the pudding. He maintained that the
Old Poor Law had been 'a simple, inexpensive and highly salutary
affair', and that the rates had been 'fully doubled'. He probed and
scrutinised the West Derby Union accounts, tabling lists of purported illegal and extravagant charges,[1] Throughout the county
there were several ready to root out embarrassing data and mourn
the passing of the honest Parish Vestry.

On the other hand, the determination to decrease the rates even
at the expense of sacrificing beneficial portions of the Poor Law,
may well have caused opposition in itself. Some blamed the incomplete nature of the New Poor Law for the troubles in the Northern
towns, while Finer has stated that the new Poor Law was 'a jejune
and clumsy caricature of the report'. It ignored Chadwick's advice
of schools, asylums, hospitals and the like, and concentrated on
cutting the rates. The consequence was 'promiscuous barracks',
the advent of 'servile war' in the North, and a revulsion from the
Workhouse which has cut deeply into the folk-memory of the
British working classes.[2]

Political agitation, especially through journalism, and non-

[1] T. Smith *Results of the Central Administration of the Poor Laws
exhibited in some of its workings in the West Derby Union* (Liverpool,
1848).
[2] Finer, pp. 93–94.

co-operation made up most of Lancashire's opposition, but violence was not unknown. The press probably played a part, for, to the Conservative, violence was the fearful consequence of a brutal law, and, to the Whig, the mark of a degraded and wild opposition. Fielden told the House of Commons in 1837 that the Poor Law Commission 'might as well attempt to conquer the world as to introduce the system into Lancashire and Yorkshire'. In the same year 'no one durst accept the office of Guardian in Oldham', and the Rochdale Guardians were condemned for taking office. The citizens of Oldham, in fact, were 'determined to take up arms'. Fletcher of Bury suggested incendiarism to the people of Blackburn, and James Cobbett armed force to the Mancunians. Apart from sporadic outbursts of violence in Oldham and Rochdale and also in Colne, there was little viciousness or destruction. Indeed, it is a strange feature of this episode that Yorkshire, and especially Huddersfield and Bradford, caused more disorder than Lancashire. Power was assaulted three times in Yorkshire. According to the *Liverpool Mercury* in 1837 he was once forced to run the gauntlet of a Bradford mob to his hotel, which left him in 'a state of considerable exhaustion from loss of blood'. The intrepid Assistant Commissioner was luckier in his trips West of the Pennines. At a meeting, the 'largest ever held in Oldham', there were bloodcurdling shouts of 'we will punce him with our clogs', and the seventy-year-old Betty Mayall, also of Oldham, swore 'she would fight to the death', but Power was subjected to no such treatment. Indeed, in the summer of 1837, Edwin Chadwick, the arch-criminal of Somerset House, visited his native Manchester—he was born in Longsight in 1800—and wandered freely amongst all levels of the populace, discussing his system of poor relief. He emerged from this ordeal unscathed, and, moreover, completely unconvinced that this prescription for pauperdom was in any fashion inaccurate, or that the opposition was anything more than the self-centred rantings of jobbers and professional agitators. The fiercest exception to this all but blameless picture is Todmorden, and it is curious that the Todmorden Union lay athwart the Pennines in an indeterminate location between the two counties, with five of its six townships lying in the West Riding. Todmorden was very much in the thrall of John Fielden, who, as well as being a violent opponent of the New Poor Law, was also an important employer. Two or three townships refused to levy the rate appointed by the Guardians, and their Overseers were fined for

this non-payment. In the November of 1838, two bailiffs attempted
to distrain the goods of William Ingham, the Langfield Overseer,
who had also refused to pay his fine. A mob from the nearby
Lambutt's factory mauled them badly, and they were lucky to
escape alive. The next demands were coupled with threats of
military action. A thousand-strong crowd gathered to greet the
military, and, when they failed to arrive, the mob wrecked and
looted the property of Guardians and Union officials. It is most
noticeable that this disorder arose, apparently, because the New
Poor Law was 'unmistakably distasteful to the bulk of the rate-
payers', and not especially through the operatives' excitement. The
influence of Fielden in Todmorden made it rather a special case,
and one might hazard the conclusion that violence in Lancashire
has been, at times, overstated.[1]

The forties were to witness more extensive disturbances but it
would be unfair to rest the blame squarely on the poor law. In the
summer of 1842 these exhibitions of public disorder reached their
peak in the gigantic turnouts and plug-pulling ventures at Blackburn, Preston, Oldham, Rochdale, Bacup, Burnley, Todmorden
and other places. But in a period of 'unexampled difficulty and
distress' the democratic aspirations of Chartism were more to the
fore, along with feelings of hostility towards the new police forces,
the corn laws and machines. The New Poor Law was but one of all
the possible cares that could be avidly grasped by hungry mal-
contents. A banner borne in Lancashire carried a typical slogan—
'What this country needs is more pigs and less parsons.'

Such commotions apart, the active opposition to the Poor Law
in Lancashire seems to have died swiftly. In the first place, the
extent of the objection has possibly been exaggerated. It has been
suggested that the New Poor Law 'drove the Northern Counties
into a frenzy'[2] and that the reaction was 'the first angry grievance
of an industrial proletarist'.[3] These statements may mislead by
being too general. Even in the journalistic field, opposition was
often cancelled by newspapers in favour of the New Poor Law.
For every *Liverpool Courier* there was a *Liverpool Mercury* and for
every *Manchester Courier* a *Manchester Guardian*. Indignation was

---

[1] T. E. Ashworth, *An Account of the Todmorden Poor Law Riots of
November 1838* (1901).

[2] Finer, p. 85.

[3] D. Roberts, *Victorian Origins of the British Welfare State* (Yale 1960),
p. 277.

probably greater in Yorkshire than in Lancashire, and seven Lancastrian Unions, as late as 1855, were branded 'agricultural' and not 'manufacturing'. The bigger agglomerations of Liverpool and Manchester appear not to have fretted unduly. A contemporary writer maintained that, despite the prolonged trade depression from 1837 to 1843, the Lancashire workers remained as patient and as stable as others were later to judge them during the Great Cotton Famine. He spoke of the 'exemplary conduct of the operatives reverencing law' in Manchester, and claimed that 'there was no insurrection to suppress', albeit 'a social commotion to tranquillise'.[1] Possibly the *Manchester Guardian* was right in its assessment in 1838, that 'the great bulk of the population care nothing about the matter'. On the whole, Lancashire's opposition was sporadic rather than general.

In the second place, the party political implications of the conflict must be noted. A once white-hot issue was soon relegated to the inner columns of the press, as first one and then another question tumbled in and out of publicity's bright but short-lived glare. Peel's Conservative Government hallowed the New Poor Law by allowing it to remain, while after 1840, the middle classes were turning to Free Trade and the Anti-Corn League and the working classes were tempted by the counter attraction of Chartism. In the third place, four good harvests and alternative employment in newer enterprises like railway construction, were instrumental in helping the economy—especially in the southern agrarian districts—right itself, and, as the standards of life improved, so did the terrors of the Poor Law recede. Even in 1836, the pro-Whig *Liverpool Mercury*, discussing the initial poor rate reductions following the Poor Law Amendment Act, confessed that 'perhaps half this great saving may be ascribed to the New Poor Law system and the rest to the prosperity of the country'. Although the early forties were unpleasant years for Lancashire, the Poor Law Commission, in showing overall declines in expenditure, seemed to many to prove their point, and this, in its turn, narrowed the opposition attack. In any event the Poor Law, in its fullest sense, was slow to reach Lancashire, and, as the years went by, the sting and austerity departed from the Commission. Chadwick left Somerset House in 1841, and with him went much of the Commission's doctrinaire drive. The change to Poor Law Board in 1847 and, with it, to parliamentary control, was a change from a

[1] H. Cook-Taylor, *Notes of a Tour of the Manufacturing Districts* (1842).

c

forceful agency to a relatively mechanical organism. The completion of Poor Law requirements in Lancashire came, therefore, under a more easy-going régime, and this must have affected the amount of opposition.

It would be dangerous to go farther than this on such a brief analysis. It is true that public indignation and passive resistance were partially successful. At the notorious Andover Inquiry George Lewis, a Poor Law Commissioner, stated: 'We cannot even get some of the northern bodies to operate the law at all, in any shape or form; already there is a cry to prevent us interfering in the manufacturing districts either through our Registrars or through our Assistant Commissioners.'[1] There is, however, one alternative factor which might help to clarify a blurred picture. It could have been that poor relief was operating in Lancashire efficiently enough to make people question the point of change, even on the Commission's premisses. Perhaps it was that some parts of the county had anticipated the Commission's proposals, so that much of the reform was, in practice, superfluous. Perhaps the dearth of opposition after the new schemes had been inaugurated in Lancashire was due, in part, to the success of obstruction, in that the county received a watered-down version; and, in part, to a realisation that, in mundane day-by-day business, the new organisation need differ little from the old. Pacifying opponents of the New Poor Law in 1840, the *Manchester Guardian* suggested that 'the change in Manchester will be extremely unimportant. . . . It will be found in practice that the same description of officers who are now employed will be required under the New Law to discharge almost precisely the same duties as heretofore'. This could prove to be a text for the whole of Lancashire, but that is to anticipate a wider discussion of the New Poor Law in practice.

ii. Character of the New Poor Law

Elective Board Principle

An inspection of the administration of the New Poor Law in Lancashire falls into a four-fold division. This comprises the relative benefits of the elected Boards of Guardians; the employment of salaried officials; the impact of a central board and inspectorate; and the degree of success of the Union scheme. In the main, and unless otherwise indicated, these sections draw liberally

[1] P.L.C., *Andover Enquiry Evidence*. Qq 21560/21561.

on the very full minutes of the appropriate Boards of Guardians. At the outset, the Poor Law Commission claimed in their 1837 Report that 'the means of an efficient administration are obtainable at a cheaper rate by the Union of Parishes' and that 'the mischievous influence of local interests' was thus avoided. Each Union had its elected Board of Guardians, and each Guardian represented a Township or Parish within the Union. As together they did not represent 'the same individual parochial interest' but a series of such interests, it was hoped that Guardians would demonstrate 'a fuller and more regular attendance' than Vestrymen had been wont to do. The latter had apparently been guilty of 'habitual secession' in times of urgency, whereas one Board could do the work of Ten Vestries. This reduction in 'the whole amount of the unpaid public service' would, argued the Commission, lead to an impartial and energetic governance 'superior in its elements to the existing machinery, economical as regards the degree of time and attention' demanded, and 'competent to act on occasions of great emergency'. Such was the fond Benthamite hope of aligning the interests of governed and governors that the public interest might prosper. Each Board was to consist of all J.P.s and of members elected by ratepayers and owners of land or property. To avoid mob excitement, voting was by secret ballot, which, in those days of partial literacy, was to cause certain difficulties. Moreover, voting was in plurality, in accordance with scales of propertied wealth. Owners and occupiers could have from one to six votes respectively, according to a rating qualification up to £250. In effect, some people had twelve votes as they qualified on both counts. It may be concluded that, in the event, with a restricted, complicated and secret ballot, farmers and principal residents were elected often without contest, and, in the words of Nassau Senior, 'a network of small aristocracies' was formed.

Such were the aims and plans for forming elected boards. The Poor Law Commission expected to revolutionise the administration of Poor Relief almost overnight and their actions have been seen as the cause of social and political upheaval as well as of violent administrative changes. The creation of Guardians has been sometimes regarded as a heavier blow at the old political order than the Reform Act itself. What evidence do the Lancashire Guardians provide for or against these somewhat dramatic statements?

Firstly, the haphazard formation of the Lancashire Unions was guaranteed to cause some inconvenience. The Unions tended to fall between the twin stools of artificiality and naturalness. On the one side, although Parochial boundaries were religiously adhered to, Unions were sometimes made up of unsuited elements. The larger Townships, for instance, wanted rather to keep to themselves. The *Manchester Courier* explains why, in its discussion in 1840 of the Manchester Union. 'The first objection which appears on the face of the arrangements, is that the Union is far too large. It will soon be found that in proportion to the number of Guardians, and the number of the poor to be relieved, the Township of Manchester will pay far more than its share towards the fund of the general Union.' Conversely, the smaller Townships, with that admixture of local pride and local self-interest which seems a constant element in municipal government, were frightened of being swallowed up by their larger neighbours. There exist countless illustrations of the parish or township within a Union struggling and obstructing in order to avoid submergence. Thus neither the tritons—fearful of overspending—nor the minnows—fearful of over subordination were entirely satisfied.

On the other side, the side of naturalness, the apparently sensible plan of using a market town as a centre contributed to this trouble. An investigation in terms of population and expenditure suggests that the Lancashire Unions were often a major core with a few accoutrements added. This was, of course, the intention, but it is none the less misleading, for the idea of Union suggests the consolidation of equals. In the harsh facts of administrative life, it is not unlikely that the much-trumpeted Union of Parishes was little more than the expansion of one or two larger entities. Just as the Unification of Germany is frequently viewed as the extension of Prussia, so, less grandiosely, may the unification of Pendlebury, Broughton, Salford and Pendleton be interpreted as the extension of Salford.

The Commissioners tended, perhaps, to get the worst of both worlds, for, where no sizeable conurbation lorded it over the rest, there was a danger—as in Burnley, Rochdale, Leigh or Ormskirk—for vacillations and rivalries to appear precisely because there was obviously no leadership. This was possibly the first and basic reason for the early failures of the Lancashire Guardians to exert the pressures desired by the Poor Law Commission. One is moved to wonder whether one or other of the mooted alternatives might have been preferable. Chief among them was a suggestion that the County be utilised for the operation of the Poor Law, and, in the winter of 1836-37, a vain attempt was made to pass a bill erecting County Boards. The County was a recognised governmental area, with an existing mode of taxation in the County Rate. None the less, the Counties were probably out of gear with changing patterns of life and settlement, and Chadwick was determined on administrative innovation. Of the existing local rule he wrote 'to talk of this as the self-government characteristic and the glory of Englishmen is despicable cant'.[1]

Another plan was based on the 'nationalisation of the Poor Rate', and the setting up of one central agency. Many, including the Manchester Ratepayers Association, favoured a national administration and rate. In 1869 William Rathbone of Liverpool drew attention to the discrepancies from town to town, and complained that the poor flocked into the large towns to take advantage of Poor Law facilities. He quoted a Manxman who had visited Liverpool four or five times to be cured of his skin disease, and one thinks immediately of the contemporary grouse about foreigners and the National Health Service. As the Liverpool Workhouse Governor so pithily phrased it, 'The Isle of Man had the benefit of his health, and we had the expense of his sickness'.[2] Naturally enough, Chadwick was keen to establish a completely national system, but the expense of (and probably, too, the absence of administrative techniques for) forming field agencies proved prohibitive. Indeed, the earliest move in this direction was the Union Chargeability Act of 1865 when the Union, and not the Parish, became the accepted area for settlement purposes, and which henceforth made 'the area of administration and expenditure the same'. Strangely enough, there seems to have been no suggestion that, for instance, a working commission be set up to organise Poor Relief throughout the country, varying the method according to the peculiar needs of differing types of problem and condition. This might, at the same time, have proved dilatory at a period when drastic action was deemed to be needed, and, given the single-minded diagnosis of the situation in terms of wage subsistence, one solution seemed sufficient.

Secondly, the very retention of the Parish at all for Poor Relief meant frequently, in practice, the perpetuation of the old rôle of

[1] E. Chadwick, 'Principles and Progress of the Poor Law Amendment Act', *Edinburgh Review* (1836).

[2] W. Rathbone, *Local Taxation and Poor Law Administration in Great Cities* (1869).

the Parish. The Townships and Parishes often baulked at the inauguration of Union work; they often obstructed that work once commenced; they often ensured that, when a Union was well under way, their influence remained considerable. With regard to the first of these three propositions, it is clear that the forming of a Union was not a signal that it would become active. Of the seven North-Eastern Unions examined by Rhodes Boyson, only Haslingden elected Guardians without delay. In Blackburn, Clitheroe, Burnley, Bolton, Bury and Rochdale there was much hesitation.[1] In December 1840, the Bolton Board applied to the Poor Law Commission to delay bringing Townships under the Board until a later date, and the first Minutes of the Haslingden Union are not recorded until June 1838. The story is the same elsewhere. In many Lancashire Unions the boundaries existed only for the Registration of Births, Deaths and Marriages. The 3rd Annual Report of the Poor Law Commission admitted that the New Poor Law had to be postponed in such areas, but that the Unions would be formed for registration purposes. It was not until 1845 that the Union of Ashton-under-Lyne became responsible for poor relief. The Garstang Union appointed no Relieving Officers until November 1838, Leigh Union delayed ten months before commencing to control relief, Ormskirk and Preston eight months, and Wigan fifteen months. Ulverstone, Warrington, Preston and Fylde seem to have moved relatively quickly, but Oldham had no Union controlled relief until the autumn of 1847. In the November of 1838, the Chorley Guardians decided 'to assume the control of the relief of the poor' and they informed the Overseers that 'they will cease to relieve the Poor on 25 December next, except in cases of emergency'. With the notorious difficulties of Todmorden, the late Unionisation of Manchester, Liverpool, Lancaster and Salford, and the problems of the Lunesdale and Barton districts, it is apparent that the New Poor Law was slow to make its mark in Lancashire. Conversely, until such times as the Unions felt obliged or were ordered to commence operations, the relief of the poor remained in parochial hands. A common formula, illustrated here by a quotation from the Bolton Guardians, was an order to the overseers 'requesting them to continue relief to the poor as heretofore until otherwise directed'. The diehard tendencies of the Parishes is further underlined by their attitude to

[1] R. Boyson, 'The New Poor Law in North East Lancashire 1834–71', *Lancs. & Ches. Hist. Soc.* (1960).

Registration. The Clitheroe Guardians proposed, for example, 'that
for the greater convenience of carrying into effect the said provisions of the said Registration Act' the Union should be divided
into districts 'which should comprise respectively the townships'.
As Power pointed out, some Unions were only quiescent because
the Poor Law Commission allowed 'a liberal compliance with
the law'.[1]
   The hiatus between the creation of the Unions and their beginning operations was partially the result of the type of persons
elected as Guardians. The elections themselves were often strange.
In Manchester three Tory Churchwardens and three Overseers of
a more reforming disposition agreed on a list of Guardians. These
were each elected with 2,982 votes or over, whilst the 264 candidates proposed by opponents of the scheme in an attempt to block
it, could muster only nine with over 300 votes each. Three others
had one supporter, and another received no votes at all. Ashton
Union went eleven years without an election, for the number of
nominees always just equalled the number of vacancies. Uncontested seats on the Board of Guardians were by no means uncommon, as Townships put forward their delegate to fight for their
interest. The Fylde Guardians, in 1845, report that there was 'no
opposition to any of the candidates nominated in any of the townships', and this is a regular occurrence throughout Lancashire.
Equally noticeable is the feature of constant re-election, and, in
practically every Union, the same names crop up time and again.
It is important to remember that these were not necessarily supporters of the New Poor Law. The Tory *Manchester Courier* welcomed, in 1841, the wholesale reappointment of the Wigan
Guardians, all of them 'well-qualified and well-disposed'. The
same journal cooled in its opposition to the Poor Law in Manchester
as the Guardians of that city were, in part, respectable Tories.
Tory Guardians were obviously not the sort of Guardians that
Chadwick would have delighted in, but, nevertheless, they were
numerous.
   On the whole, however, the Guardians of whatever political
creed or social complexion had in common a decided lack of keen-
ness to see the wheels of the New Poor Law set in motion. Alfred
Power constantly drew attention to this difficulty. He reported the
anti-Poor Law feelings of the Rochdale Guardians and the split of
the Preston Guardians, which was a 'nearly equal division of

[1] Power-P.L.C., 17 Dec 1838, P.R.O. M.H. 32/64.

friends and enemies'. He was also alarmed at the 'political feelings' ruling elections at Wigan, Bolton, Clitheroe, West Derby, Todmorden and Lancaster, and he yearned for a more effective supervision of the Guardians. Perhaps the most meaningful characteristic of the new species of Guardian was his continuity with the ancient régime. Over and over again, the Church Wardens and the Overseers of the Parish became the Guardians of the Union. They were obviously the ones with the time to spare and the interest to serve; they merely changed the name of their office. Townships often elected their paid Overseers as Guardians and at Clitheroe they formed a majority of the Board. 'Many of them are ignorant, inefficient persons', claimed Power, 'sent by the small Townships to oppose the law', ready to 'struggle to the last' for their 'own situations and salaries'. This avowedly Benthamite urge made no appeal to the Assistant Commissioner, who attacked the Warrington Union for working 'largely through the influence of the old Overseers'. He later tried to prevent Preston from having too many Overseers as Guardians, and he was especially hard on the smaller towns, where, he felt, the Overseers were of 'inferior stamp'.[1] In brief, the Guardians, politically and socially, ran true to form. Rarely can elected Boards have been so diffident about their purported revolutionary functions. Apart, perhaps, for Unions, like Barton, which appear to have flourished with a commendable briskness, little anxiety to forge ahead was shown.

Salford and Liverpool are prime examples of many of these tendencies. In Salford the case of Francis Wrigley, an Assistant Overseer, excited considerable local attention. He was apparently caught up in the struggle between the Salford Whigs and Tories. He was suspended for 'dereliction of duty', but, while his Tory friends put this down to 'strong political prejudices', the Whigs claimed he had 'perverted his office for political purposes'. Charles Mott, then the Assistant Commissioner in the North-west, reported to the Poor Law Commission that, on obtaining a majority, the Salford Tories had replaced the Whig sympathiser— a man named Wakefield—with Wrigley. An 'unpleasant enquiry' followed, complete with lengthy reports and an extended correspondence. Six months after Wrigley had been discharged, John Hope, Clerk to the Salford Union, told the Poor Law Commission of his 'mortification and regret' over the Commission's 'protracted

[1] Power-P.L.C., 27 April, 17 Dec. 1838, 13 and 26 Feb. and 12 Apr. 1839, P.R.O. M.H. 32/64.

neglect' of the case. Probably the Commissioners were none too keen to see a Tory reinstated, and, at this point, the case seems to have faded out of the limelight. During those six months, however, the Salford Union was so preoccupied with this squabble that over half its correspondence with London concerned Wrigley.[1] Liverpool managed to journey through three phases of Poor Law history with scarcely a tremor. In April 1841 the *Liverpool Mercury* rejoiced at the advent of the New Poor Law, but, in the same edition, the Tory Overseers advertised their hope that 'the feelings and wishes of the great body of ratepayers . . . will have their due weight'. Indeed, the bill to procure an independent system for Liverpool was already under preparation but, in any event, the Guardians elected in May 1841 were chiefly Tories, and the Commissioner noted that 'the election of the Guardians took place without a contest'. In July of the next year Raymond Houghton proposed, under this new Act, twenty-one Select Vestrymen of whom fourteen were Guardians, and practically all of whom were Tories. The Rev. A. Campbell was chairman of this trio of ostensibly different committees; J. Mellor, E. Ford, J. Hand, J. Wilkinson and W. Foster were present in all three lists; and some twenty others appeared in two.

When the Unions did eventually swing into action in Lancashire, their work was checked and barred by the Townships and Parishes. Given Guardians of the unenthusiastic calibre indicated above, it will be realised how much of a brake upon action they could be. It would appear that, on occasion, a Gilbertian situation must have arisen, with the Guardian hoping to gain control of a Parochial Workhouse, and the Overseer, trying to prevent this, one and the same person. In their obstructionist attitude, the Parochial authorities enjoyed two practical advantages in that they normally owned the amenities necessary for the continuance of poor relief and in that they still operated the rating and rate-collection system. Rhodes Boyson has shown how the seven Unions he studied hung on to Township Workhouses and to relief as a 'Township charge' until 1866,[2] and the same story is repeated in much of the county. When the brisk Barton Guardians began their régime in 1849, they found sets of cottages still in use at Urmston and Flixton for Workhouse purposes, and their bid of £1,800 for the Barton Workhouse had to be raised to £2,000 in 1850. The Rochdale Overseers

---

[1] Salford Poor Law Correspondence, 1841–42, P.R.O. M.H. 12/6220.
[2] Boyson, op. cit., p. 36.

ordered the local Overseers to look after the Workhouses, for they
felt 'compelled to recommend the continuance' of the Township
institutions. Newton Township refused to allow Warrington Union
to take over their Workhouse, and the Warrington Workhouse
itself was rented for some £300 per annum only after hard
negotiating. Burnley, which was to distinguish itself by having
eleven Townships in 1838 which returned no Guardians, insisted
on Township rather than District collecting of rates, and this was
a generally uniform pattern. The dependence of the Unions on the
Townships is illustrated by the constant inclusion in the various
Minutes of such formulae as 'orders were made upon the following
Townships' or 'transfer to the establishment and to each Township
the appropriate charge'. Sometimes the Guardians sound even
more pathetic and their finances quite unstable, as when Clitheroe
Union admits that 'as the funds of the Union are very nearly
exhausted, there must be a further call on the various Townships'.
Earlier in the same Minutes, one reads a proposal 'that the clerk
do forthwith adopt legal proceedings against all Overseers of
Townships who have neglected to pay the amount of the orders
made upon them for carrying into effect the purposes of the Union'.
   These first two types of Township continuance are not, perhaps,
as important as the other way in which the Parish or Township
perpetuated its rôle in the new scheme. Even when the Unions
functioned smoothly, freed from checks and obstacles, there is
ample evidence to show that, very often, the Township supervision was paramount. In the North-East of Lancashire, local
Townships continued 'to decide the amount of such relief'. Only
the Clitheroe and Haslingden Guardians met as a full board, and
then they reviewed cases 'in a definite order according to settlement', so that Guardians needed only to attend during the times
that paupers from their own Townships were being inspected. In
Rochdale, Bury and Blackburn, the Guardians deteriorated into a
set of unofficial sub-committees for relief in the respective Townships, and in Bolton the Townships committees demonstrated a
range of attitudes from liberality in the urban, to stinginess in the
rural areas. The Lancaster Guardians employed the Townships in
a most detailed manner, and the laying of charges upon them was
done in a niggling week-by-week fashion, with items like '2s. 2d.
from Adcliffe for provisions' being plentiful. In Ormskirk, the
Overseers continued to be used extensively in settlement and relief
cases. The Ormskirk Relieving Officer was asked, in 1839, to

'request the Overseers of the several Townships in the Union to ascertain and report in writing' those willing to take on apprentices. In Oldham, the Relieving Officers had 'to divide the applicants for relief into divisions and arrange the times of their attendance at different times' in order to avoid 'present pressure and confusion'. It is apparent that each such district had its own chairman and miniature Board, chosen from the Guardians of the corresponding Townships, to resolve the problems of relief and to check the Officers' 'books according to the general principle of relief adopted before the division of the Board'. Most of the Unions created sub-committees to supervise Workhouses or organise rating charges, and, automatically, these duties fell to the Guardians in the areas concerned. On the whole, therefore, the Township continued to wield much of the practical power of the Poor Law. With the rate-payer continuing to associate his financial burden with the Parish or Township in which he resided, the Boards of Guardians slowly declined in significance. Just as a contemporary citizen may know which hospital to visit in time of sickness but can barely name its Regional Board, one is bound to ask whether the Victorian man-in-the-street had a much less hazy idea of his Union as compared to his Workhouse, his Relieving station or his Parochial rate-collector.

These two general factors—the awkwardness of Unionisation and the continuance of Township influence—almost certainly militated against the success of the elective Boards of Guardians. Much was expected of them and their theoretical power was high, and yet they proved, especially in the initial stages, largely unsatisfactory. One last feature remains to illustrate this overall lack of impetus and control from the elected Guardians. Perhaps the most astonishing element about the Boards of Guardians in Lancashire was the incredible absenteeism from meetings. This chronic lack of attendance must certainly have enfeebled the whole new apparatus of the representative committee. It is not a case of one or two absentees, but of regular and consistent non-attendance throughout much of the county and over a period of some years. It is absenteeism to an extent that makes it difficult to avoid the conclusion that, in many Unions, the Guardians were all but nominal in their authority. One example must suffice. In Haslingden the eighteen Guardians, in their first year of office from June 1838 to June 1839, attended meetings as follows: 15, 9, 3, 1, 0, 1, 1, 3, 1, 4, 2, 1, 1, 1, 0, 7, 3, 3, 6, 9, 5, 5, 3, 4, 3, 3, 3, 3, 3, 4, 5, 4, 5, 5, 8, 1, 3, 4, 3, 6, 8, 3, 11, 4, 3,

3, 5, 4, 4, 3, 4, 1, 3. It is possibly unkind to add that the higher
numbers are sometimes on the days when the meetings were held
at the Commercial Inn rather than the Haslingden National
School.

Lancashire suggests a picture of years in which Guardians had
not taken over their proper functions followed by years in which,
with the Poor Law more and more unimportant politically, the
Guardians were too lethargic to undertake their duties correctly.
A fairly rigid pattern of action emerges from a study of the Boards.
They resolved the problems of Registration divisions and Relief
and Medical districts; they appointed Relieving, Medical and
other officers; and they inspected the Workhouses and set up
Workhouse sub-committees. These tasks completed, they tended
to sit back and, unless urgent emergencies arose, they merely kept
a rather skimpy eye on accounting procedures. Attendance became
slacker, and the number of reasonably important motions passed
unanimously by quartets, was astounding. Over and over again,
the Boards of Guardians degenerated into dull, rubber-stamping,
money-checking mechanisms. A watch on accounts, however
sketchy, is not without its place, but the Lancashire Guardians
soon lost all flair for initiating action.

The doleful narration of the Lancashire Guardians' shortcom-
ings is a vivid example of the national story. Finer has suggested
that, in the critical 1839–1842 period, the Boards rebelled. He has
shown that there were party Boards, Boards of 'jobocrats', and
anti-Poor Law Boards, and that Chadwick was no longer able to
use the Guardians as a lever against his opponents in the Cabinet
and the Poor Law Commission—'the great manufacturing middle
class had thrown their weight' behind opposition to the New Poor
Law.[1] Mutiny amongst the Lancashire Guardians was a sin of
omission, not of commission; rather was theirs a negative rebellion
of apathy. Moreover, as the New Poor Law was only on its way
into the County Palatine as this crisis arose, it is fair to suppose
that its roots were at a shallow depth. Guardianship in Lancashire
certainly accords with what might be termed the 'older' view.
The Webbs wrote of 'a prompt and almost universal falling-off in
the quality of the Boards', after some enthusiasm to reduce the
rates, because being a Guardian became a 'dull and irksome
business'.[2] Certainly Power was well aware of the maladministra-

[1] Finer, pp. 83–84.
[2] Webb, p. 229.

tion and some of the reasons for it. Until his transfer to Malvern in December 1840, he campaigned against the Vestry appointment of Overseers, the eligibility of paid officers for the post of Guardian, and the identification of Electoral or Relieving Districts with Townships. He suggested that 'contentment with the Poor Law' existed simply because it was 'not in fact the same law which was at first so much spoken of and dreaded'.[1] The Lancashire Guardians were not, perhaps, alone in their defects; few, none the less, could have surpassed them in doing nothing in particular, and doing it very well.

Use of Expertise

The upholders of the New Poor Law laid much stress on the employment of salaried officials. It was supposed that a regular and competent Poor Law service would replace the amateurish and haphazard Parochial workers, and that cheapness would be substituted for prodigality. 'The Assistant Overseers of several Townships', wrote the Poor Law Commissioners in 1837, 'will often be superseded by one Relieving Officer.' The Assistant Overseers, they admitted, would still carry out 'the most onerous part' of rate collection, whereas the Relieving Officers would concentrate on the control of relief. This 'separation of duties', so they argued, would lead to 'a considerable reduction of officers employed'. In supporting the idea of the Union official, they eschewed the suggestion that 'accurate knowledge' was the prerogative of the rulers over 'a small district', and claimed that 'the paid and permanent officer' on a large scale was a more sensible proposition, for he would prove more energetic and impartial.

Apart from Overseers accepting honorariums, Lancashire had some 228 paid Assistant Overseers in 1834. To those must be added the various other groups of officials, such as Workhouse personnel, and part-time medical officers. In 1849 a return of officers was demanded by the Poor Law Board as for 24 April of that year. The total of officers paid by the county Unions was over a thousand, and of these some five hundred were employed on a full-time basis. Their wage bill amounted annually—if one allows for Oldham making no return and for non-unionised areas— to over the £50,000 mark. Power calculated, in 1837, that ten of the Lancashire Unions spent £8,900 on Assistant Overseers and Workhouse supervisors. The same ten Unions, in 1849, had a

[1] Power-P.L.C., 17 Dec. 1838, P.R.O. M.H. 32/64.

salary bill of £19,000. Some minor points help to account for this
increase, such as slight rises in population and the fact that Power
did not consider employees outside his two major classifications.
None the less, there were few officers who did not fall into the
categories of Assistant Overseer or Collector and Workhouse
Master or Matron. It would seem that the New Poor Law caused
a proliferation rather than a reduction of officials. The bulk of the
part time appointments were for Registrars, to implement the
Registration Act, and Medical Officers. There were also teachers,
but these were especially based on the new Industrial Schools of
Liverpool and Manchester. One does not condemn the encouragement of medical, educational and statistical services—one merely
demonstrates that the New Poor Law begat its own species of
officials.

Sometimes Relieving Officers replaced Assistant Overseers and,
with the reduction of Workhouses, there was a corresponding
reduction in Workhouse Superintendents. Many of the Assistant
Overseers, however, were part-time workers, and the replacement
of several by one full-time officer did not necessarily lead to great
savings in expenditure. Again, a consolidated Workhouse programme, while leading to a smaller demand for Masters and
Matrons, still required a number of employees such as porters and
seamstresses. There was an increase rather than a decrease in
Workhouse capacity, although the actual number of Workhouses
was lessened, and overall employment was probably scarcely
altered. Nor did the appointment of Relieving Officers automatically sound the death-knell of the Overseers, the Assistant Overseers, the rate-collectors and the numerous other Parochial
Officers. There were, in 1849, seventeen in Ashton, eighteen in
Bolton, ten in Bury, twenty-two in Chorlton, and thirty-one in
Burnley. It has been remarked to what extent the Townships, and
thus their officers, carried on many of the duties, especially
financial, of the Poor Law. The Commissioners' 'separation of
duties' led, not to a reduction of officers, but logically enough, to
an augmenting of the numbers. It is scarcely an exaggeration to
claim that the Relieving Officers were not replacements but additions. Recollecting the employment of medical officers, registrars
and teachers, the conclusion must be that, in Lancashire, the
numbers of staff and the amount of salary expenditure both rose.
Alfred Power noticed 'the continuance in office of the old paid
officers' and admitted that the 'Relieving Officers have merely

been superadded to the Unions'. This was probably no more nor less than developments elsewhere. In 1846, when the Commissioners published records of officers by counties, one finds a total of 8,240 officers employed at a cost of £407,000. There was one officer to every 2,000 inhabitants, earning an average income of £50, or 6d. per head of population. In Lancashire the figures are slightly above the mean, with 1,005 officials paid £53,500 per year; that is, one officer to every 1,700 inhabitants, with an average income of £53, or 7d. per head of population.

This is a narrowly statistical conclusion. The Poor Law Commission promised to reduce the number of Civil Servants and the expenditure on them, and the reverse was true. Not only did Parochial government maintain its position, probably retaining officers who naturally do not figure in Union returns, but appointments and salaries grew considerably. What Oliver MacDonagh has called 'the momentum of government itself', or its natural tendency to procreate in its own image, had become quickly established in the New Poor Law. But it would be unfair to leave the matter simply as a broken promise or a vain hope. The broader question must be faced of whether or not this new bureaucracy increased the competence of the Poor Law. The answer quickly resolves itself into a discussion of the Relieving Officer. Other officials, of course, cannot be discounted, but they may be more rapidly disposed of. The Medical Officers, for instance, were doctors who merely extended their professional duties on a part-time basis; and the Guardians frequently paid them less than the Poor Law Commission, anxious to obtain sound medical services, would have wished. The quality of medical attention may be judged from the report to the Clitheroe Guardians in 1853 that, owing to his father's 'infirm health', the medical officer's unqualified son was cheerfully doing his rounds.

A more important officer in each Union was its Clerk, generally a local solicitor, who acted as general secretary to the Board. When, as so often happened, the Board was lax and irregular, the Clerk assumed a prominent position, handling the sometimes voluminous business of the Union with considerable independence. In the main, clerks carried much of the Guardians' burden of administration, and were lynchpins of Union administration. Needless to say, many of them had held a similar kind of office during the old dispensation, such as N. Gardiner, one time Director-Overseer of Manchester, who became Clerk to the newly formed Manchester

Union in 1841. Several also acted as Superintendent Registrar. The only other officers worthy of comment are the Workhouse Masters and Mistresses. One might guess that, with fewer Workhouses, the efficiency of the Masters and Matrons—invariably a married couple in each establishment—would rise through competition. The condition of Workhouses, however, remained notoriously poor, and the Workhouse Masters and Matrons seem to have lacked the character and quality to run their institutions efficiently. The Commissioners and the Guardians must accept much of the blame for bad Workhouse management, but few Workhouse Masters rose above a very ordinary level of competence. They were not well paid; they received no training; and, in practically every case, the incumbents of a retained Workhouse remained there after the coming of the New Poor Law. Some were unable to hold down their post even so. The Lancaster Guardians resolved to hale their Master before them 'that he obey the orders and directions of the Guardians in all respects'. He was later forced to resign in 1840. In 1841 John Slater was dismissed from his post as the Salford Workhouse Master because of an 'absence of courtesy'. Most of them worked unimaginatively and according to the definitive lines laid firmly down by their superiors. Some of the character of their labours will be evident in a later discussion of the Workhouse System.

The most important group were the Relieving Officers. Their functions were the making or breaking of the scheme: applications for relief were normally made to them; the necessary investigating and interviewing of cases was their responsibility; the decision as to treatment was chiefly theirs; the actual payment of relief when granted was their job; the keeping of the appropriate accounts was also part of their task; and, in many cases, they supervised the rate collection and other aspects of Township administration. At every turn of the New Poor Law's progress, the Relieving Officers were indispensable to its furtherance. They were a silent service, and their history has remained unsung, but of all the salaried experts of whom the Poor Law Commission boasted and in whom historians have seen precedents for our present-day governmental services, they had, by far, the greatest share in the everyday running of the New Poor Law Unions. One of the determining reasons for their import is a negative one. The Elective Board Principle had proved so decrepit in the county, that the onus for Poor Law management fell squarely on the Relieving Officers. Practically all the Boards did little except rubber-stamp the decisions and the accountancy of the Relieving Officers and it is difficult, on a reading of almost any of the Lancastrian Boards' minutes, not to conclude that these officials were the key-figures of the whole system.

The realities of the situation meant that they could only operate against the background of the continuing Township government. In some places, like Lancaster and Ormskirk, where the Parochial Officers maintained a high level of Poor Law activity, the Relieving Officers appear to have acted as checkers over these officials. In Wigan it was announced that the newly-engaged Relieving Officers and—as some of them were still called—Assistant Overseers 'shall forthwith assist the present Overseers'. The procedure was blatantly frank in the Bury Union. Ewbank, the Relieving Officer for Heap, was told to relieve the poor there and also in Ashworth, leaving Hopwood, Birtle and Pilsworth, ostensibly within his district, to fend for themselves. Relieving Officer Ramsbottom was told to relieve the poor in Bury and 'to attend upon the Overseer of Walmersley to see the poor paid there', leaving Tottingham Lower and Elton outside his sway. Pilkington's Relieving Officer, by name Lancashire, was ordered to leave Radcliffe and Ainsworth to their respective Overseers. It was a candid exhibition of legerdemain. The Bury Union was divided into three districts, but the three officers acted in only one or two Townships within that district, and the remainder carried on as before. The picture is complete when one discovers that Ewbank, Ramsbottom and Lancashire were, in fact, the late Assistant Overseers for Heap, Bury and Pilkington respectively. Power reported that 'in several Unions' the Guardians renewed the appointment of the old officers, as the rate-payers preferred the 'indulgence' of a native of their township. Sometimes—as in Burnley and Haslingden—Assistant Overseers and Relieving Officers remained one and the same. Although limited by the township pattern of rule, the Relieving Officer enjoyed considerable authority. One or two extracts from the Haslingden Minutes may serve as examples of what was fairly general practice. With little or no ado, it might, for instance, be passed 'that a check for £54 15s. 0d. be given to Charles Nuttall', the Relieving Officer for Haslingden and Henheads. It would seem to have been an arbitrary and haphazard procedure. Their influential authority is similarly self-evident from another favourite formula; to wit, 'the new applications for relief were reported by the respective Relieving Officers and were

D

decided upon by the Guardians'. Again remembering that a meeting of Guardians might possibly number but three or four, the
often complete reliance on the Relieving Officers is once more
underlined.

A picture slowly emerges of Relieving Officers doing the
donkey-work for each Union, with the Guardians merely keeping
a more or less watchful eye on them. Who exactly were these indispensable servants? Four of Manchester's seven officers were
Visiting Overseers in the old régime, or, as the Overseers themselves had prophesied, 'if we substitute Visiting Overseer for
Relieving Officer and Overseers for Guardians, the routine is the
same as has been in vogue in Manchester for more than a quarter
of a century'. The Assistant Overseers of Liverpool, E. Gray and
J. Evans, sailed smoothly through their city's vacillations between
Union and Vestry without a tremor. In desperate situations, the
Guardians did show their mettle, for John Newton was dismissed
by Ashton Union for 'gross neglect and inhuman conduct' in
causing the death of a two-year-old child, Noble Paget, in 1846.
Blackburn had three Relieving Officers, backed by eight salaried
Overseers employed 'for the purpose of collecting the rates and
performing the ordinary duties of overseer', and of these eight,
six were actually Guardians. Of Bolton's five Relieving Officers, at
least two were late Assistant Overseers, and both Clitheroe's
Relieving Officers were one time Assistant Overseers.

In 1846, the 82 Relieving Officers of Lancashire were paid
£8,000 annually, an average of less than £100 each. Considering
the extent, the clerical burden and the unpopularity of the duties
it was not an especially attractive proposition. The Webbs have
pointed out that no 'Device of the Prescribed Qualification' was
used by the Poor Law Commission, and no attempt was made to
train Poor Law staff or ensure an adequate standard of entry.[1]
The Poor Law Commission was not always in a position to enforce
its objections to individuals. It objected strongly to Samuel Ramsden becoming a Relieving Officer for Oldham on the grounds of
his misconduct when an Assistant Overseer in Manchester. The
Oldham Board merely said 'he will make a good Relieving Officer',
and there the case ended. A second instance concerned the death
of a Salford pauper, William Andrew, caused by 'a decline from
want of the necessities of life'. As with the Wrigley affair, this precipitated a full-scale enquiry and it involved the Home Secretary

[1] Webb, pp. 236–7.

as well as the Poor Law Commission. Despite grave doubts expressed both by the Home Office and Somerset House, the Relieving Officer, William Armitt, was merely cautioned. The testimony certainly points to a body of men, untrained and unqualified, selected to perform functions that, through the exigencies of the situation, were more important in practice than they had been propounded in theory. They were not, however, completely inexperienced. Indeed, the strongest impression gained of the Relieving Officers is their continuity with the old order. It is not always possible to judge the past histories of many of them from the Guardians' Minutes, but, over and over again, the purportedly new Relieving Officer was the Assistant Overseer with a fresh label. This might be expected, of course, for with no training establishments nor professional examinations, the Assistant Overseers were the only ones with the experience and, probably, the desire to participate in such work. Expected it might well be, but it does tend to mock a little at the much-vaunted idea of a salaried bunch of experts handling Poor Law matters.

Chadwick blamed his failure to get 'the administrative principle as set forth, acted upon' on the government's retention of the elective element. He felt that the Boards obstructed the efficiency of the paid officials. In a sense, however, the failings of the Boards in Lancashire left a wide vista of influence open to the so-called new officialdom. But this salaried staff was, in the main, the old guard redressed, and, in so far as administration is necessarily limited by the capacity of the administrators, it is not surprising to find the quality of Poor Law government remaining more or less constant. The Relieving Officers had a fair chance to make good, but they had neither the urge nor the wit to do so. Many of them, in fact, had common ground with the Guardians, in that they both represented the Old Poor Law and were frequently intent on sustaining its character. It was either a folly or a pretence to brand the old stewards of the Poor Law as experts and to assume that ignorant or corrupt local management had been replaced. It is surprising that Chadwick developed no scheme of training nor system of competitive entry for Union officials. Presumably it was felt that the pressure of Guardians and Assistant Commissioners would be enough to maintain a competent standard. However, the everyday managing of Poor Law affairs could barely be overseen to that extent, and, after all, the lowest levels of administration require a certain capacity for responsible action. Once more the

Poor Law foundered on the Parochial rock, while, at the same
time, the Union was too small to inaugurate training schemes, in
the way that a county or national organism might have attempted.
In Lancashire at least the early years of the New Poor Law reveal
the boasted use of expertise as little more than a myth.

Centralisation and inspection
The most important contribution of the New Poor Law to
British administrative history was the creation of a central authority. In 1833 England had one of the smallest state bureaucracies in
Europe. In 1854 no nation 'intervened so decisively' in the affairs
of its inhabitants. The construction of the Poor Law Commission
was one of the first and most extensive steps in this process, and
yet, in a sense, it was an inadvertent development. David Roberts
has written 'certainly neither central inspection nor the regulation of commerce were strange to the English in 1833. Quite the
contrary, they were known only too well, and for that reason
deeply hated.'[1] None the less, while the clime of English thinking
was as individualist as it has ever been and with practically all
political groups opposed, for one reason or another, to centralisation, the Poor Law Commission was built. There was thus an
abiding suspicion of the central board and obstructionist tactics
were often adopted towards it. Some of these have already been
observed, in Lancashire, and they were to continue many years.
The unreceptive and unenthusiastic welcome accorded the Poor
Law Commission's brief in the county is the first feature of any
consideration of the effect of one upon the other. The impact of
the central board upon Lancashire must be seen against the canvas
already painted of querulous Guardians and unimpressive officials.
This is particularly meaningful because of the new idea of an
hierarchy. The major innovation was the establishment of a direct
link between central power and its local operation by elected
boards. The dichotomy of central department and local department formed Chadwick's tutelle. It was a marriage of state dis-
interest and provincial self-interest which was intended to produce
social equipoise and solidity. And having noted some ways in
which the one side of the equation had fallen short of its requirements, the great difficulties of the other side may be visualised.
The fact that the newly growing self-satisfied towns of industrial Lancashire were energetically in the van of opposition to

[1] Roberts, op. cit., p. 315.

centralisation only adds piquancy to the point. Indeed, in the case of Liverpool, one finds a vivid example of completely triumphant objection.

Besides a somewhat unwilling and incapable partner, the poor Law Commission had troubles and weaknesses purely its own. Its inner dissensions apart, the Commission was enfeebled by its lack of potency. There was, in fact, insufficient centralisation, for, despite many wide-ranging powers, the Commission could not, for instance, coerce the unions into raising rates to build Workhouses, and, without this, the Workhouse Test was doomed to failure. The central board could make the local Guardians initiate nothing. As late as 1909, the Royal Commission on the Poor Law, speaking of the Central department, concluded that 'its powers of initiation' were small and that apropos the Guardians, it was powerless to force them to act. The Poor Law Commission was never intended to be authoritarian in the extreme. Ideally, it did not halt but reform local government. Beginning in theory with no more than compromise powers, it had its teeth further drawn in the face of opposition and frustration. When 'the bureaucratic formalism' of the Poor Law Board replaced the Commission, much more of the sting was removed. The more uncompromising and embattled Poor Law Commission faded into the mechanically formalistic Poor Law Board, and, it must be emphasised, many parts of Lancashire saw little of the New Poor Law until the declining years of the Commission. 'The central authority', wrote Rhodes Boyson, 'was prepared to wait until the agitation against the New Poor Law had lessened, before compelling the Guardians to administer relief', according to the Commission's wishes.[1] Having waited thus long, the central authority found the complexion of the problem changed, in terms of increased prosperity, a reaction against centrifugal forces, and so on. In brief, the influence of the state department is in direct proportion to that of the local authorities. Having noted the tenacious manner in which localism retained its sway in the Poor Law, the reverse must follow; to wit, the power of the central authority was correspondingly weaker.

To place the ideal of centralisation in its proper perspective, it is only just to add a reminder that the New Poor Law was not a piece of Collectivist legislation. It was not an attempt to widen the scope on intervention into the individual's life. The fallacy of

[1] Boyson, op. cit., p. 35.

automatically confusing centralisation with overgovernment has several times been underlined, and the New Poor Law was a case in point. A scheme of Poor Relief, operated by a form of public authority, already existed; this was an effort to make it more efficacious; it was not an expansion of public authority, rather was it a centripetal shift in the nature of public authority. There was even a possibility, as its protagonists were quick to demonstrate, that the New Poor Law, precisely because it clarified a messy, chaotic pattern, would reduce the actual sum of governmental interference. There is, in short, no reason to suppose that the population of Lancashire had their civic privacy much more disturbed by the New than the Old Poor Law. Where, perhaps, the Poor Law Commissioners erred was in making a fetish of uniformity. They attempted to impose a rigid blueprint on the entire country, and, as the opposition in Lancashire exhibited, they normally refused to consider local characteristics and idiosyncrasies. They, in turn, herein failed to find a balance in the tricky relationship between local and national authority.

The main instruments employed by the central body to make its presence felt locally may be tidily summarised as visits from the Assistant Commissioner and a flow of regulations from Somerset House. It was typical of Victorian times and typical of Chadwick that a voluminous correspondence of an earnest, solemn and verbose variety was religiously maintained. The amount of paperwork undertaken by Somerset House, the Assistant Commissioners and, to a lesser extent, the Clerks to the Unions reached fantastic proportions, as the welter of reports, records, schedules and data was scrupulously compiled. It is to the credit of Somerset House that they maintained a first rate level of office management, and, judging from the Minutes of the Boards, it is rarely that their reply to a given letter misses the next weekly meeting. The ferreting out of information was as unabashed as it was detailed. The Lancashire Unions received, for instance, a communication in 1838 'requiring information of the name and age of any pauper afflicted with stone in the bladder'. This massive documentation heralded the coming age of government by clerks and forms. The Gradgrind-like hunger of Chadwick and his minions for facts is in itself characteristic of the new scientific statistical approach to administration. The officials of the Lancashire Unions, along with their confrères throughout the country, were perpetually called upon to furnish tables and returns to the Poor Law Commission, just as, in return, the Commission flooded the Unions with one set of regulations after another. Obviously a surfeit of mail could not possibly keep the Unions on the straight and narrow path, and, therefore, the much more significant development of inspection took place. In the whole of Lancashire, excepting Ulverstone, and for the West Riding of Yorkshire, it was Alfred Power and later Charles Mott who made the regular visits from Manchester.

In the eighteen-thirties the precedent of inspection was being made elsewhere—the new Factory Inspectors served as one example. It is now an accepted part of public life that each sphere of civic service has its set of itinerant overlookers, who examine and test it against the prescribed standards. It was much less the norm when Power travelled about Lancashire and Yorkshire, forming Unions and then following up with visits of inspection. In 1841 the twelve Assistant Commissioners were issued with precise instructions. Special enquiries apart, they were told to attend meetings of the Boards of Guardians 'not less frequently than twice in each year' and that they 'should not on any account omit to visit the Workhouse of each Union once in six months'. They had also to take averages and 'collect and diffuse information'. It meant that each Assistant Commissioner had about fifty Unions to supervise, and such an extensive task meant that they were reduced to stand-bys for emergencies and referees for conflicts. The twelve districts were soon reduced to ten, and with unreliable communications, the Assistant Commissioners, like the Factory Inspectors, had a superhuman task to perform. Nor was Chadwick's desire to form an audit system realised. One of the main features of inspection was obviously a check on finance, but Chadwick's plan for district auditors was slow to reach fruition. Each Union had its accounts audited, either by a departmental or by a Board nominee, but it was largely an arithmetical device. It was merely a confirmation of calculations entered, as opposed to a hounding out of illegal charges and the like. The Assistant Commissioners, or, as they were later called, Inspectors, supervised this audit, but it was not until 1868, following the passage of the Union Chargeability Act in 1865, that audit districts were finally completed and the District Auditors came under the full control of the Poor Law Board.

A full account of Power's travels may be found in his own letters to the Poor Law Commission. His quarterly returns cover the fifteen months from the autumn of 1837 to the end of 1838,

during which period he made 134 visits to the twenty-two Lancashire Unions under his control. The incidence of these visits was
most irregular. Eighteen were to Todmorden, ten each to West
Derby and Burnley, and nine each to Preston, Rochdale and
Prescot. Bury had but two visits; Ormskirk, Ashton and Bolton one
each, and Oldham none at all. The visits were also very bunched,
doubtless due to supervising the inauguration of new Unions or
conducting special enquiries in others. Todmorden's difficulties, for
example, probably explain the ten visits in one quarter, followed by
eight in the next. It would appear that all Unions, with the exception of West Derby and Blackburn, went at least six months
without inspection during this time, and not one Union was
visited in each of the five quarters. Power had as many Unions
again in Yorkshire to supervise, and he proved an assiduous and
courageous proponent of the New Poor Law. None the less, his
erratic progress, although not chiefly his fault, makes clear the
unsatisfactory nature of inspection in those early years.[1]

Sample studies of the Poor Law Commission's extensive
archives reveal few signs of strong and masterful influence.
Correspondence from and to the Unions was usually formal.
Clitheroe was an average sort of Union, and its communications
with the central authority were dull, repetitious and uneventful in
the extreme. Normally some three dozen items of correspondence
were sent to and from the Poor Law Commission or Board annually, often including a demand for a return, the return and an
acknowledgement. Sometimes, as in 1847, the number reached as
many as seventy-seven, while, in 1841, it was no more than thirteen. The exception seems to prove the rule. About the only unorthodox letter was a direct approach to the Commissioners by a
hawker, William Martin, who related a long tale of the misfortunes
of his sick wife, his five small children and himself, and of the
Guardians' refusal to assist him. All the Commissioners could do
was admit frankly their complete lack of powers to interfere.
Little wonder that, in 1855, H. B. Farnall, an Assistant Poor Law
Inspector, told the Clitheroe Guardians that they were 'wholly un-
fettered' and 'entirely masters of your position'.[2]

It is difficult to gauge the overall effect of centralisation and
inspection in Lancashire. Intangibles, like the personal relations

[1] Power-P.L.C., 1838–1840, P.R.O. M.H. 32/64.
[2] Clitheroe Poor Law Correspondence 1834–56, P.R.O. M.H. 12/5752;
12/5753; 12/5754 and 12/5755.

of Power and Mott with Guardians and officials or the psychological impress of a newfangled department and its inspectors, are
too numerous. It would, of course, be foolish to suggest that the
impact of state intervention on Lancashire's Poor Law was anything but a substantial one. At the same time, Poor Law administration is strictly a matter of humdrum, day-to-day cases and accounts.
Given a service which was, of necessity, widespread in area and
erratic in action, it is difficult to believe that the influence of this
'provincial prolongation of the Board's secretariat' could have
been as profound as Chadwick might have wished.

Work of the Unions
The remaining sub-section inspects the techniques employed by
this combine of Guardians, officials and Inspectors, to realise the
aims of the Poor Law Commission. They attempted to reduce
pauperdom by the Principle of Less-Eligibility, which entailed
reducing Outdoor Relief and making the Workhouse System
function properly, and by financial stringency in general.
    a. Outdoor Relief. Although some felt that all Outdoor Relief
should end, it was not interrupted, and, indeed, the prohibition of
Outdoor Relief, never completely obtained, tended to slacken as
the years drew on. In the northern industrial areas an embargo on
Outdoor Relief was impracticable, for the stresses of an industrial
economy affected large numbers at a time, and Workhouses,
spacious enough to accommodate massive outbreaks of temporary
distress, would have lain empty for months on end during periods
of prosperity. Of the seven North-Eastern Unions, only Blackburn
and Bolton tried a Workhouse Test, and they soon abandoned it,
so that their Workhouses were 'largely voluntary almshouses for
the sick and aged'. One or two other Unions attempted the Outdoor Labour Test, notably Chorlton, which at all times was more
favourably inclined towards the New Poor Law than most Lancastrian Unions. In the early forties, fifteen acres of Chat Moss
were cultivated by husbandry. J. Latham, Clerk to the Guardians,
spoke of 'a successful undertaking' that 'deters the idle and worth-
less'. Over two years, the cost, on balance, was but £176, and the
'hundreds of idle persons deterred' helped the Relieving Officer,
Watkinson, to ply his trade for a populace of 93,000 without undue
difficulty. Mott recommended the scheme to all manufacturing
areas.
    Two towns, Rochdale and Bolton, were particularly troublesome

to the Poor Law Commission. In October 1841, Assistant Commissioner Tufnell reported on distress in the former. While admitting that affairs were not as bad as in the south, he pointed out that 'the germ of abuse' of the Allowance System was evident. In 1846, Mott made a report on the Macclesfield and Bolton Unions. He gathered much incriminating testimony concerning the relief of Bolton's poor. The Clerk, J. Woodhouse, and a Relieving Officer, B. Brown, admitted that, with so many manufacturers among the Guardians and with insufficient Workhouse accommodation, there was extensive relief based on insufficient earnings. Woodhouse, saddened by 'the impropriety of yielding indiscriminate relief', claimed that Guardians visited the unemployed telling them to apply for relief. R. Haslam, another Relieving Officer, resigned because he was ordered to ask men if they wanted relief, and Brown felt that a sounder Workhouse Test could reduce the rates by one third. There is, in fact, the hint here that Bolton never operated an Allowance System until after the coming of the New Poor Law.

Irish immigrants, as well as other vagrants, aggravated the problem. The *13th Annual Report* of the Poor Law Commission in 1847 recorded 80,000 Irish in Liverpool alone. By switching from central to district relief, the Liverpool authorities managed to lower cases relieved from as many as 25,000 a week to a figure between 4,000 and 10,000 a week. In the first quarter of 1847, 144,000 Irish landed in Liverpool, and only 16,000 moved on to the United States and Canada. Despite the unwearied exertions of the Liverpool Vestry, mortality amongst the pauper Irish sprang from seventy-nine in April 1846 to 586 in April 1847. The figures of Irish cases relieved in other parts of the country reflect the tragic impact of the Irish Potato Famine, and the figures for rural Unions, like the Fylde and Garstang, or for smaller Unions, like Prescot and Rochdale, are particularly notable. Manchester, like Liverpool, tried to deal competently with 'the influx of Irish', and some of them were given work in the stone-yards. All in all, the peculiar social and economic issues of Lancashire, coupled with the attitudes of the Poor Law authorities and the people at large, militated against any halting of Outdoor Relief. The Cotton Famine of the eighteen-sixties was to be but the most impressive example of the fact that, when distress hits a manufacturing area, it hits it hard and extensively. In such circumstances, talk of a free labour mart became irrelevant.

The fruits of this policy may be investigated in the successive reports of the Poor Law Commission and the Poor Law Board. For the quarter ending Lady Day 1839, Lancashire had 18,195 out-paupers, the highest figure in the country. For the same quarter in 1840, 21,263 were on out-relief, out of a national total of 121,852. Yorkshire was the only other county to pass the 7,000 mark. Throughout the forties, the number of Lancashire paupers fluctuate violently, but they never fall below a level of about five per cent of the population. Nor do any great inroads appear to have been made in the number of paupers on outdoor relief. For the year ending March 1842 and 1843 the respective figures of paupers in and out of Workhouses were 6,000 to 60,000 and 8,000 to 80,000 approximately. Many of these paupers, of course, were aged, infirm, juvenile and sick. The quarter ending Lady Day 1845 offers a normal pattern of 81,000 relieved in Lancashire, of whom 24,000 were able-bodied. Only 2,000 of the 8,000 Workhouse residents in this period were drawn from the able-bodied group. The Workhouses, therefore, catered for but one-twelfth of the able-bodied poor, as opposed to one-ninth of the remainder. Yet very rarely does Lancashire appear in such a bad light with regard to pauperism as the nation in general. Apart from one or two occasions— notably with regard to able-bodied out-paupers—Lancashire was always well above the national mean, sometimes two or even three times above. Although pauperdom remains a definite issue in Lancashire and although little headway appears to have been made in connection with outdoor relief, the picture looks almost rosy compared with other parts of England and Wales.

Per head of population, Lancashire certainly had less total paupers and less able-bodied paupers than the rest of the country, and, indeed, the Poor Law Commission had forlornly admitted in 1839 that 'four-fifths of the money now expended on relief is still out-door relief'. It had never been suggested, of course, that the problem was as acute in the northern as in the southern counties. However, by the mid-forties, extravagant claims were being made for the New Poor Law in the south, and it was Lancashire and the West Riding that were held in scorn by the Poor Law Commission for their refusal to co-operate and for all the apparent obstacles to the operation of the Poor Law Amendment Act.

The eighteen-fifties saw no radical alteration in this pattern, although there was a happy slackening in the numbers of paupers as a whole. In 1854, on New Year's Day, there were 60,745 paupers on out-relief and 11,702 on in-relief in Lancashire, and of these the able-bodied numbered 11,493 and 1,490 respectively. At this time one eighth of the nation's paupers and one seventh of Lancashire's paupers were indoor, and one seventh of the nations able-bodied paupers and one ninth of Lancashire's able-bodied paupers were indoor. In brief, Lancashire was drawing on a par with the rest of England and Wales. The overall totals favour Lancashire once more in 1854, and the following percentages of paupers to populations indicate this:—

	Lancs.	England and Wales
Indoor	2·2	2·8
Outdoor	4·5	9·25
	6·7	12·05

In 1869, the Poor Law Board felt that 'relief in aid of wages is given to a greater extent in Lancashire than in any other county'. In so far as this may be true, then the wheel had indeed turned full circle. By 1860, however, the picture is one of a county which has maintained a reasonably steady pattern of indoor and outdoor relief, with the New Poor Law having few general effects. Moreover, the pattern, despite Lancashire's special characteristics, seems scarcely out of true with that of the nation at large.

   b. *The Workhouse System.* The maintained strength of Outdoor Relief finds its converse in the defects of Workhouse accommodation. Workhouse administration was a bone of contention amongst the Poor Law Reformers. Chadwick and Nassau Senior favoured a group of four specialist houses in each Union, but, 'the Poor Law Commission found themselves convinced that the Assistant Commissioners were right' in wanting a single Union house. The difficulties of distributing a whole family to varied establishments or obtaining sufficient inmates and specialists to justify them were pointed out to the Commission, whilst the economic effects of 'well-arranged and sufficient Workhouses' were underlined. Unfortunately, the classificatory system failed disastrously within most of these Union houses, partly because the Union populations were often too small, and the General Mixed Workhouse ineluctably rose again 'as the localised dump-heap for all kinds of destitute persons'.

   Lancashire had, said the Poor Law Commission in 1837, always felt 'a general feeling of the necessity of resort to some Workhouse

establishment', and, Todmorden apart, all the Unions in the
country had several Workhouses at their disposal. One of the first
tasks of the newly appointed Guardians was to conduct surveys of
the available Workhouse accommodation. Sometimes the reports
of the Workhouse sub-committees are included in the Board
minutes, and they leave little doubt that, however bestial and
horrible the Union Workhouses were to become, Oliver Twist
would have been little better off in a pre-Union establishment. Of
Bury's seven Workhouses, six were acceptable to Gregg, the investigating Guardian, but Hopwood Workhouse was 'a filthy,
miserable, discreditable place', and it had been reported earlier
that 'the Governor had no control over some parts of the Workhouse, and that in that part the inmates were abusive in their
language and turbulent in their dispositions'. At Rochdale the
Butterworth Workhouse had its bedrooms 'open to the roof' but
the committee felt 'compelled to recommend the continuance'. At
Spotland Workhouse, idiots slept in the dayrooms so that 'their
dirty and offensive habits at night cause quite an unpleasant smell
in these rooms throughout the day'. The Leigh Guardians were
remarkably well-pleased with their Workhouses, although the
reported diet appears unappetisingly monotonous—one pint to one
quart of porridge and wheaten bread for breakfast; bacon and
potatoes or lobscouse or pea soup for dinner; meal porridge and
buttermilk for supper. Clitheroe's visiting committee to Holden
Workhouse 'found the Houses and inmates generally in a very
filthy state and in our opinion the establishment is under very bad
discipline', with the bedding 'horribly infected with vermin' and
the bedrooms 'quite nauseous'. A lengthy report was submitted to
the Lancaster Guardians in 1840. The Lancaster Workhouse had
four 'damp and badly ventilated storeys', with 'a dark cell for
refractory inmates' and with 'the accumulated dust and filth of
the whole house' swept down through gratings and piled high in
the bottom corridor. Twenty-eight and often more old women
were assembled in the largest day room which was but 28 feet by
15 feet, while the only men's room was 20 feet by 15 feet. The
210 inmates subsisted on dreary dinners of potato stew on four
days, offal on two days, and meat on Sundays. The bathroom 'is
never used excepting under medical directions', and the attics
contain twenty beds apiece with 'at least two occupants'. They
found the 'common privies' or cesspools in 'an abominable state',
and fourteen children had died the previous month. Finally, 'one

of the outbuildings is occupied as a sleeping apartment for a few infirm old men'.

It was, in the main, Workhouses like these that were taken over by the Lancashire Guardians in order to carry out the New Poor Law. The immediate reaction of the Unions was to trim the existing Workhouse situation, rather than to embark on heavy capital expenditure. Wigan retained 3 Workhouses to serve 3 separate areas, Rochdale kept 4 out of 7 Workhouses; Preston kept 6—later 4—of its 9 Workhouses; Oldham 4 from 6, Chorley 2 from 5, and so on. It is unlikely that such Workhouses could show much improvement, particularly with an eagle eye on finances and all provisions contracted by cheapest tender. Even Charles Mott was constrained to complain of the 'inefficient state' of the Chorley and Leyland Workhouses, and, in the former, he discovered 20 women and 30 children in 14 beds in a room 28 feet × 24 feet. Again, Clitheroe retained only two Workhouses, when the Commission wanted them to use three for classification purposes, and the Clitheroe Workhouse system was still judged inadequate in 1856.

Not all the Unions failed to achieve Workhouse efficiency. Many of these inherited a fairly competent administration which was easily adaptable to the Commission's requirements. Manchester is perhaps the clearest example of this, for all admissions had to be on a written order, classification was followed rigidly, rules concerning diet and refractory inmates were adhered to strictly, visiting regulations were harsh and well-kept, and all paupers were inspected half-an-hour after rising. The retiring Board in 1841 were of the opinion that the New Poor Law 'is calculated to induce greater vigilance and watchfulness over the Workhouse, the officers and the expenditure of the public money, and that the comforts of the poor are likely to be much better attended to under its operation'. Despite the vigilant efficiency of the Workhouse in Manchester, there was a total of 756 deaths in the 107 weeks beginning December 1842. Barton, like Manchester, operated their Workhouse strictly, once they had overcome their difficulties with the Barton Parochial authorities. They classified rigidly and were in constant consultation with the Poor Law Board and with the Assistant Poor Law Commissioner, Austin.

On the whole, nevertheless, the first response of the Lancashire Unions was to make use of their often decrepit heritage of Workhouses. The streamlining of the Workhouse System by a scheme of closures meant, obviously enough, a reduction in accommodation. Coming at a time when pressure was supposed to be placed against out-door paupers, this seems paradoxical. It could scarcely have been believed that the very threat of the Workhouse Test would end pauperdom, both indoor and outdoor, overnight. Even on the Poor Law Commission's own premises, it would have been sensible to expect at best, a slight and temporary increase of Workhouse inmates, as the abolition of Out-door Relief was attempted. The reduction of the old Workhouses was due to an enthusiasm for administrative neatness and to an interest in cutting down expense. 'Very few will ultimately find it desirable to retain more than one establishment,' announced the Poor Law Commission, in 1839. Frequently closures were necessary because Workhouses were so tumbledown or useless that no other course was open to the Guardians. There were also several areas in which the accommodation was much too extensive. In 1836, for instance, 270 inmates shared room enough for 1,582 in the Ulverstone Union. And yet, in 1847, the Chorlton, Manchester, Wigan and West Derby Workhouses were reported full, and, in 1848, there were no vacancies at Ashton, Chorlton, Preston, Wigan, West Derby and Warrington. Nor was there any restriction on out-door relief in these areas at this time. Both in terms of classification and for the economic utilisation of accommodation, the need for which varied so considerably, a much larger area of administration, such as the county, was required.

The evolution towards a unitary Workhouse System in Lancashire was a muddled venture. The decrease in the number of Workhouses within a Union was an avowedly disastrous development. Although, on the surface, a Union could claim its own one or two Union Workhouses, there was no gainsaying the limitations placed on the New Poor Law by the sheer fabric of such institutions. Bricks and mortar can often, like people, make mockery of the intentions of legislators, and many of the Lancashire Workhouses were either too antiquated or too unsuited to the needs of the New Poor Law. Slowly, a second wave of response can be seen to emerge, as, doubtless urged on by the central authorities and by their own Victorian pride in erecting civic and institutional symbols, the Guardians decide to build new Union Workhouses. The limiting factor in Workhouse construction had been a legal one. The Poor Law Commission was permitted to order alterations or enlargements, and in 1841, the Manchester Assurance Company

had advanced the City's Guardians £11,000 for just such a purpose. In each Annual Report of the Commission, a list is included
of Unions so commanded; Fylde, Ormskirk and Burnley are mentioned, for example, in 1839. New Workhouses, however, could
only be constructed with the consent of the Guardians and the
rate-payers, and, needless to say, it was several years before
suspicions of the New Poor Law had sufficiently died in Lancashire to bring this about. By then the necessity for the large Workhouse had either vanished in some areas, or increasingly, distress
was the consequence of large-scale fluctuations which could throw
whole communities on relief.

Few Unions erected new Workhouses during the lifetime of the
Poor Law Commission. Manchester, Lancaster, Liverpool, Chorlton and West Derby began building in the eighteen-forties, but it
was well into the fifties and even the sixties before most Boards
were under way. Ashton's £12,000 Workhouse was opened in
1850, and, in the same year, Warrington and Leigh were granted
£7,050 and £7,000 respectively for Workhouses of a capacity of
some three hundred. In 1855, the Poor Law Board reported that
Chorlton and Bury had opened new Workhouses, and that Bolton,
Manchester, Blackburn and Wigan were engaged on them. At the
same time, it was 'greatly to be regretted' that Rochdale, Burnley,
Haslingden, Chorley, Todmorden, Clitheroe and Garstang were
not involved in any such enterprise. Later in 1855 Clitheroe did
decide to build a Workhouse, costing £4,500, for 300 inmates. A
startling feature of the new Union institutions was the high sums
expended upon them. In 1842, Manchester's Guardians decided
to build a Workhouse for 1,500 people at Peak's Farm, Swinton.
The cost was to be £25,000, but successive additions of nearly
£20,000 had to be made before it was completed, and, in 1846, no
less than £46,000 was granted for the enlargement and adaptation
of the existing Poorhouse. The Liverpool Vestry wished to construct a Workhouse capable of housing 1,800 paupers. Its initial
cost was £20,000 in 1842, but, once more, further loans of £2,950,
£3,632 and £5,000 were soon needed. The money was usually
found by the Exchequer Loan Bill Commissioners, and rising
building expenses, coupled, perhaps, with the local politicians'
wish to cut a dash, added heavy interest burdens to the Poor Rate.
Preston's story is typical of most Lancashire Unions. Following
desultory closures, enlargements and controversy, it was decided
to supplant all Workhouses, save Ribchester which was to be set

apart for imbeciles, with one large Workhouse. It was opened in
1868, and it could take in 1,500 paupers. By 1870, the loan charges
against it stood at £87,761.

The creation of a Workhouse System in Lancashire largely
proved to be a fiasco. No one seems to have decided which was the
cart and which the horse. Should Outdoor Relief be prohibited
before an adequate and classified system of Union Workhouses had
been constructed, or vice versa? One must conclude that Lancashire essayed hardly one step towards an embargo on out-main-
tenance, and that her efforts to reform in-maintenance were half-
hearted and later expensive. It is important once more to recollect
that humane feeling was not the strong point of the Victorian
middle classes, that their social outlook was a rough approximation
to *laissez-faire* and that to delve into their pockets for public funds
was anathema to them. Frankly, they were opposed to paupers, and
regarded them, indoor or outdoor, as nuisances and criminals—
they wished to offer the paupers neither subsistence at home nor
hospitality in the Workhouses. Caught up in the vortex of industrial poverty—a stark problem that could not be ignored—the
Lancashire Guardians dithered, uncertainly and dismally, between
the two types of treatment. The Workhouse Test and Outdoor
Relief were, none the less, mutually exclusive. The logic of the
theory and the logic of the circumstances made it impossible to try
both and arrive at Chadwick's goal. Unwittingly, the Lancashire
Poor Law authorities were forced, by the social conditions of the
area and by their own predilections, to continue both modes of
treatment. They inherited a dual system of Poorhouse relief and
residential doles, and, in general, the net result of their work was
to perpetuate this dualism. Some abuses and discrepancies were
doubtless ironed out of the relief mechanisms, but the provision of
outdoor maintenance remained at a similar kind of level. By the
eighteen-sixties, many Unions had replaced small and ill-con-
structed Workhouses by larger single units. These, by 1870, were
often run on stricter, cleaner lines than hitherto, but their functions
had changed only slightly. Without much classification and without
the stress upon them of prohibited Outdoor Relief, they were
'hidious agglomerations' and little more. The large-scale projects for
building Union Workhouses were, in practice, a mere renewal of
dilapidated and uneconomic premises. The paupers in the Union
institutions were precisely the same mixture and variety as before,
and, purely in numerical terms, accommodation was probably not

E

much more extensive. Lancashire's distressed were provided with
a haphazard and arbitrary selection of Workhouses and Outdoor
allowances in the thirty or so years after the passing of the Poor
Law Amendment Act. Those who had the misfortune to suffer
under both dispensations might have found it difficult to describe
the differences between the old and the new.

   c. The Financial Issue. On their own admission, the acid test for
the Poor Law Commission was ultimately financial. The general
aim of the Poor Law Amendment Act was to reduce the heavy
burden of the Poor Rate. It is certain that the New Poor Law,
whatever its other defects, improved upon the old régime in respect
of financial controls. The mechanics of audit were gradually introduced; the Guardians maintained some checks on the weekly
expenditure of their Unions; and the central authority was unend-
ing in its demands for carefully compiled statistics. The accounting
techniques of Poor Law management were slowly over-hauled,
but these could not be expected to lower the rates substantially.
It is evident that Lancashire fared much more cheaply than the
remainder of the country. Indeed, every year, Lancashire had the
lowest expense per head of any county. In 1834, she was 1*s.* 4*d.*
behind Cumberland's next lowest of 5*s.* 1*d.* Ten years later Cumberland still came next in the list, but the gap had narrowed to one
penny. In 1843 Sussex had a *per capita* rate of 8*s.* 1*d.*, while, in 1844,
Wiltshire had the unlucky distinction of the highest rate with
10*s.* 6*d.* per person. In 1832, when the nation's poor rate topped
seven million pounds, Lancashire expended 4*s.* 6*d.* per head—the
nearest England and Wales came to this figure was the 5*s.* 6*d.* of
1853. These figures lend evidence to the argument that Lancashire
was in no dire need for the New Poor Law. The black years of 1847
and 1848 apart, Lancashire's Poor Rate hovered around the four
shillings mark, both before and after the introduction of the
reformed Poor Law. The national figures were drastically reduced
from the nine or ten shillings of the early thirties, but they were
never to drop much lower than six shillings. Ironically enough,
Lancashire's most propitious totals were in the late thirties, when
much of the country was supposedly benefiting from the New
Poor Law and when Lancashire was annoying the Poor Law Commissioners by its stalwart opposition. In the March of 1837, just
as Power was carving Lancashire into Unions, it was calculated
that, in the previous year, the *per capita* rate had fallen as low as
2*s.* 9*d.* It would not be impossible to argue a case for Lancashire's

poor bill rising in the late forties and early fifties, exactly at the time the New Poor Law was purportedly taking effect. This would, however, be leaning too enthusiastically on statistics, and other factors must not be precluded. Generally speaking, poverty failed to subject itself to Chadwick's arithmetical laws—the most that can be said of Lancashire's Poor Law expenditure is that, although it varied from 2s. 9d. in 1837 to 6s. 11d. in 1848, it maintained a steadily constant level throughout most of the twenty-three years under review. In other words, what variations exist are explicable in terms of differing economic and social conditions. The financial consequences of a changed system appear to have been, on the whole, negligible. Poverty, unemployment and distress demanded treatment, whether from Overseers or Guardians, and a novel form of administration was no guarantee of more prosperous days for the workers of Lancashire. Just as many commentators have demonstrated that the fall in the national rate was due to other forces apart from the New Poor Law, so would it be dangerous to blame a rise in the Lancastrian figures solely on the amended organisation. The Poor Law Commission's reports were not always fair to Lancashire. The Secretary and the Assistant Commissioners were keen, if honourable, men, and although they probably distorted the figures but rarely, they were not averse to mapping the correct numbers into partisan patterns. Although Lancashire's Unions were slow to gain control over the managing of Poor Relief, the usually healthy Lancashire figures helped to lower the national averages and reflect glory upon the executors of the reformed law, despite their attacks on the obdurate northerners.

An interesting minor illustration of this phenomenon occurs in a list, published in 1837, showing what decreases had been achieved by the New Poor Law. Non-unionised Lancashire was contemptuously relegated to thirty-fourth out of the forty-two county areas, for her decrease from 1834 was only 27 per cent. Sussex, where the innovations were in full flower, stood triumphantly at the head of the list, having dropped 53 per cent since 1834. A rapid calculation helps to dispel a misleading picture, for whereas Lancashire's *per capita* rate had fallen from 3s. 4d. to 2s. 9d. that of Sussex had been reduced from 18s. to a little short of 9s.

The financial angle on Lancashire's Poor Relief programme illustrates convincingly the dictum that the New Poor Law, whatever its proud boasts, was a system of treatment rather than of prevention. Possibly more so than elsewhere in England, distress in Lancashire, occurring so frequently in the manufacturing districts, was never touched at its roots. Like the Old Poor Law before it, the Whig revision of 1834 quickly became little more than the abatement of the nuisance of destitution. That it was sometimes done more clinically or more harshly cannot affect the basic truth of this.

Summary

It would be folly to pretend that this account is an exhaustive study of the Poor Law in Lancashire. Its purpose was to glance cursorily over a broad field in an attempt to detect trends in the development of a major social service in an important region. We have scriptural recognition of the permanence of the poor, and yet, when the fabric of a society is altered, the problem of poverty takes on a slightly novel colour. The coming of industrialism and urbanisation to Lancashire at the time of the Industrial Revolution was such a change, and it demanded a new response to reckon with the spectre of industrial distress. The Poor Law Amendment Act of 1834, hailed both then and now as an epoch-making and drastic piece of legislation, hardly provided this answer for Lancashire.

Minor reasons and minor conclusions have been noted along the way. Most of them point towards the generalisation that Lancashire was fundamentally untouched by the New Poor Law during the thirty years following its inauguration. The superficial trappings of Unions, Guardians and Relieving Officers were introduced, but the bases remained largely as before. Many forces interplayed to bring about this consummation, but two truisms are of outstanding significance. Firstly, the Old Law in Lancashire was not unlike the Commission's model version. Many Townships had competent Vestry government and many of them employed salaried officials. They were not, of course, subject to central inspection, but they managed, along with schemes of out-relief, a series of Workhouses, and the Poor Rate was lower than the Poor Law Commission ever achieved. Secondly, the New Poor Law in Lancashire did not aspire to the Commission's model version. The Townships continued to play a prominent rôle in Union affairs, the Guardians tended to be the same types, if not always the same faces, as the late Overseers; whilst the new salaried officers were frequently the late employees with a different label. Central intervention did not disturb the tenor of Lancashire's ways unduly, for it was too intermittent and frail, and the dichotomy of outdoor and indoor maintenance continued. The monetary load on Lancashire's rate-payers certainly remained steady, and, if anything, it increased. Unionisation, inspectoral and accounting procedures, and other administrative devices helped to clarify and purify the system, but, all in all, the more Lancashire's Poor Law changed, the more it stayed the same. On examination, the gap between the pre-1834 and the post-1834 Poor Relief service closes considerably, and, in the mundane passage of everyday Poor Law affairs, it is difficult to visualise any startling changes of officer, pauper or rate-payer.

Lancashire rode out the dogmatic and vigorous reign of the Poor Law Commission without undue alteration, and, after 1854, the centralising proclivities that had existed since 1834 gave way to an era of localism. It would appear that the pattern of Union management and Workhouse construction did not crystallise until the eighteen-sixties, nor did the partnership between local and central boards become effectively close before then. It was 1868 when the ordering of the Poor Law audit organisation was completed, and it was 1865 when the Union Chargeability Act made the Union area the proper ambit for revenue and expenditure and for settlement. On the face of it one might be permitted to guess that the New Poor Law in Lancashire only reached full stature as the prevailing mood of the country swung towards the Collectivist tendencies of Gladstone's Liberals. Certainly it must be concluded that Chadwick's so-called tutelary governance, in so far as it applied to the Poor Law, had an indifferent welcome in Lancashire.

The continuum between old and new in the country's Poor Law management comes as no surprise. Nevertheless, it must be demonstrated, or the general significance attached to a dramatic Act of Parliament may be allowed to conceal the character of its humdrum practice at the local level. Nor must the Poor Law Amendment Act be underestimated, for it was indeed a pioneer work, in which many of the origins of contemporary government may be discovered. It created precedents for central authority for inspections, for expertise, and for the entire evolution of a scientific attitude towards administration techniques. All that may be finally said is that, in Lancashire, for thirty or so years, its practical manifestation in the present never approached its theoretical value for the future.

The abiding feeling evoked by a study such as this is a sad
awareness of the miseries of Lancashire folk throughout all the
dreary years considered, and of the chilly appraisal of misfortune
by those more prosperous and in authority. A letter in the *Liverpool
Courier* of 12 May 1837 makes the point sharply. Its laconic
writer reminded Liverpudlians that the weekly cost of food per
man in Kirkdale Gaol was 5*s.* and that, in Liverpool Workhouse,
the weekly diet cost 2*s.* o½*d.*

III. Public Health

i. Introduction of Public Health reform

General propositions
Public Health has been defined as 'embracing all activities which prevent disease and enhance the health of members of the community, and which can be carried out more efficiently by communal than by individual or family action'.[1] It is a necessarily vague definition, for such activities are open to a wide variety of interpretation—communal action, for instance, had been adopted in the middle ages, when the Black Death threatened, and the Tudors had instigated vigorous health policies. The Industrial Revolution, however, produced a health problem of such proportions that state activity on a hitherto unprecedented scale was required to meet it. By altering much of the social fabric of Great Britain, the increase of population, of heavy industry and of urbanisation created a new and disturbing type of medical environment. State influence on the health of the community was largely unnecessary until this new situation occurred. From that point the history of Public Health has been a tale of ever-increasing governmental intervention, culminating in the erection of the National Health Service during the post-war Attlee administration. The first major step in this movement was the 1848 Public Health Act, which was the result of agitation begun in the early thirties. This section will attempt to describe the conditions of Public Health in Lancashire during the initial period, and also to analyse the early practical work of the Public Health movement. Firstly, however, it would seem valuable to outline the general propositions of Public Health reform.

There was, needless to say, more than one remedy for the desperate medical problems of early Victorian England, just as the

[1] J. J. Clarke, *The History of the Local Government of the United Kingdom* (1955), p. 109.

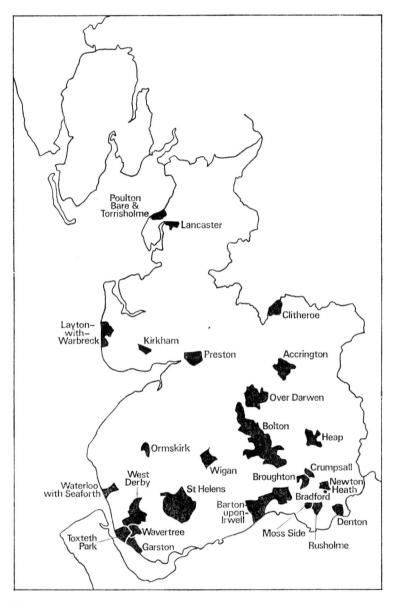

Map 2.

The County of Lancaster showing the administrative areas of the Local Boards of Health formed under the Public Health Act, 1848 (1849–58).

adherents of health reform were moved by more than one motive. Humanitarian feeling did, of course, play a useful rôle in urging different attitudes on the public and in supporting the various measures put forward. The popular appeal of the humanitarian perhaps fails to do justice to a less attractive but probably more significant element, namely the work of Edwin Chadwick and the Utilitarian creed he preached. Many commentators are prepared to give most of the credit for the Public Health movement to Chadwick and his companion.[1] Some writers have tended to equate Utilitarianism with humanitarianism. 'The stimulation of the public conscience . . . was largely the work of one man. . . . To Bentham belongs the credit for having drawn attention to the need for Public Health legislation; he was indeed the Father of Modern Preventive Medicine.'[2] Although Chadwick and Shaftesbury worked closely together and although Benthamism need not exclude a social conscience, the Utilitarian analysis was a characteristically hard-headed one. A clear account of this analysis is to be found in Chadwick's Report in 1842 on the *Sanitary Condition of the Labouring Population of Great Britain*.

Chadwick was alarmed by the economic waste involved in disease and death, and it was no concidence that Public Health reports should be initiated by the Poor Law Commission. The 'voluntary' theory of pauperism was breaking down as more and more evidence suggested social causes were to blame. If, as William Farr, the father of social statistics, had calculated, the 'minimum value' of the population was £159 per head, and if one quarter of the deaths and thirty times as many cases of sickness were preventable, then the loss to the national product was colossal. The causes of such wastage were, therefore, obstacles to the free action of economic man. Families were left destitute; productivity was impaired, and resources were eaten into by medical needs. No less than the Workhouse Test, the prevention of disease was an attempt to unshackle the individual that his economic efforts be ever more fruitful in the interests of greater happiness for a greater number. It was an artificial instrument to clear the ring for *laissez-faire*, and the idea that 'sanitary neglect is mistaken parsimony' was to be strongly urged at a local and mundane level as well

---

[1] R. A. Lewis, *Edwin Chadwick and the Public Health Movement 1832–1854* (1952), Finer pp. 210–38; B. L. Hutchins, *The Public Health Agitation 1833–1848* (1909).

[2] D. Guthrie, *A History of Medicine* (1945) pp. 286–87.

as in theorising Benthamite circles. This thrifty notion did, of course, make some appeal to the earnest Victorian middle class, and the Christian view that 'Cleanliness is next to Godliness' was an added fillip to the cause.

The concept of enforced medical well-being—Chadwick's 'perpetual bathnight' as *Punch* nicknamed it—had three distinct facets. In the first place, there was a steadfast belief that disease and filth went hand in hand, and that, if the filth were cleansed, the disease would automatically vanish. Chadwick argued in the 1842 report, that 'the annual loss of life from filth and bad ventilation is greater than the loss from death or wounds in any wars in which the country has been engaged in modern times . . . that these adverse circumstances tend to produce an adult population shortlived, improvident, reckless and intemperate, and with habitual avidity for sensual gratification', and that 'the most primary and most important measures . . . are drainage, the removal of all refuse of habitations, streets and roads, and the improvement of the supplies of water'. Chadwick and his supporters accepted the prevailing view that exhalations from decomposed matter poisoned the atmosphere. It was thought that gases arising from refuse mingled with atmospheric gases to form a contagious or contaminated 'atmosphere' for the spread of Cholera and other diseases. The Miasmatic or Pythogenic theory, as it was variously called, held sway until the Germ Theory of Disease was developed by Pasteur and Koch much later in the century. It vindicated the 'sanitary idea' as practised by the Environmentalists, and the danger from 'emanations of decaying organic matter' was urged nationally and locally.

In the second place, Chadwick realised that shocked protestations were not enough, and that administrative agencies must be created to grapple with the unsanitary environment. The English were 'living on a dung-heap' and yet the administration of towns was medieval, with a tremendous diversity of authorities. Chadwick's 'ideal was a compact commission, appointed by the government, executing or supervising public works through a competent full-time engineer, and working in co-operation with a qualified Medical Officer of Health'.[1] As with the Poor Law, he argued that the supposedly disinterested amateurs in local government must be replaced by experts and that out-of-date divisions must be replaced by more realistic ones—he even suggested that the area of

[1] Lewis, op. cit., pp. 55–59.

jurisdiction should be the natural drainage basin. Chadwick flirted temporarily in 1845 with the idea of the private utility, for he so despaired of the municipalities that it seemed a Joint-stock venture might prove more competent. Apart from this momentary lapse, his supporters and himself fired dozens of their 'verbal missiles' in favour of central control, competent local bodies with qualified assistance, and a system of inspection. That famous pioneer of sanitary legislation, Professor Johann Peter Frank, had tried to awaken a 'hygienic conscience' in Germany with his elaborate régime of a medical police, and certainly some of Chadwick's views—with regard, for instance, to a public funeral service—have a distinctive German flavour. This Teutonic influence apart, the administrative techniques mooted by the Utilitarians were squarely based on Chadwick's tutelary ideal.

In the third place, these bodies were to be provided with a ready technical answer to insanitary conditions. The key to the problem was the immediate removal of deposits of filth, both domestic and commercial, before decay polluted the atmosphere. Increased population and speculative building had, in many urban areas, led to a monstrous situation. Towns had neither the administrative nor the technological equipment to tackle the problem, and the end-product of inefficient scavenging and ineffective sewers was massive accumulation of sewage at terminal points. A report on Ardwick presented to the Chorlton Guardians referred to these as 'dung mountains', and the Old Hulme Hall manure depot at Manchester contained 25,000 tons of solid deposit. Little wonder that Chadwick decided that 'the most primary and most important measures, and at the same time the most practicable, and within the recognised province of public administration, are drainage, the removal of all refuse of habitations, streets and roads, and the improvement of the supplies of water'. He advocated 'arterial-venous' drainage, which was a comprehensive and articulated system based on hydraulic power. High velocity water would cleanse the streets and houses of the towns, and sweep the final deposit into the countryside as liquid manure. The chemist Liebig had calculated that one man in one year could produce enough nitrogen to assist the growth of 800 lbs. of wheat, and, argued Chadwick, the revenue so obtained would help offset the costs of the system. The sanitary circle was thus completed, with 'public sewers as the arteries pumping out the rich town guano, and the water pipes as the veins returning the excess moisture of the countryside'.[1] Two engineering devices were necessary for the implementation of such a scheme. Firstly, a constant flow of water at high pressure was required, as opposed to the intermittent supply which most areas received. Thomas Hawkesley had developed such a system at Nottingham, and, using this experience, Chadwick calculated that the average house could be equipped for £16, the equivalent of 5½d. per week—1½d. from the tenant, the rest from the landlord—over thirty years. Secondly, the introduction of small earthenware pipes was felt to be essential. These egg-shaped, steeply graded tubes, modelled by the engineer John Roe, were preferred to the flat, large sewers, made out of brick and with slight gradients. This older type impeded flow, and were generally ineffectual—given increased water supplies, it was doubted whether they would cope at all. The dogma of the small earthenware pipe, especially shaped to hasten flow, was soon to become an important item of Chadwick's stock-in-trade.

These three theories—one medical, one administrative, one engineering—formed the central thinking of public health practitioners in mid-nineteenth century. Other solutions were suggested, just as there were other sides to the problem. One further aspect of the difficulties was the disposal of the dead. The report on Intramural Interments of 1843 drew attention to many abuses, not least the dangers of corpses left too long unburied and of grave-yards overcrowded to the extent of 11,000 bodies per acre. There was, of course, a direct link with the mainstream of Chadwick's reasoning. Corpses, like dung, gave forth poisonous exhalations, and therefore quick and cheap disposal was necessary. As far as Chadwick was concerned, public intervention for the disposal of decaying matter was the crux. The uncompromising assertion of his plans naturally led to widespread opposition and although, as with the Poor Law, the resistance was quite diverse, the main three attacks were on the medical, governmental, and technical theories promoted by Chadwick and his friends.

The anti-contagionist beliefs of the Chadwick school were roundly criticised by many physicians. The College of Physicians and Surgeons led the assault which made some play with the capricious incidence of Cholera. As its extent was not always proportionate to the amount of filth present, the accepted idea of infection by bodily contact remained plausible and the efficacy of curative treatment and quarantine was not completely lost. The

[1] Lewis, op. cit., p. 54.

spasmodic nature of epidemics was, of course, to be explained later by Koch and Pasteur. Water-borne Cholera bacteria might, for instance, strike at a river or a well, thus giving the then baffling 'thick' and 'thin' contagion. In actual fact, the emphasis laid by Chadwick on filth disposal was incidentally correct, for the breeding grounds for germs were automatically reduced. The principal disadvantage lay in a lack of emphasis on the purity of water, particularly if a river was used both for water supply and sewage removal. For their part, the contagionist physicians argued at length over the most successful cures. Tobacco enemas, saline injections, mercury, opium, emetics and purgatives were but a few of the grisly remedies for Cholera, which could, some felt, be induced through 'depressing passions' and terror. Faced with such fanciful discussion, the environmentalists were loudly scornful of the orthodox medical men and suspected them of axe-grinding.

The opposition to the administrative policy of Public Health reformers followed predictable lines. Briefly, local government was not itself over-eager to act. Torpid authorities together with a half-hearted parliamentary interest, which sometimes broke into outright opposition, slowed the development of Public Health considerably. The inertia of local government and its usual outcry against state intervention was probably at its worst in the health field. Established authorities, jealous of their independence; parliamentary agents, afraid of losing their profits from private bills; even Boards of Guardians—they all contributed to 'a dead-weight of apathy'. Rarely was health a dramatic enough issue to force the pace, save when Cholera threatened. It was highlighted by no straightforward conflict between church and chapel, Whig and Tory or manufacturer and landlord. The whole social atmosphere acted as a blanket on progress. Nor were the rate-payers always enamoured of the orthodox 'clean party' argument that communal health was financially a sound proposition. All in all, insufficient people were prepared to think in public health terms, therefore, from Tory to Manchester Radical, in Parliament and in Council Chamber, the necessary administrative urgency was often lacking.

On the technical side, Chadwick and his supporters were faced by a bewildering array of self-interest. Irresponsible private companies were anxious to maintain their hold on water-supplies, gas undertakings and sewage concerns, and, in the case of water, companies tried to strengthen their grip on supplies. Building speculators, profiting from the demands of increasing population, and slum-owners, unwilling to invest in improvements which could raise their rate-levies, joined in the resistance. But the spearhead of technological opposition came from the civil engineers themselves, of whom Chadwick wrote 'a more ignorant, or a more jobbing set of men . . . I have rarely met with'. The hospitality of the Institute of Civil Engineers to the Board of Health gave a lead to the dissatisfied rate-payers and slum-owners. Many engineers rejected Chadwick's terra cotta pipe dogma and they resented his committal of the General Board of Health to an untested idea through the use of friendly engineers. Their irritation at unfair competition and their quickness to spot faults in Roe's techniques were widespread enough to slow down any efforts at radical change in sewering and watering. There were, of course, errors to be uncovered in the work of Chadwick's engineers, and his circulatory ideal was weakened not only by practical difficulties but by the introduction of guano and chemical fertilisation. However, it is difficult, in retrospect, not to see a large measure of undue conservatism and vested interest ranged against the new Public Health technicians, an opposition aggravated, no doubt, by the abrasive personality of Chadwick himself.

The first faltering attempt to implement Public Health reform on a national scale was the General Board of Health, established in 1848. This brought to a head the wide expression of objection to sanitary reform, and it united politicians, professions and commerce in protest. But, despite opposition, the Public Health problem gradually forced its attention on Society. It was an overwhelming problem, and the sheer gargantuan pressure of filth was probably a main reason for action. The oppressive and offensive physical inconvenience of insanitation was a prime impulse to the Public Health movement. And to indescribable discomfort was added the fearful dread of disease like Cholera, Smallpox and Typhus. In the four Cholera epidemics of 1831–32, 1849 and 1866, over 15,000 died in Lancashire alone—in 1849, four in every thousand Lancastrians died. Cholera came to Liverpool in 1831 via Hull and York and 1,523 out of its 4,912 cases were fatal. On one ship alone in Liverpool docks eighty-three died out of a complement of 349. Thirteen other areas had Cholera cases, with 706 fatalities in Manchester and 216 in Salford. In the 1849 epidemic there were 8,184 deaths, and the dreadful total of 5,308 in Liverpool. Of those who died in Liverpool in 1848 it has been claimed that seven-eighths were Irish. In the earlier epidemic hospitals were hastily established—like Swan Street and Chorlton-on-Medlock Hospitals in Manchester; Lime Street and Toxteth Park Cholera Hospitals in Liverpool; and the Warrington House of Recovery to serve the victims from 'Sewer Island' as the stricken Lower Bank Street area was known. An unhappy aspect of the first outbreak was the breakdown of trust between doctors and people. A riot occurred in Manchester over the mangled body of a child subjected to a post mortem. The *Liverpool Mercury* reported in 1832 that 'amongst great numbers of the lower classes in this town the idea is prevalent that the Cholera is a mere invention of the medical men to fill their pockets' and that hospital patients were 'victims of experiments while living and subjects for the dissecting knife when dead'. Crowds assembled to prevent removals to hospitals and surgeons were mobbed. 'The very disgraceful outrages to which the medical gentlemen of Liverpool have been subjected' led doctors to threaten 'to leave the people to their fate'. It is sometimes forgotten that the dramatic incursions of Cholera were not the only feared diseases in Lancashire. Typhus—the 'Irish Fever'—was another killer, affecting the cotton towns which normally escaped Asiatic Cholera. Liverpool, Manchester, Salford, Bolton, Wigan and Chorley were the chief victims, and, in 1839, 1,343 died of Typhus in Lancashire. In the North Western Registration District of Lancashire and Cheshire 9,076 died of Typhus in 1847. Smallpox accounted for 7,105 Lancastrians between 1837 and 1840.

The gigantic problem of filth in Lancashire was unpleasant enough; associated with frightening diseases it became more and more pressing. Soon action could be no longer prevented.

Public Health Prior to Reform

An estimate of the efficiency of Public Health reforms in Lancashire obviously requires some description of the medical and administrative problems that existed. It is possible to compose such an account from the official papers of the period. These include the flood of governmental reports on Public Health during the eighteen-forties, which contain data submitted by local observers. There are also the reports of Inspectors investigating particular areas under the 1848 Public Health Act, and the Annual Reports of the Registrar-General. In addition, local records exist, notably concerning the work of Improvement Commissioners. Surprisingly, the newspapers of the age are more reticent about

Public Health than they had been earlier about the Poor Law. The political arguments were bandied about with the usual journalistic enthusiasm, but the social detail seems to have been played down perhaps because the middle-class reading public was not unduly concerned with such detail unless it was directly affected, as in the case of epidemics. Perhaps the editors felt that the material was too raw and crude for their sheltered readers. Doubts have been expressed about the validity of the official sources. It is certain that, as in all his crusades, Chadwick loaded the case as much as possible. Occasional inaccuracies and statistical misrepresentations are apparent, and the picture was painted as black as possible. Doubtless sunny items which might have lightened the horrors of the situation were omitted. But although official reports were propagandist, they relied on reasonably accurate information, so that the general situation was depicted vividly but, in the main, truthfully.

Four major reports were published in the eighteen-forties. The first was the work of the Select Committee on the Health of Towns in 1840. It claimed that 20 per cent of the Liverpool and 12 per cent of the Manchester working classes dwelt in cellars, and Richard Cobden, on behalf of the Manchester Statistical Society, estimated the Manchester figure at 14,960. J. R. Wood, a colleague in the Society, said that fever in Liverpool 'principally prevailed' where 'cellars abound', and, he said, 'I was generally obliged to carry my handkerchief to my nose.' Dr. W. H. Duncan of Liverpool told of his city's 2,400 closed courts with thirty-six inhabitants to each privy, and of the 38,600 cellar dwellers. Spencer Court was singled out for special mention as a fever-trap, and it had, according to an Irishman living there, 'a smell bad enough to raise the roof of his skull'. Dr. Robertson of Manchester, J. Fletcher of St. Helens and E. Ashworth of Bolton were other observers in Lancashire towns who testified to the 'malign influences' of buildings more 'economic in the outlay than convenient to the inhabitants' and to 'the pallid and careworn appearance' of what Fletcher called 'a deteriorated race'. All agreed that 'municipal institutions are quite unfitted for Public Health work', and that 'new laws and regulations are becoming necessary for sanitary purposes in the civic government of towns'. The Committee suggested a General Building Act and a General Sewerage Act to meet the case, and, in a typically Victorian passage, they sternly pronounced that 'the effect of this utter prostration of energy . . . has been to reduce multitudes, who might otherwise have passed with credit through their humble spheres, to have recourse to ardent spirits'.

This was followed in 1842 by the Poor Law Commission's *Report of the Sanitary Condition of the Labouring Population*. It sold well and enjoyed much popularity and, as might be anticipated from its authorship, it constructed a more formidable statistical case than its predecessor. This was especially true of disease, for Chadwick was now able to use the results of the Act for the Registration of Births, Deaths and Marriages, which had come into force in July 1837. In Lancashire, for example, 29,690 had died of Epidemic, Respiratory, Brain and Digestive diseases in 1838. Eighteen in every 1,000 had died of such causes, whereas the United Kingdom figure was only fourteen in every 1,000. Believing these diseases to be 'most powerfully influenced by physical circumstances under which the pollution is placed', Chadwick mustered considerable evidence that suggested a relation between disease and filth, much of it based on Lancashire sources.

Item by item the causes of filthy conditions were inexorably assembled. Dr. Baron Howard found the neglect of street cleaning 'a most harmful influence' on fever incidence. Some Manchester streets were so filthy that recovery vehicles could not negotiate them—they were 'impassable from depth of mud, and intolerable from stench', 352 of Manchester's 627 streets were clogged with ordure, and the privies of the Little Ireland area were 'disgusting and offensive beyond description'. Mott, the Assistant Poor Law Commissioner, criticised water supply. There were numerous pumps and tanks 'in this proverbially rainy district' but the water was 'frequently like ink'. Riddell Wood emphasised the dangers of overcrowding, which apparently were gravest in Manchester, Liverpool, Ashton-under-Lyne and Pendleton. Three or four in a bed was a common occurrence, with many examples of women 'being common to men'. Riddell Wood told cautionary tales of women fallen into easy virtues as a result of overcrowding, which, he claimed, was not confined to the poorest classes. Baron Howard felt that lodging-houses were 'the most malignant foci of infectious fevers in Manchester', and he confessed 'the abominable state of these dens of filth, disease and wretchedness'. Attention was called to the weakness of local authorities. Little Bolton paid £80 to a surveyor whose responsibilities comprised lighting, paving, cleaning, sewage, fire, nuisance and encroachment. He was unable, it was reported, to obtain an order for the expense of clearing a pool

F

of stagnant water in a populated area, which covered 9,000 square feet, was 2 feet deep and was littered with dead animals. J. R. Wood produced frightening mortality figures. Of 4,629 deaths among the labouring classes of Manchester in 1850, only 429 were over twenty years of age. 3,597 died in Liverpool the same year, and the average age was fifteen. 'One twenty-eighth', he calculated, 'of the population is annually swept away', and Lancashire, with a death-rate of one in thirty-two, had the worst record of any county in the kingdom.

These two earlier documents, however, were overshadowed by the two reports of the Buccleuch Commission set up in 1843 to enquire into the health conditions in large towns and populous districts. A massive weight of testimony was assembled which, together with the evidence of the previous documents, pointed inexorably toward the need for drastic action. Fifty towns with a mortality rate of over 2 per cent were investigated. The appendix to the First Report tabulates the answers obtained to a host of questions concerning health matters in the fifty towns, and it also includes commentaries on a number of them. Not surprisingly, ten Lancashire towns appear in the list, and four—Liverpool, Preston, Chorlton and Ashton-under-Lyne—have special mention made of them. 1,132,000 were, according to the 1841 Census, living in these areas, and, as the county's gross total was 1,667,000, the emerging picture was reasonably representative. 31,670 of this number died in 1841, a percentage mortality of 2·8. The questions on sewage, drainage and nuisance disposal reveal a hotch-potch of circumstances, ranging from the seemingly sufficient arrangements in Ashton, Oldham and Bolton to the laconic negatives of Wigan and the lamented inadequacies of Salford or Bury. The myriad types of administration are very noticeable, along with constant criticisms that these are inept or too limited in their powers. A clearer picture is apparent with regard to water supply. Simply, private companies monopolised the field, save where wells or pumps were used, and the supply of water to the poorer classes was disgracefully inadequate.

Dr. Duncan once more contributed a statement on Liverpool; 'the most unhealthy town in England'. A third of the working classes lived in courts and an eighth in cellars, and only four miles of the twenty miles of working-class streets were sewered. 32,000 houses had seven or more inmates: lodging houses sometimes had thirty sleeping in their cellar; and so called dames' schools often

operated in cellars with upwards of forty children. In the period
1835–39 there had been 17,469 cases of fever and fifty-three out of
every 100 children died before they were five. In the 1,982 courts
in Liverpool—629 closed at both ends—one person in thirty-seven
had contracted fevers, and one in thirty had died. The Irish were,
he claimed, 'especially exposed'. That well-known social observer,
the Rev. J. Clay, spoke of the 'very insufficient' drainage in Preston
and the 600 inhabited cellars there. Midden-pans nearly four feet
deep were emptied only twice a year, and the water company
provided only half of Preston's 10,000 houses, at an annual rental
of 10s. to £8—a high rate even by today's standard. Dr. P. H.
Holland stated that two-thirds of Chorlton's houses had 'separate
necessaries' without drainage, and that sewering was only possible
at the owner's expense. Some 'always steal their water' and the
water company was irregular with supplies. The River Medlock
provided a receptacle for the refuse not only from 100,000 people
but from several factories—'the vilest compound of villainous
smells'. J. R. Coulthart spoke of the 110 cart-loads of night-soil
collected in Ashton-under-Lyne per week, and of how many
refused to have a collection made more than once in four months.
'The worst-conditioned housing' was found by Coulthart to have
floors 'covered with water, ashes and excrementitious nastiness. . . .
If the stranger were to turn up the clothes of the unmade beds with
the ferrule of his umbrella he would perceive that they were black,
filthy and odious.' Mortality in Ashton was a dreadful 3 per cent.
   The second report includes the famous commentary by Dr.
Lyon Playfair on large towns in Lancashire. He commenced with
the general proposition that 'the congregation of masses of beings
into confined spaces necessarily causes the production of large
quantities of animal and vegetable refuse', and he argued, sensibly
enough, that, irrespective of whatever medical theory was correct,
such filth 'by reducing the general tone of the system remained a
most powerful predisposing cause'. He carefully examined the ten
critical Lancashire towns, with reference to sewering, scavenging,
accommodation and water supply. Scavenging appeared to have
been fairly regular in six towns, but Playfair added the rider that
courts, alleys and 'undedicated', that is unadopted, streets were not
'within the province of the public scavenger'. Practically all courts
had 'a practice unknown in the metropolis' of having an open
cesspool, dunghill or midden within their precincts. The nuisance
was aggravated by the 'reckless conduct' of 'nightly prowlers'. In

the St. Georges Road and Oldham Road area of Manchester there were only thirty-three privies amongst 7,095 houses. In Liverpool forty houses normally shared one privy, and, in twenty-six streets of 1,200 houses, 804 had no convenience at all. The city also boasted 'a regulation peculiar to Liverpool' of forbidding the connection of water closets to sewers. The cellar population of the towns was estimated at 67,736—about 6 per cent of their total population. Crowded cellars were not the only fault in accommodation underlined by Playfair. He discovered in Manchester ninety-four cases of six sharing a bed, twenty-seven of seven sharing a bed, and two of eight sharing a bed, while the average number of inmates per house in Liverpool was seven. Water supply looked a little more impressive superficially than in actuality. The value of constant water had not yet been realised, and none of the towns had adequate fire protection. Manchester, Liverpool, Wigan and Bolton had intermittent supplies. Two companies supplied Liverpool and, between them, they claimed to serve 1,424 more houses than there were in the borough. Water was piped for an hour or so on alternate days, while in Manchester water was piped for one to four hours per day. Wigan's eight stand-pipes worked only an hour daily, and Bolton's public pumps were insufficient. Playfair recorded an incident in which 63 people were queueing at one such pump. All in all, concluded Lyon Playfair, the facts pointed to 'consequences so serious to the Public Health as imperatively to call for the interference of the legislature'. Of Lancashire's 102,025 deaths in 1841, 83,616 were under twenty, and the average age of death was twenty-two years. 11,000 deaths were of active labouring adults. Playfair calculated that 14,000 deaths and 398,000 sicknesses had been preventable, and the financial loss to the county he estimated at £5,133,557. It has been said that the Buccleuch Commission 'was to sanitary science what the 1834 Poor Law Report was to public assistance'. Most of these official accounts referred to the larger towns. One can, however, learn a little of the smaller towns through the investigations made by Board of Health inspectors in those townships which applied for permission to set up Boards of Health. These reports were often minor best-sellers, and several in Lancashire were prepared by Robert Rawlinson, one of the leading engineers of the age. Although the enquiries were completed in a day, they give a succinct view of Public Health in small townships.

Crumpsall had no system of drainage nor of government. Cleaning was 'left to those who like to do it' and was rarely accomplished 'excepting by a thunderstorm'. Its 3,151 inhabitants shared 622 houses, their well-water was 'tainted by foul matters'; their death rate was twenty-one per thousand of which a quarter was due to zymotic diseases. The township of Rusholme had nuisance spots where 'the air is tainted by an offensive privy, pig-sty and midden' and foci of fever along the Irwell, Irk, Medlock, and Cornbrook, which 'natural water-courses were contaminated with refuse'. Even rain was 'the colour of ink'. Appendices to this report spoke of 'dung-mountains' in nearby Ardwick, of streets 'impassable from the depth of mud and the intolerable stench', and of the 'dead sea' of sewage. Broughton, with a death-rate of fifteen per thousand, was in a happier state, but its cesspools were 'very palpable to the senses' and both sewerage and water supply stood in need of radical overhaul. Pendleton was much worse. The death-rate sometimes rose to twenty-two per thousand for the 14,000 people crowded into less than 3,000 houses. 200 cellars were inhabited, and there was a 'damp and foul atmosphere at all times, and modern rivers of refuse for the former rivers of water'. There were only three or four pumps, and pits and canals were used by many 'seeking water hither and thither'. The water was claimed to be the worst in Lancashire. 'A black ditch' stood instead of sewers, and fifty-three streets were unpaved. The chapelry of Much Woolton was a mix-up of some hundreds of crowded dwellings, slaughter houses and lodging houses. Ten in a room, five in a garret and five in a coal-hole were among the cases of overcrowding. Rubble drains, 'dumb wells' and closed cesspools were used for sewage, and marl-pits and even a stone quarry were used for water. The average-death rate was a dreadful thirty in each thousand. In a later report on Moss Side, one learns a little of conditions in a relatively pleasing residential area, but even here ditches were used for sewage and housing had fast overtaken the availability of wells.

By and large, therefore, Lancashire was a county in which human habitation, not exclusively in the larger towns, was beset by filth. Grossly insanitary surroundings and disturbingly seamy water supplies created an unprecedented health problem. What administrative devices were operating to deal with the issue? The variety of administrative attempts formed a veritable bureaucratic spatchcock. In this it did no more than reflect the national complexity, including numerous Paving Trusts, Commissioners of

Sewers, Highway Committees, Municipal Corporations, Courts
Leet and Improvement Commissions. 276 towns in the United
Kingdom of over 5,000 had neither Corporation nor Local Act;
ninety-two Corporations had no powers and in 158 towns powers
were divided. John Simon wrote that there was 'no general law
of sanitary intention' and that the government 'had nothing to say
in regard to the Public Health, and Local Authorities had but the
most indefinite relation to it'. Said Simon, 'the householder stored
his filth as he liked, or got rid of it as he could'.

The position in Liverpool illustrates the confused situation.
In 1835 the new Corporation gave its Watch Committee the
responsibility of street-cleaning, but left the Highways Board and
the Toxteth Park Improvement Commission to continue their
allied tasks. In 1842 a Health Committee was set up which looked
after court drains but not court sewers. The Commissioners of
Paving and Sewering controlled those two services. They watered
the streets, but the Council cleaned them. Similarly, they controlled
the water used for fire extinction, but the Council supervised the
Fire Brigade. To cap this, there were two competing Water Companies. Private exertions compensated a little for this chaos. The
Liverpool branch of the Health of Towns Association was one of
the most active in the country, with Dr. Duncan, Samuel Holme
and William Rathbone among its leading members. A monthly journal—*Health of Towns Advocate*—was published by the Association. The Liverpool Guardian Society for the Protection of Trade
was also interested in health, especially in water supply. There
was also the legendary Catherine Wilkinson, who, supported by
William Rathbone, organised baths and wash houses in the city;
Liverpool was the only place in Lancashire with public baths.

Most towns either with or without borough status benefited
from Local Acts, some of which established Improvement Commissions. These were severely restricted in their mandate, and
cleansing was motivated not so much by health reasons as by the
necessity of keeping the wheels of commerce moving freely
through the main thoroughfares. Later, Commissions in places like
Fleetwood and Bury were to perform similar functions to Boards
of Health. Before 1840, however, their powers were few and
their opportunities limited. Local Acts were also concerned
with granting rights to commercial undertakings, such as the
Manchester Road and Street Cleansing Company, with the
engineer Whitworth the key figure, and his cleaning machine its

chief implement. Either by sub-contraction or independently, private enterprise operated the standard utilities, with the water companies the prime illustration. The Poor Law Unions were the only other civic bodies with an interest in health. They were the units selected to implement the Registration of Births, Deaths and Marriages, for statistical analysis was to be of the utmost value in health reform; they were in charge of much of the defence against Cholera, and they helped in that remarkable Victorian exercise, the free vaccination service.

The health conditions in Lancashire left nothing to the imagination. They were appalling in the towns and alarming in the countryside. The administrative machinery was archaic and confused beyond measure. A strange mixture of public bodies and private undertakings made no large impression on a huge problem, despite the endeavours of dedicated individuals. By the early eighteen-forties, neither central nor local authority had made any spectacular move towards reform.

Establishment of Public Health Authorities in Lancashire 1848–58
The neat pattern of the reformed Poor Law, established by and through a single legislative set in 1834, was not emulated in the field of Public Health. The problem was, in a sense, a more complex one than either pauperism or crime. Both these social dislocations were more open to judicial test—the pauper before the Board of Guardians; the criminal before the Magistrates' Bench. Public Health difficulties were communal rather than individual, and the consequent variety of environmental factors affecting differing areas made a common policy impossible. Whereas a pauper or a thief remained a similar kind of legal issue whether he appeared in the back-to-backs of Bolton or in a Fylde village, the problems of health were more intricate. Here it was over-crowding; there it was poor water-supply; elsewhere it was lack of sanitation. A proliferation of problems over a widely varying geographical region resulted in a hotch-potch of attempts. The mixture of devices tried could have been a distinct advantage. The Poor Law Unions had a tendency towards rigidity—Chadwick's set formula was sometimes too inflexible for especial issues. The less structured Public Health mechanisms could well have meant proper adaptation to local needs. Any such merit, however, was to be more than balanced by the makeshift nature of the devices used and by the permissive nature of legislation in the period under review. With

local initiative practically the only lever, many areas remained completely unaffected by any action. The New Poor Law and the New Police covered Lancashire throughout, whilst Public Health reform was at best haphazard and slow.

If the incidence of reform was *ad hoc* and its growth lethargic, its character was similarly variegated. So many bits and pieces had been tried for so long, that it is difficult to judge where reform begins. By the late eighteen-forties the major forces for reform were based on the idea of prevention through sound and united administration. The 1848 Public Health Act stated the case clearly, '. . . it is expedient that the supply of water to such towns and places, and the sewering, draining, cleaning and paving thereof, should as far as is practicable be placed under one and the same local management and control'. It was only in this period that governmental organs obtained the wholesale power to undertake practical engineering steps to facilitate the supply of water and the removal of sewage. Hitherto powers had been restricted and petty, with minor adjustments and negative tactics uppermost. Such radical essays in reform came in two fashions. There was a group of towns which took advantage of the 1848 Public Health Act. There was also a group of towns which obtained local statutory powers of a similar nature to General Board of Health requirements.

'No moment in the world's history has been more significant for Public Health than the year 1848.'[1] In so far as the 1848 Act initiated a long line of health legislation, this verdict must be accepted. It was singularly important because it laid the foundation for the extensive Public Health services of today. Space forbids a pursuit of the labyrinthine steps that led via vain Bills and ineffective Acts to this first major statute. Its only notable predecessor was the Town Clauses Consolidation Act of the previous year. This model Act was designed to save faulty private bills by offering an acceptable *pro forma*. Parliamentary consent was still required and it failed to curtail legal expenses, but, worst of all, it left most towns unmoved. The 1848 Act was normally permissive, but there were exceptions when it could become compulsory, and, once established, a Board of Health was obliged to implement a comprehensive series of requirements. A tenth of the rate-payers were required to petition for the creation of a Board of Health in their locality. Where the mortality rate

[1] C. F. Brockington, *Medical Officers of Health 1848–1855* (1957), p. 4.

exceeded an average of twenty-three per thousand over the preceding seven years, the creation of a Board was compulsory. According
to the value of his property, each rate-payer had from one to six
votes, and the Boards were normally twelve strong. The work of
each Board was guided by no less than forty formidable clauses.
The Boards were obliged to appoint a Surveyor and an Inspector of
Nuisances. They were required to arrange for an ordnance survey,
to maintain streets and to construct sewers, and owners and occupiers were to be required to cleanse, drain and provide water in
their properties. They became the licensing authority for slaughter
houses and lodging houses, they were to control cellar habitation,
and they could, if they so wished, appoint a Medical Officer. The
Nuisance Removal and Diseases Prevention Act of the same year
gave summary jurisdiction against dangers to health, and wrested
control of Cholera jurisdiction from the Superintendent of
Quarantine. A general frame for complete coverage of health
problems, as then defined, was made possible. Wide rating and
loan powers were provided in order to implement these positive
proposals, for financial as well as legal inadequacy had been a
feature of previous legislation. The expense of creating a Board was
between £88 and £136, much cheaper than the normal private bill
with its cost of some £2,000. The General Board of Health was
established to supervise the Act. It had three members—a political
head and two others, both unpaid—and it was given an initial life
of five years. Provided old acts or standing boundaries remained
undisturbed, an Order in Council was all that was needed to create
a Board of Health. Otherwise a Provisional Order was required;
that is, it required a decision in Parliament.

This foundation for 'a sanitary revolution' has had many critics.
Many criticised the permissive nature of the Act. Others found
fault with a plan based on the Poor Law pattern, with a Board
reminiscent of the Guardians and with both the General and
Special District Rates based on the Poor Law assessment. The
President of the Board was Lord Morpeth, First Commissioner of
Woods and Forests. Lord Ashley and Chadwick were his colleagues.
Dr. Southwood-Smith was made the first medical member of the
Board in 1850. Although Chadwick's hope of a petition from one-
fiftieth of the rate-payers was vanquished, it was still felt that the
authority which could be established by only 10 per cent of the
rate-payers was alarmingly intrusive. The right-wing press strin-
gently opposed 'this new Imperium in Imperio', with the 'new

triumvirate' replacing the one 'dislodged from Somerset House', as the *Manchester Courier* put it in May 1848. After many travails, the General Board of Health had its powers transferred to the Privy Council under the Local Government Act of 1858 which

Table II: **Local Boards of Health in Lancashire 1848-1858***

Name of Board	Authority	Date of Inauguration	Pop. (1861)
Accrington	Provisional Order	1853	20,000
Barton, Eccles Winton and Monton	Order in Council	1854	11,146
Bolton	Local Act	1855	70,396
Bradford	Order in Council	1856	3,900
Broughton	,,	1856	4,448
Clitheroe	,,	1850	7,000
Crumpsall	,,	1854	4,285
Denton	,,	1857	3,335
Garston	,,	1854	4,720
Heap	,,	1854	17,359
Kirkham	,,	1852	3,380
Lancaster	Provisional Order	1849	14,487
Layton-with-Warbreck	Order in Council	1851	3,907
Moss Side	Provisional Order	1856	2,695
Newton Heath	Order in Council	1853	14,000
Ormskirk	,,	1850	6,426
Over Darwen	Provisional Order	1854	16,492
Poulton, Bare and Torrisholme	Order in Council	1852	2,337
Preston	Provisional Order	1850	82,000
Rusholme	Order in Council	1851	6,400
St. Helens	Local Act	1851	18,866
Toxteth Park	Provisional Order	1855	4,000
Waterloo with Seaforth	,, ,,	1856	4,500
Wavertree	Order in Council	1851	5,392
West Derby	,,	1850	16,215
Wigan	Provisional Order	1850	37,658

* Information is taken from Privy Council, *Returns of Districts where the Public Health Act 1848 or the Local Government Act 1858 are in force*, 22 February, 1867.

also established new arrangements for the setting up of Local Boards.

During the ten years the General Board of Health lasted, only twenty-six townships in Lancashire took any advantage of the Public Health Act (see table II). Four boroughs—Preston, Wigan,

Lancaster and Clitheroe—grasped at the Act. Another—Bolton—
was incorporated in 1838, and, in 1850, an extensive Improvement
Act was obtained, with provisions both of the 1847 Town
Improvement Clauses Act and the Public Health Act. The powers
extended not only to the Parishes of Great and Little Bolton but to
nine other smaller townships as well. The Council was empowered
to act as a Board of Health over this territory, to undertake the
running of the Great Bolton Waterworks, and to have super-
visory powers in connection with the Bolton Gaslight and Coke
Company. A later Act in 1854 dealt with lighting and water.
Where a Borough formed the area of control, the Borough Council
undertook the duties of a Board of Health; otherwise the Local
Board of Health was specially elected. Eight of these remaining
Boards were clustered around Manchester. These were Barton,
Bradford, Denton, Moss Side, Newton Heath, Crumpsall,
Rusholme and Broughton. Five Boards were in the Liverpool area.
These were Garston, Waterloo with Seaforth, Wavertree, Toxteth
Park and West Derby. Layton with Warbreck and Poulton, Bare
and Torrisholme provided two interesting coastal examples. The
remaining Boards were dotted about the county at random. They
were Accrington, Over Darwen, Heap, Ormskirk and Kirkham.
St. Helens, composed of four townships, required special legislation in 1851. Some 400,000 Lancastrians were by 1858 supervised
under the Public Health Act—a mere handful compared with the
county's tally of two and a half millions in 1861. Only seven of
the Boards catered for populations above 15,000. Only Bolton,
Preston and Wigan topped 20,000. Conversely, ten Boards had less
than 5,000 inhabitants.

Considering Lancashire's stricken health conditions, this
amounted to a poor response, and one that apparently became
extremely feeble after Chadwick's departure from the Board in
1854. Eight Provisional Orders—quite a large proportion—were
required in the county, all of which necessitated parliamentary
action, while some townships, such as Bacup, Pendleton and Much
Woolton, underwent investigation, were recommended for Boards
of Health but never obtained them. Another point is that many of
these Boards of Health were not responsible for the poorest and
most needy areas. Layton and Poulton were both coastal villages.
The Liverpudlian Boards were principally on the fairer Southern
side of the city. Of the Mancunian Boards, Moss Side, Crumpsall
and Rusholme were chiefly middle-class environs. It is sad to note

that, few as the Boards were in Lancashire, fewer still catered for the desperate cases. This is, of course, balanced by alternative legislation for the bigger conurbations which housed the majority of Lancashire's poor. A glance at the map, however, reminds one of several industrialised parishes—Ince, Gorton, Bootle, for instance—which had neither Board nor any other form of municipal control of its health hazards.

   Liverpool and Manchester were in the forefront of those towns who made private statutory arrangements concerning Public Health. The newly formed Manchester Corporation was slightly earlier—if slightly feebler—in its first positive action. The 1844 Police Regulation Act argued 'the powers at present possessed for the good Government and Police Regulation of the Borough of Manchester have been found to be defective and insufficient', and it thus included wide-ranging powers to remedy this. All house-owners were obliged to provide a 'fit and proper privy', only to be emptied and cleared 'as the Council may think fit'. A fire, police and slaughter house registration were among measures introduced by a whole string of bye-laws and a new Building and Sanitary Regulations Committee was created to supervise them. This inaugural Improvement Act was reinforced by no less than ten other Acts by 1858. Liverpool's Sanitary Act of 1846 was the first piece of comprehensive Health legislation passed in England. It made the Town Council responsible for drainage, paving, sewerage and cleaning, it permitted the appointment of a Borough Engineer, an Inspector of Nuisance and the first-ever Medical Officer of Health. The old powers of the Highway Board were taken over by the Council, and a Health Committee appointed. W. H. Duncan was the first Medical Officer, and, alongside the new Health Committee and its officers, he led the attack on one of the most intensely difficult health problems in the country. The complete and well-rounded nature of the Liverpool Sanitary Act warrant the praise heaped upon it, and it has tended, perhaps a little unfairly, to dwarf the less broadly based Manchester Police Act. In 1847 the Liverpool Corporation Waterworks Act gave the city power to purchase existing undertakings, and this was supported by frequent amending Acts in 1850, 1852, 1853, 1855, 1856 and 1860. Liverpool, therefore, had obtained practical control of its major Health utilities before the Public Health Act was under way.

   What of Lancashire's other large towns? The remaining seven

large towns took certain steps to adapt their municipal organisa-
tions to Public Health needs. Six of these became Boroughs in the
period under review. Salford was incorporated in 1844, and
Broughton and Pendleton were to become part of Salford in 1853,
but its administrative issues were becoming more and more involved with Manchester. This is especially true of water-supply.
Warrington attained Borough status in 1847, and Sanitary (Scavenging, Watering and Cleansing), Sewerage and Street Improvement
and Lighting sub-committees were recommended. Not until
1854 were the responsibilities of the Improvement Commission
taken over by the Council. A year later Ashton-under-Lyne
became a Borough, and in 1856, the Ashton Corporation purchased the local Water Company. In 1849, Oldham was incorporated and, in February 1850, the Oldham Town Council extended its control of Public Health agencies. Blackburn became a
Borough in 1852, and, two years later, the powers of the Commissioners were transferred to the Town Council. The Town
Council quickly authorised a Highways and General Drainage
Committee to drain and sewer the town, and additional powers
were obtained in the 1854 Blackburn Improvement Act. Finally,
Rochdale was incorporated in 1856, and, by an Act of 1857, the
Council adopted the manifold powers of the somewhat complex
Rochdale Improvement Commission.

The seventh remaining large town was Bury. The Bury Improvement Commission was not created until 1845, and it was
designed to promote 'the health and convenience of the inhabitants'. The sewering of the towns was considered along the lines
suggested by Chadwick, and the Commission maintained its
authority until Bury was incorporated in 1876. Only a few other
Lancashire towns had Improvement Commissions of post-1830
vintage. One was in Fleetwood, under the 1842 Fleetwood Improvement and Marketing Act. The Fleetwood Commissioners
ruled until 1894, when the Urban District Council came into
being, and they, too, operated along fairly positive lines, introdu-
cing schemes of sewering and the like. It is interesting to note the
other instances of coastal areas indulging in Public Health activities. In 1846 Southport established an Improvement Commission.
Legally speaking, Southport was a village within the Township of
North Meols at this time. Similarly, in 1851, Blackpool obtained a
Local Act, although officially part of Leyton with Warbreck, one of
the Local Boards of Health. Burnley and Colne were the only other

two townships to have pre-1845 local acts still extant, and these
both applied to water supplies.

Thus by the time of the 1858 Local Government Act, some
three dozen towns in Lancashire had adopted forms of organisation which could enable them to reform Public Health services
radically and progressively. Although this meant that, by 1858,
some three-quarters of the county's population had administrative
coverage for Public Health, there were still over 400 parochial
authorities without mechanisms for advanced work in this field.
The great majority of these had experienced growing populations
over the preceding decades, and the problems of water supply and
sewage disposal were facing the small village as well as the large
town. Doubtless the large urban areas had the greater need, but,
in 1858, half a million Lancastrians lived without administrative
intervention into their Public Health needs. Whether the Lancastrians who did enjoy such intervention benefited from it, and to
what extent, is the theme of the following sub-sections.

ii. Work of the Public Health Authorities 1844-1858

Administrative techniques
Public Health work during this period involved four elements.
These were the administrative machinery erected to grapple with
the issue; the two technical problems of water supply and sewage
disposal, and the unavoidable question of finance. To avoid confusion it would seem simpler to deal at length with the centrally
supervised Local Boards of Health, and then much more briefly,
to complete the picture with short surveys of the work of the
Borough Councils and Improvement Commissions. It is possible
to build a picture of Public Health work from the minutes kept
by the Local Boards, the Improvement Commissions and the
Borough Council Committees, as well as from varied other
sources. There is certainly sufficient evidence to track the development of Public Health utilities from the Manchester Act of 1844 to
the Local Government Act of 1858.

    a. Local Boards of Health. The Local Boards attempted many
techniques pioneered by the New Poor Law. They included
elective committees, the employment of salaried experts and
central control. It is intended to examine each of these in turn.

    As well as being sparsely distributed, the Boards of Health were
slow to become established. With fourteen days' notice of the

inspection, a month's respite, an occasional supplemental enquiry, a draft order, the final official order and a complex electoral procedure, dilatoriness was to be anticipated. A typical example is that of Crumpsall. The petition was presented in 1851, the inspection was conducted in the following July, and the Board first met in March 1853. Rusholme's enquiry occurred in August 1849, but it was April 1851 before the Board first assembled. Again, one is reminded that administrative enactments, like the Public Health Act, are far from being reforms completed by the stroke of a pen. The legal ritual was seldom less than laborious, and this is one reason why Lancaster was the only Board in Lancashire to be inaugurated before 1850. Despite delays, Boards came slowly into existence. With a minimum of one-tenth of the rate-payers in support, the Boards began their work. Their permissive basis gave them an impetus often missing from the compulsory Poor Law. There had to be an initial enthusiasm for a petition, and this was possibly maintained when the Boards were formed. Certainly the Board members had a better record of attendance at meetings than the chronic absentees amongst the Poor Law Guardians of Lancashire. The Committees were, of course, smaller than the rather weighty Boards of Guardians, and, given relatively tiny areas, journeys to meetings were scarcely the same problem. Generally speaking, however, the meetings normally attracted a hard core of members, usually about five or six. As with the Poor Law, there were times when the Boards were short-handed or even unable to meet, but the chief impression gained from a study of the available Minutes is of small groups of men working quite assiduously.

There were disadvantages. Elections were often uncontested, and the same names run on and on with neither new blood nor challenge at the hustings. There were occasional complaints about the filling of casual vacancies without elections. Two Crumpsall Board members, Simpson and Pendlebury, were disqualified in 1859, and their places filled by appointment. Robert Whyatt, who had been chairman since the inauguration of the Board, resigned, and acrimonious objections were made to the Board. Not all Board members were as keen, for instance, as Eccles Sharrock, who was member and Chairman of the Over Darwen Board for many years and who went so far as to make a 'liberal offer' of interest-free loans for private improvements in Darwen. Edward Wilson was disqualified from the Poulton Board because of non-attendance and

for the non-payment of eleven years' rates. H. P. Ree resigned from
the Moss Side Board, unable 'to share the responsibility' of the
Board's 'extravagant expense' in sewering certain streets. At
Rusholme, John Billington led strong attacks on sewage schemes,
and they were passed by only seven votes to four. As the Local
Boards were required to act in respect of such expenditure, it is
difficult to interpret such opposition as being anything other than
deliberate stalling. The closeness of voting in cases about which,
theoretically, the boards had no legal choice suggests the presence
on Boards of members avowedly opposed to the Public Health Act.
As with the Poor Law Guardians there was a certain overlap from
old to new. The Toxteth Park Board superseded the old Toxteth
Park Commissioners, and the Chairman was Councillor Gregson
of the Liverpool Council. The members' declaration included a
mention of the 'powers and authorities reposed in one as a Commissioner by virtue of the remaining powers', of the 1842 Act, and,
in July 1856, the Minutes record a general meeting at which six
'Commissioners' were present for the election of five new 'Commissioners'. Kirkham provides a classic example of administrative
continuity, for the Board of Health was highly reminiscent of an
earlier Committee of the Householders and Rate-payers Meeting,
which, in 1849, had moved 'that it is expedient to drain and sewer
the town in a substantial and effectual manner'. Five of this eleven-
strong Committee were to be found amongst the first Board of
nine members, including three of the Birley family. This is not
recorded critically, but rather as a reminder that administrative
machines need men and that, in local government circles, it is
simpler to change the machines than the men. The Public Health
Act gave teeth to interested parties, and it would be wrong to
suppose that, because the Boards were novel, their personnel was
fresh.

The cases of Borough Boards of Health have a special interest.
In Preston, a Council Sanitary Committee, formed 'to watch the
progress of Lord Morpeth's Bill', had reported it as a threat, and
a petition was launched against 'odious and inquisitorial interference'. The 'startling facts' that Preston's mortality figures
averaged out at twenty-eight per thousand (thus rendering the
town liable to compulsory legislation) stimulated the Council into
an application for a Board of Health. This 'most painful evidence'
resulted in a local Board created in 1850, to which was transferred
the powers of the Improvement Commission. Very little is then

heard of the Board of Health. Despite its being co-identical with the Council, no mention is made of it in the Council Minutes until 1853, and, even after this date, relevant entries are sparse. The Clitheroe Council, on the other hand, had shown immense interest in Public Health. From November 1848 to August 1850, meetings were often concerned with nothing else, and, in December 1848, the Council became 'The Sanitary Committee', to act upon the precepts of the Nuisance Removal and Disease Prevention Act of that year, 'especially at a period when a formidable Epidemic Disease has made its appearance'. Three Medical Officers were appointed, although only one was a medical practitioner, and the town was divided into eight districts for nuisance purposes. Meetings were sometimes daily, and reports constantly referred to the correlation of 'malignant Cholera' and 'stinkingly apparent' filth. St. Helens was, like Bolton, an extraordinary case, it comprised the four townships of Windle, Parr, Sutton and Eccleston, and it was well governed, for health purposes, by an Improvement Commission set up in 1845. In 1851 a further Act incorporated most of the provisions of the health legislation of the late forties, and additional powers were added by an Act of 1855. An important clause of the 1851 Act gave the General Board of Health sanction over loans desired by the St. Helens' Commissioners. The general tone of the Improvement Acts and the crucial loan-sanction clause place St. Helens in the centrally-supervised group of authorities, rather than with the independent Boroughs and Commissions.

Although the membership of the Boards was so small, most of them formed a series of sub-committees, thereby adding considerably to the regular demands on time and energy made by regular monthly Board Meetings. A typical instance is Newton Heath, where Building and Sanitary, Paving, Sewage and Scavenging, Gas and Water and Finance and Office Committees were formed. The net result was that, in small areas, small groups of men—either a half-attended Board or a sub-committee of two or three—were often making far-reaching decisions. Preston and Clitheroe were the only two authorities with any intermediary body, between Local and General Board, which might have acted as a check, and the General Board of Health was decidedly limited in its compass for a number of reasons, and especially so in Bolton and St. Helens. The upshot was tight little oligarchies with considerable influence. One example illustrates this vividly. Four men

G

levied a Special District Rate of 9*d.* on the Crumpsall rate-payers
in 1858.

So much for the Elective Board principle. One of the first
responsibilities of these bodies was the appointment of full-time
officials, in line with Chadwick's ideal of administrative expertise.
Local investigations show how difficult this was to realise. These
officials were frequently untrained and poorly paid, and their per-
formance was often unsatisfactory. At worst they were abjectly
inefficient. James Bell was appointed Inspector of the Poulton,
Bare and Torrisholme Board in June 1852, but, in October, he was
replaced by a man called McKie, and three men held the post
during a little over a year and a half. Crumpsall sacked their
inspector, John Berry, for 'inattention to the duties of his office',
and he refused to yield the 'plans and papers in his possession'
until challenged by the superintendent of police. Thomas Booth,
Surveyor and Nuisance Inspector for the Newton Heath, resigned
after only eight months, and a sub-inspector, P. Travis, had to
be discharged. W. Gregson, the Kirkham Surveyor and former
Township Committee man, was criticised for the 'improper mode'
of his work, and he was later called upon 'to attend to the works and
to the service of the Board more sedulously and steadily than he
had done. . .'. But a month or so later he was in bed when he
should have been attending a meeting. He tried to resign, but,
owing to the 'unsatisfactory state of his accounts', this was not
accepted. He refused to perform his duties, and, finally, he lost
three months' salary to compensate for his deficient accounts.

The most surprising feature of the compulsory appointment of
certain officials was the pluralism practised by many Boards. At
Garston, the same man, James Standing, was Surveyor, Inspector
of Nuisance and Rate-Collector. At Rusholme the jobs of
Inspector, Collector and Surveyor were combined. Clitheroe,
Over Darwen, Crumpsall, Wavertree and Moss Side combined the
posts of Surveyor and Inspector of Nuisance. Newton Heath
appointed John Needham as Clerk and Collector and James Booth
as Surveyor and Inspector of Nuisance. Apparently such pluralism
was in order, and it surely made for economy, but it leads a suspect
air to the ideal of the full-time expert, for, given the needs of these
areas and the functions outlined for these officers, each task was a
man-size job. One example may perhaps underline this point. The
Over Darwen Board of Health Minutes include catalogues of the
duties to be undertaken by the Surveyor and the Inspector of

Nuisance. The former had forty duties of a most comprehensive nature, and the latter's duties ran to twenty-three sections. The energetic Mr. Brady performed both functions. The financial rewards for such endeavour were unattractive. The same Mr. Brady earned only £100 per annum, although the post had been advertised at £150. Brady resigned in 1858, and the new Inspector, Mr. Rigby, was paid only £70 a year. Given a sudden demand for Surveyors and other officials it is scarcely surprising that Boards had to resort to hiring professional help and using part-time labour, or, indeed, that officers were often unsatisfactory. On the whole, there seems to have been too many who were overworked, too many on a part-time basis, and too many who were inefficient.

The question of Medical Officers of Health is an important one. Despite the long list of compulsory items in the Public Health Act, there was no obligation, strangely enough, to appoint Medical Officers. Many people felt that theirs was an essential rôle, and Liverpool had given a lead by appointing the first-ever municipal Medical Officers during Cholera outbreaks, but the lack of permanent Health Officers was woeful. Only two Boards seem to have made such appointments. Two men, Wright and Baines, were made Medical Officers for the Poulton Board, although it must be admitted that it is not clear from the records whether they were qualified doctors or not. Dr. John Pegge was appointed Medical Officer of Health for Newton Heath in 1855, and he appears to have been a qualified medical practitioner. All in all, the character of expertise in Lancashire was not encouraging, and the Boards of Health seem not to have sought out worthy officials and paid them well. Perhaps the urgency of Public Health reform tended to blow hot and cold. It was, for instance, probably no coincidence that, when the Cholera scare grew in 1853, the Rusholme Surveyor's salary was doubled from £60 to £120 and the pressure of his work mounted accordingly.

The third administrative element was the position of the General Board of Health *vis-à-vis* the Local Boards. Although the General Board mailed 100,000 letters in its first five years, relations between central and local bodies do not appear to have been as close as one might expect. Not all the Board's records are fully available—some, like the Layton with Warbreck Minutes, were lost on active service as war salvage—but only a few instances of direct contact have so far been uncovered. These were a couple of visits by Henry Austin, Secretary of the General Board, to Clitheroe, and of A. L.

Dickens, an Inspector of the General Board, to Crumpsall and Newton Heath. Apparently Robert Ranger also paid visits to Moss Side and St. Helens. Apart from the initial inspections and a few supplementary inspections, there was little direct personal contact between London and the localities. The clauses of the 1848 Act were complex, and the Boards were frequently demanding elucidation, or, for example, 'urging an early attention to the improvements of Kirkham'. Rusholme went to the extent of hiring a solicitor, Nicholas Earle, to explain the legal issues. He forwarded six foolscap sheets in answer to fifteen complicated queries posed him by the Board. Rusholme had to call on the General Board to define the status of streets developed from 'green fields', for house-owners 'contended that the streets were highways', and thus not eligible for action by the Local Board. Indeed, the General Board of Health was normally asked to meet complaints and objections of one kind or another. Alfred Dickens' visit to Crumpsall in 1856 was 'to promote a better feeling' following rate-payers' complaints. The General Board also had to rule on charges of voting forgeries and rating difficulties. Daniel Fleming, a Moss Side rate-payer, made such vehement criticisms of his road charges, that Robert Ranger was despatched by the General Board to report. Boundaries and bye-laws were a further matter of concern for the General Board. The proximity of Local Boards to one another around Manchester and Liverpool and their relation to the parent cities caused several boundary problems. Lists of bye-laws were forwarded for confirmation to the General Board. They were carefully studied. Rusholme's bye-laws for street cleansing and slaughter houses 'appear meagre' according to the General Board, and had to be revised. Over Darwen published several sets of bye-laws on lodging houses, slaughter-houses, street cleaning and so on. They included zealous and modern sounding projects for daily visits of refuse carts, the use of 'deodorizers', and a 'dust box or other movable receptacle for each house-hold', but these schemes were not implemented. The major feature, however, of central control lay in the loan-sanction clause, by which the General Board supervised borrowing by the Local Boards. This enabled the General Board to bring pressure to bear on the Local Boards to adopt Chadwick's own techniques and plans of, for instance, sewage development. The General Board of Health was an active agent in the new Public Health arrangements, and it supervised every item of the Local Board's work. There were few positive leads, however, and the General Board appears to have been occupied in the humdrum business of confirming bye-laws and plans, and in sorting out mundane queries. The obvious lack of itinerant inspectors and the reliance on the mails as the main mode of communication meant that the General Board's rôle, while insistent and constant, always seems rather aloof and distant.

It is, however, in the correspondence now held in the Public Records Office, between the General Board of Health and the Local Boards, that the answers to certain questions may be found which are not readily available in the more local sources. The minor mystery of how the Boards actually were initiated is partially solved. In Ormskirk the Sanitary Committee of the Ormskirk Poor Law Union was responsible. The Chairman, William Welsby, wrote to the General Board asking for information about the 1848 Act. He raised the petition, he posted the posters; he arranged the meeting in the Town Hall which was 'under my control'; he suggested possible witnesses; he reminded the General Board when it was slow to act; he acted as Returning Officer; and he was a member of and Clerk to the Board until well after 1858. This instance offers a vivid illustration of Public Health work arising from the Poor Law agencies. Another approach was in Layton with Warbreck, where James Heywood, the local M.P., organised the inception of the Board. He forwarded the petition, appending to it a most friendly letter addressed to 'My dear Chadwick', and he badgered the General Board when it delayed operations. Motives became a little clearer as well. The Ormskirk reformers were obviously disturbed by Irish Lodging-Houses which were 'quite a pest to the town', and their first action was an anxious and hasty effort to establish necessary bye-laws for such institutions. In Layton the importance of Blackpool—'the great sea-bathing place of North Lancashire'—is underlined. The Board was opposed to Babbage's plan for watering the area and was only half convinced of the need for wholesale sewering. Rather was it obsessed with bathing machines, hackney cab stands, pleasure boats, donkey carriages and other early paraphernalia of the nascent sea-side resort. Patiently the General Board persuaded the Local Board not to include extraneous bye-laws in its proposals, and, eventually, the Blackpool Improvement Act was passed to cover its especial needs.

Opposition to the Public Health Act is illustrated in the correspondence. When the Ormskirk Report was published in 1850, Thomas Worsley complained bitterly that there was 'scarcely any

truth', in these 'unfounded statements', and that the petition had
been got 'by misrepresentations'. A solicitor, M. Edge, forwarded
a counter-petition of 760 signatures, the consequence of an anti-
Public Health meeting. This assembly of 'ignorant dupes' was
attacked in turn by Thomas Hutton, who told the General Board
that the meeting was the work of those interested in the sale of
water. (He also ground his own axe—his shop was so poisoned by
an open sewer at the front and a slaughter-house at the back 'that
parties have been obliged to leave' his premises.) Thomas Ker-
shaw submitted a list of the slum cottage-owners who had requisi-
tioned this same meeting, advising the General Board that seven
out of the fifteen had already been summoned for nuisance.
Welsby, the Ormskirk Guardians, the local Justices, and the Union
Medical Officer, Dr. Symonds, sent memorials to the Board claiming that the report was 'not in the slightest degree exaggerated' and
praying for immediate action. The heat was little diminished when
elections were held. Welsby obviously ran the elections in cavalier
fashion, for he was returning officer, candidate and teller, and he
refused to allow anyone to scrutinise the count. He was criticised
for his selective distribution of voting papers and it is scarcely a
surprise to learn that men like Thomas Worsley were not returned.
These complaints occurred yearly, but the General Board contented themselves with non-committal acknowledgements and
claims that they had 'no power of interfering'. This seeming
impotence of the General Board is characteristic of its correspondence. It told the Layton Board that the extent of reform
would 'rest entirely with the inhabitants', and it contented itself,
in the main, with answering queries and shielding itself from the
bombardment of complaints with its formula of having 'no power
whatever to interfere'.

This, then, was the type of organisation created under the
Public Health Act. Small groups of more or less dedicated rate-
payers, a few over-worked, underpaid and often incompetent
officials, and an omnipotent but somewhat faraway body were the
chief characteristics of this organisation.

b. Other Authorities. The six Boroughs in Lancashire which
were in no way concerned with the Public Health Act organised
their Public Health affairs along much the same lines as a Local
Board of Health. The division of municipal activities into Committees was the obvious mode of approach to the pressing troubles
of unhealthy towns. Manchester formed a number of such Com-

mittees over the years and despite its varied difficulties, Manchester Corporation—'which has hitherto done its duty well'—
was praised by Playfair, and each new Act and each new Committee
brought fresh clauses and bye-laws to bear. In Liverpool the 1846
Sanitary Act allowed the Council to so consolidate the several
functions of several agencies at one fell swoop, and it vested the
whole of these powers in the newly formed Health Committee—
a triumph for the Benthamite concept of an all-purpose local body.
The Health Committee was a large body of between thirty-eight
and sixty-four Councillors, and it divided itself into five sub-
committees of twelve, thus emulating, in practice, the Manchester
pattern. Usually only a dozen or so attended the main committee
meetings, and enthusiasts like William Rathbone and J. A. Tinne
were on two or three sub-committees. Blackburn, incorporated in
1851, took on the tasks of the Improvement Commission in 1854,
establishing a Highway and General Drainage Committee for the
purpose. Oldham had a Surveyor's Committee, and, later, a Gas
and Waterworks Committee. Rochdale had four Committees for
Lighting, Scavenging, Hackney Coaches and Fire Engines, and
Warrington had Sanitary, Sewerage and Street Improvement
and Lighting Committees. The Improvement Commissions also
worked through Committees. Fleetwood had its Lighting and
Watch Committee, its Road Committee and its Sanitary Committee, whilst Bury had a Paving Committee, a Lighting, Scavenging
and Nuisance Committee and a Sewage Committee, together with
two sub-committees 'to inspect the state of the roads and lamps'.
    If anything, the officials appointed by these bodies have earned
more fame than the elected members, and they were certainly an
improvement on their counterparts on the Local Boards. Most
famous of all, of course, was Dr. W. H. Duncan of Liverpool, but
John Newlands, the Borough Engineer, and Thomas Fresh, the
first inspector of Nuisance, enjoyed considerable repute. R. L.
Gossage and as well known a personage as Robert Stephenson were
to aid the development of Liverpool's water supply. Manchester
was equally lucky in its initial choice of officers in John Francis, the
General Surveyor, James Walker, the Consulting Engineer, and
F. Bateman, the Water Superintendent. Naturally enough, the
Borough Councils and Improvement Commissions were quick to
appoint a variety of officials and sometimes there was continuity
from the Improvement Commissions to the Borough Councils, and
Rochdale, for instance, retained ten of the Commission's officers.

In the important respect of Medical Officers of Health, however, these authorities were no more enlightened than the Local Boards. Liverpool was, with Dr. W. H. Duncan, the notable exception. Manchester followed much later in 1868, but Blackburn had no Medical Officer until 1874 and Oldham none until 1871. The major difference between the Boards and the authorities lay in the absence of a central agency. The major towns were happy to proffer evidence to governmental commissions, and, during the Cholera epidemic of 1854, Liverpool had some slight connection with the General Board of Health. Bury was in touch with Chadwick on occasion, and Rawlinson inspected the town's drainage, but otherwise Manchester's alarm at centralisation—Heron, Manchester's Town Clerk, led a deputation in 1848 to explain to Lord Morpeth the Corporation's hostility to the Public Health Act— was fairly characteristic of the Lancashire Councils and Commissions. They were suspicious of bureaucratic interference and inspection and they doubtless felt, with some justification, their efforts were sufficiently effective. Although the relation between the Local and the General Board might not have been unduly strong, the other authorities were completely independent of state intervention, save that their powers were all authorised by Local Acts of Parliament. For the greater part of Lancashire's inhabitants, there was no extra-municipal watch or check on Public Health organisation.

The major advance in state interference came after 1858. Under the Local Government Act of that year, dozens more townships established Boards. In the ten years of the 1848 Act Lancashire had twenty-six areas with some allegiance to the central government, two of them of a sketchy variety. In the following ten years the number rose to eighty-six. This included Liverpool, by a Local Act of 1863, but Manchester still remained aloof. The consolidation and completion of this tendency was accomplished by the Public Health Act of 1872, which, amongst other decrees, made Medical Officers compulsory. Urban and Rural Sanitary Districts were erected, and, of Lancashire's sixteen Boroughs at that time, only Barrow had neither local nor national sanitary powers. When the County Councils Act of 1888 came into force and the county enjoyed a supervisory capacity in respect of these Sanitary Districts, Lancashire had 135 Districts, apart from the eleven major Boroughs. It is of interest to note that of the twenty-six original Local Boards, twenty-one remained more or less intact, whilst the other five had become absorbed in the larger cities and towns. In terms of administration, therefore, it must be concluded that central control of Public Health in Lancashire had made relatively little headway by 1858.

Control of water supply

a. *Local Boards of Health*. Water was the key to the Public Health problem. Water was needed for normal consumption and commercial purposes and the population explosion had obviously increased the demand extensively. The tendency towards urbanisation made the difficulty even greater, for reliance on springs, wells and pumps was bound to be undermined by the cramped housing of industrial towns. Water was needed to combat the filthy state of streets and drains, and the widespread introduction of sewerage schemes was yet another burden on resources of water. In modern times the average consumption of water per head is often as high as forty gallons a day, including commercial and civic usage. In the eighteen-thirties the citizens of Manchester and Liverpool used six and eight gallons respectively each day, although the range between the amount consumed by rich and poor was quite wide. Even allowing a paltry daily ration of eight gallons, the rise in population in Lancashire between the beginning of the century and 1831 implied that an extra 5 million gallons of water were required each day. In 1801, on a reckoning of eight gallons per day, the country's total requirement was roughly 1,985 million gallons per annum, and, by 1831, the figure was an astronomical 4,200 million gallons. With civil engineering still in its infancy and with little public pressure, thirty years was a brief spell in which to expect many advances. Nor was this a problem restricted to large towns, for the rise in population was evident, if less spectacular in smaller towns. The pre-1858 Boards in Lancashire do offer, in fact, a wide range of examples from tiny Moss Side to an ever-growing Preston. This enables one to observe the reaction to the demand for water on local governmental units both large and small. The overall striking feature, of course, is that by 1858, roughly 400,000 of Lancashire's 2,429,000 were under the supervision of the General Board of Health, which, under the Public Health Act, required property-owners to provide water for their buildings. So late was the Public Health Act, in comparison with the Poor Law Amendment Act and the Acts relating to Police Reform, that it would be unfair to expect giant inroads into the problem by 1858, especially

as many of the Boards were formed in the mid-fifties. None the
less, the issue was a pressing one, and, if the reports of the various
Commissions and Committees be believed, one of some standing.
What steps had been taken by 1858 to supply with water the
400,000 Lancastrians living under the General Board's jurisdiction?
Preston, Bolton and Wigan were by far the largest towns concerned. Preston, its Board of Health formed in 1850, made no
move in any direction for three years, and one of the first mentions
of the Board's activity is its annual expenditure for the year ending
May 1853. This was a paltry item of £80, which is an indictment
in itself of Preston's sloth in this matter. It must also be remembered that, according to John Clay and Lyon Playfair, only about
half of Preston's 10,000 houses were supplied with water and that
the annual charge was as exorbitant as £8 per year. In 1853, however, the Preston Corporation, acting as the Board of Health,
purchased the Preston Water Company at a cost of £135,225. By
1855 the Board met and kept its own minutes separately from the
normal Council Meeting, a move dictated by the growing weight
of business. In 1856 John Newton was engaged at a handsome
salary of £250 to improve water supplies, and, in 1858, his first
annual report suggested that such improvements were, at last, on
the move. George Thomas Clark's Report on Wigan's Public
Health needs in 1850 said that no town was 'better suited for
complete and cheap supply of water'. Pumps and springs were,
however, the main source of water, with one well—Boy's Well—
serving 10,000 people. The Wigan Waterworks Company had two
reservoirs, with a supposed reserve of 1·75 million gallons, serving
one-fifth of Wigan's houses, either through house taps or communal court taps. Clark reckoned the supply would last only thirty-
three days, whereas one hundred days was, he felt, the minimum
safety margin. Robert Rawlinson was also asked to report on
Wigan's mammoth difficulty in 1852, two years after the foundation of the Board of Health, and he advised the Borough to begin
a major scheme based on the impounding of the Seven Stars Brook
in the Douglas Valley. In 1853 the Wigan Waterworks and Police
Act enabled the Board of Health to purchase the privately owned
waterworks, and, under the Waterworks Act, uniform rates were
established beginning at 1s. 6d. for tapped water and 4s. if a bath
or water-closet was used. But, eventually, the Board succumbed to
the urgent necessity for a large-scale solution, and Rawlinson's
scheme was promulgated by the Wigan Waterworks Act of 1860.

It was ten years, in fact, before the Wigan Board of Health applied itself vigorously to the Borough's needs. The Bolton Waterworks Company was established in 1824, with holdings at Dady Meadow Springs. Six other reservoirs and watersheds were developed before the Corporation took them over. The Improvement Act of 1850 extended the corporation's powers considerably, and the big Heston Reservoir was completed under the Council's supervision in 1857.

Eight Boards had, by 1861, populations of between ten and twenty thousand, and a sample of these may next be studied. B. H. Babbage reported on Accrington's drainage and water needs in 1850, but no extant local material suggests that the resultant Board of Health made any moves to improve the supply of water before 1860. Lancaster's water, with the 'sooty taste' and 'dingy colour', had been roundly condemned in the Report of James Smith in 1849, and he recommended the four million gallons Scotforth Reservoir, which would provide twenty gallons a day for each person. Like Preston and Wigan, Lancaster certainly had plans well in hand in the middle eighteen-fifties. These aimed to provide 600,000 gallons per day from Millstone Grit Springs, at a weekly cost of 3s. 4d. to each household. The Newton Heath Board deliberated for over four years before forming a committee 'to consider the best means of obtaining a supply of water to the township'. In 1859 the Board were still wrangling over water supply with Manchester Corporation. The Over Darwen Board undertook but few negotiations with Darwen Waterworks, its only concern with water being a lengthy row with the local company about fire plugs. This began in 1854 and was only resolved in 1859. It reached a climax in 1857 when the Board suffered the indignity of having its fire-plug water cut off, which forced the Board to purchase a meter. It is a comical reflection on the times that the body, purportedly responsible for watering the town, could be held to ransom in this way. St. Helens gives a more complete illustration of Boards of this middling size. The St. Helens Water Company had operated since 1843, but in 1851, the Commissioners (although subject to General Board rulings, the St. Helens Improvement Commission retained its label) obtained control of the workings with the sanction of the General Board of Health, and made some slight improvements. The next year, 1852, Hawkesley presented a larger scheme to raise 550,000 additional gallons a day at a cost of £11,850. Again, the General Board gave its sanction. An amending

and consolidating Act was passed in 1855. This included a contract
with Liverpool Corporation for supplies from the Rivington
works. The Act laid down uniform Water-rates and ensured that
the four townships would be fully supplied with water, wherever
possible. New works went on apace, extending pipes to the limits
of Sutton and Parr and building up storage space of over one
million gallons. Once more, with General Board confirmation,
borrowing of £30,000 was empowered. The measures for improv-
ing St. Helens' water supply were well carried out to the satisfac-
tion of the General Board of Health.

A dozen or so smaller townships, with populations less than
10,000, remain to be examined. No mention of water occurred in
the Rusholme Minutes for three years after its inauguration. In
1854 the Board petitioned against the Manchester Waterworks
Bill, and forced the insertion of clauses to 'preclude a power of
compulsory rating' on Rusholme. It was left to the Board to
'Contract and agree' for such water as they desired from Manchester.
The Crumpsall and Moss Side Boards had no discussion of water
supply before 1858, despite Crumpsall's water being 'tainted by
foul matters' and Moss Side's housing fast outrunning its wells. In
the Liverpool area, Toxteth Park appeared to do little or nothing
about water, while Garston and Wavertree initially contented
themselves with enquiries to Liverpool Corporation. The Kirkham
and Poulton Boards of Health took no account of water-supply at
any of their meetings before 1860. Clitheroe was soon anxious to
establish a water-works at Waddington Fell, and the report of an
engineer, Philip Park, was accepted in 1850. The cost would be
£7,671 and the cubic capacity would be 538,444 gallons daily. A
civil engineer, James McLansborough, estimated the cost at
£6,714. Later the energy seemed to fade. The Board asked the
General Board whether a private company might not be preferable,
and that twelve months would be needed to draw up plans. The
General Board, understandably enough, could not comprehend
this delay and frowned on the idea of private enterprise. The
Surveyor, John Robinson, was then asked to map out a cheaper
scheme, and he proposed a £4,000, 1½ million-gallon reservoir.
This plan was generally approved. Ormskirk, with its populace of
some 6,000, was the first Board to complete a major project.
120,000 gallons of spring water were steam pumped to the
Greetby Hill Reservoir and served, via covered tanks, to householders at a cost of 1d. or 1½d. per week. Rawlinson, who had

inspected Ormskirk for the General Board, returned to earn £400 for supervising this £4,500 scheme, which was reported completed in May 1854. This successful venture demonstrated what enthusiastic action could produce in a small town.

Such unequal progress at all grades was hardly sensational, but three provisos must be made. First, water-supplies existed however inadequately, whereas sanitary services were often negligible. In spite of the demand for water to implement sewerage schemes, it is to be expected that sanitation should loom larger than water-supply with the Local Boards. Second, the Boards contained only three towns over 20,000 strong, and it was obviously in over-crowded and rapidly expanding areas that water was less accessible to private individuals. Third, most of the Local Boards were patently too small to manage large-scale undertakings. They were based on political rather than geological boundaries, and the sheer chance of parochial frontiers coinciding with drainage basins was a slender one. Even St. Helens, with four townships, failed to do this. Many tended to rely either on private initiative, be it commercial or individual, or on purchase from larger towns. One can see the beginnings of yet another of the complex overlaps characteristic of English administration. This was the first direct governmental interference in water-supply and, because the administrative spheres were so rigid, water reserves were often outside the area of demand, namely, in another's administrative sphere. The implicit decision to leave water undertakings to local resolution, rather than to plan on a national scale, was to be one of the causes of the century-old struggle between town and country for water supplies, of which Manchester's constant attempts to invade the Lake District are a prime instance.

b. Other Authorities. If the watering of small towns was to give rise to anxiety, the troubles of the bigger towns and cities were correspondingly larger, and some of them tackled the problem with relish. The Manchester and Salford Waterworks Company had eked out rainwater rivers and pumps to the tune of some 1½ to 2 million gallons per day. In 1851 the Corporation gained control of this rather feeble company, and, under the powers allowed by the 1847 Manchester Corporation Waterworks Act, they began the huge Longdendale scheme, which was planned to provide no less than 30 million gallons per day. The cost was enormous; there were squabbles over rentals with Salford and other Local authorities; there were financial and engineering embarrassments; and the profits of the prosperous gasworks were used to offset the water-rate. Despite land-slides and floodings, the waterworks attained solvency by 1862 and the beginnings of a gigantic concern, which was to supply water not only to Manchester but to its environs, was under way.

The story of Liverpool's water-supply has attracted many writers, possibly because it is a tale of wrangling and conflict over many years. Two companies—the Bootle and the Liverpool and Harrington—supplied Liverpool on a haphazard and wastefully competitive basis. In 1845, the Highway Board ordered a Special Committee to take evidence 'on the alleged dearness and insufficiency of water'. Five thousand signed a memorial of complaint against the trading companies. It was reported that ten courts in Banastre Street had had no water for three years, and that, in Charles Street, each tap served thirty people—for half an hour on three days in the week. The press joined in, with the *Liverpool Mercury* attacking the 'grasping avarice and tyrannical oppression' of the water companies, which were, in turn, defended by Harwood Banner. The Liverpool Corporation Waterworks Act of 1847 gave powers of purchase of existing undertakings, which was accomplished in the following year. Still the sounds of battle were heard, for there then ensued an almost legendary conflict between the Pikists and the Anti-Pikists. The former wished to promote a giant scheme at Rivington Pike, drawing on the river Douglas and Riddlesworth, while the latter preferred a programme of local works based on sandstone springs. An investigation by three engineers, including Hawksley, favoured the Rivington scheme, and this was approved by Parliament. The Anti-Pikists obtained a Council majority, but the contracts had been sealed, and, after a court of enquiry, the work was begun. Chorley waterworks, which was sited at Rivington, was acquired, and, by 1857, a constant water-supply was tapped from 500 acres of reservoirs containing 3,000 million gallons.

The other Boroughs were by no means as thorough, nor were, of course, their problems so extensive. A Parliamentary return, dated 1857, shows that of thirteen water companies in Lancashire, only four—Bolton, Wigan, Liverpool and Chorley, and Manchester—were publicly owned. The list was not a comprehensive one, but it does show that Ashton, Accrington, Blackburn, Bury and Radcliffe, Clitheroe, Colne, Darwen, Rossendale and Warrington were served privately as late as 1857. Given the notorious inadequacy of privately supplied water, it would seem sensible to adopt public ownership as the threshold of advance in this field. Ashton purchased the local trading company in 1856, Oldham took over the two Strinesdale Reservoirs from the Oldham Gas-Lighting and Waterworks Company in 1853 and constructed further ones of 700 million gallons capacity; and Rochdale began control of its water-supply in 1866. Blackburn, well served by its local company, which provided a daily supply of around twenty gallons, did not purchase this going concern until 1875. Warrington, like Blackburn, had no water-company until the eighteen-forties, and it was remarkably late—1890-91—before it was purchased by the Corporation. Of the non-boroughs, Fleetwood flirted with the Fylde Waterworks Company for several years without making any headway; a private Company was floated in Southport in 1853; and it was not until after lengthy argument and squabbling that Bury purchased the Bury and Radcliffe Waterworks in 1872. New private companies, like the Widnes Gas and Water Company, were still being floated at the end of the period. Public control of water was thus the exception rather than the rule before 1858. One of the strongest motives for a change of supervision was the need for agencies sturdy enough to join in the scramble for gathering grounds, which the localised management of water-supply was to initiate.

Apart from Local Acts, there was no general legal pressure on these towns to provide water-supplies. Again it must be pointed out that the Commissions and Corporations were governing bodies of a general kind, with no special interest in Public Health. Like the work of the Poulton and Layton Local Boards, activities in Fleetwood and Southport concern the growth of the West Coast holiday centres, with piers, bathing machines, promenades, donkeys, pleasure boats, hotels and sea walls prominent in discussions. Towns like Bury and Blackburn were naturally concerned with gas-lighting, traffic and markets. In so far as the use of incorporation or of the older Improvement Commission was motivated by tradesmen and business people, commercial reasons tended to be primary. The well-lit, well-made street, leading to the spacious market-hall, was more direct an influence than the long term need for water-supply. Indeed, the justification of suing for municipal status was sometimes avowedly political, as in the cases of Manchester or Bolton, or specifically connected with policing, as in

Oldham and Salford. Public Health was never the sole and rarely
the leading cause of Incorporation, and Councils lacked the relative
single-mindedness, impetus and oversight of the Local Boards of
Health.

Control of Sanitation

   a. Local Boards of Health. Prevailing medical theory and the
more pragmatic judgement of the senses combined to make the
removal of filth the premier duty of Public Health authorities.
Cleanliness was the essential prerequisite for a healthy community,
and deposits of filth, especially of sewage, were rightly deemed to
be a frightening threat to social well-being. As with the constantly
flowing tap of today, so with the modern lavatory flushing system;
a simple twist or tug makes for familiar acceptance, and it is
difficult not to take such services for granted. It is salutary to delve
back not too many decades to a time when these problems suddenly loomed large; when, indeed, the necessity of solving them
was a literal matter of life and death.

   Of the largest towns, Preston had a mixed record. Its Improvements Commission, which included the Mayor and eight of the
Council, had kept the streets in repair, and, through the offices of
the Preston Gas and Light Company, Preston had been the first
provincial town to have gas-lit thoroughfares. And yet Preston
was lackadaisical about its water-supply and not very enterprising
in terms of main drainage. It was six years before the Board of
Health began the necessary and obligatory surveys of the town's
drainage, and it was 1858 before the General Board of Health
signified approval of the Preston arterial drainage scheme. By 1862
about two-thirds of Preston's houses drained into main sewers.
Clark had reported that sanitation in Wigan had reached a
dramatically low level. One privy to twenty-four houses was the
norm and forty-five two-roomed cottages in Wallgate shared four
privies and had their first floors below ground level. Only 100 yards
of street out of a possible 28,979 yards were sewered, and flat-
bottomed sewers 16 feet square were usually the only type. It was,
none the less, 1857 before the Wigan Board of Health published
bye-laws for the cleaning of streets and the emptying of water
closets, privies and cesspools. By 1853 Wigan had drainage plans
accepted by the General Board, but it is not until the 1874 Improvement Act that the Wigan Corporation obtained the right to
enforce a uniform system of sewerage, with proper management of

privies, cesspools and middens. Bolton was slow to deal with its problem of sewage disposal, and the Hacken and Burden Sewerage Works were not completed until 1884, when many were still without adequate sewerage. In 1873 there were, in fact, less than 500 water closets in the town, and the bye-laws of 1861, significantly enough, have much to say about ashpits and cesspools, but very little on water carriage sewage. Bolton had been given sanction to borrow £16,000 but only £400 could be raised, and it was decided to use chief rents and rate revenue for sewage disposal, rather than a capital loan.

Newton Heath, Over Darwen and St. Helens may serve as examples of medium-sized Boards. The 'proposed sewerage' of Newton Heath was planned by Clement Trapp in 1855, a year after the establishment of the Board. Holland Street and Albion Street were each 'declared a highway' the following year, when their drainage was completed. Legal problems caused some hold-up later, but the Newton Heath Board had set off to a brisk start. Over Darwen were also fairly quick off the mark. Comprehensive sets of bye-laws were swiftly published, and the Scavengers' Refuse Cart was to pass daily through the streets. Baths and Wash-houses were purchased and sewage plans submitted. Brady, the Inspector of Nuisances, promptly wrote a sewage report, and notices were served on householders needing privies. A Bristol Tumbler Cleansing Cart, priced £29, a dray horse and six whale-bone brooms were purchased, and the Board bought 2,000 yards of piping from Ingham and Sons, stressing 'that they would have to supply the smaller pipes'. Sewage tenders were invited. Edwin Knight's tender was accepted, then turned down in favour of John Isherwood, and, by November 1856, the Board was embarking on side-street sewage. Unluckily, this vital spark of Public Health energy came near to extinction. Isherwood was guilty of breach of contract, for he delivered several ton loads of materials to Wood Street as much as sixteen hundredweight short, and this was still causing difficulties in 1858. There were also considerable troubles with James Greenway, concerning the easement through his land for the main sewer, and this continued over half a year, while other duties distracted the Board from the main task of sewerage. It was not until December of 1859 that, at long last, a decision that the firm of Trapp and Helis should survey Darwen and plan a complete sewerage system was made. St. Helens had been empowered by the Local Act of 1845 to construct common sewers

H

in any street and provision was made for the communication thereto of private drains, especially in new houses. By 1851, when the Act was replaced, £1,272 had been spent on sewering. The 1851 legislation gave the St. Helens authority compulsory powers to oblige owners to sewer. Facilities at 'a reasonable sum' had not been used. By 1855 another £1,967 had been spent, and 12,993 lineal yards of sewer had been laid. Unfortunately, the sewerage found its main outlet into the Sankey Brook, and the Local Act of 1855 made provision for a main arterial sewer of some 3,000 yards at a cost of £10,000.

Of the smaller Boards, Ormskirk was again the only one of all Lancashire's towns to have completed a full scheme by 1854. Again Rawlinson was the planner. The cost was £5,500, and over 15,000 lineal yards of secondary drains and four outlet sewers were laid. In Rusholme the firm of Barber and Worthington were hired to build a main sewer, and it was also decided that twenty-two streets should be 'sewered, levelled, paved, flagged, and channelled'. Yet over a year later only in Moore Street had work begun. All previous proposals on sewage were rescinded, and owners were requested to 'level, pave, flag, sough and sewer'. A year later privies and ashpits 'required in almost all cases emptying and cleaning, and in many altering, reconstructing and draining'. In 1854 Moore Street was still uncompleted, and, as late as 1859, notices to culvert and sewer were still being issued in an attempt to deal with open brook sewerage. The Crumpsall Board employed Jesse Grundy to extend sewerage in Lower Crumpsall. Occupiers exhibited a 'determination not to comply with the notices and resist any claims' on specified work, and Grundy was threatened with proceedings for non-fulfilment of contract. These sewers were completed in July of 1855, but 'the work was done in a slovenly manner'. Although new contractors—John and William Worthington—were employed, the sewering of thoroughfares was a slow and laborious business, and the rate-payers and occupiers were most unco-operative. Moss Side's survey suggested 'good and deep drains' for all streets, and seven streets were decided upon for sewering in 1856. Moss Lane, Withington Road and Whalley Road were the three most important of these, but rate-payers opposed these moves strenuously. It was June 1858 before contracts were negotiated with Messrs. Worthingtons, and, in December 1859, Moss Lane was still not completed.

In Kirkham Robert Hull's tender was accepted in July 1853—

over a year after the inception of the Board—but soon he was being threatened with legal action for incomplete work. At one stage, Hull was ordered to complete his work in one month or continue at his own expense. Six months later the work was still not finished, and it was 1855 before Hull's initial account was settled. It was decided that the 'sewerage of the town still be taken direct to the brook', but, more sensibly, arrangements were made to construct private drains at the same time as the relevant public sewers. Such drains had to be of glazed tiles, laid in tubular columns under the supervision of the Surveyor—a move very much in line with Chadwick's thinking. The Poulton Board was formed in 1852, but drainage plans were refused by the General Board and it was June 1854 before the first bill for sewering—a paltry £98 18s. 0d.—was paid to the firm of Johnson and Son. In the period 1855–57, however, several schemes based on tubular earthenware and iron pipes were mooted, although by 1859 the Board seemed to have lost some of its energy for sewering with some areas of the town as yet untouched. Sewering in Layton was a most protracted business, especially the main drainage of South Shore, Blackpool, which gave rise to a correspondence which had not ended in 1858 and which involved both Dickens and Austin of the General Board.

The record is not encouraging. Certainly the Boards had other tasks to perform, like street cleansing and the licensing of new buildings. The coastal authorities seemed remarkably attracted by the idea of repairing coastal roads, doubtless with an eye to their future as holiday resorts. Problems of nuisance, of lodging-houses and slaughter-houses were other tasks with which the Boards had to contend. Gas and markets also attracted the attention of some Boards. None the less, sanitary progress was abnormally slow, and, ten years after the Public Health Act, which supposedly ushered in the era of sanitation, there was little to show. The story is one of lengthy negotiations and hesitant planning, with few major proposals urged forcibly and firmly sustained. The lack of strength in the elected Boards; the frailty of the Boards' officers; and the vigorous opposition of many rate-payers were sufficient to delay most schemes. The Boards were not entirely to blame for the dilatory nature of their work. Practically every authority was troubled by its contractors. At Rusholme the firm of Barber and Worthington managed to sewer and pave five out of a proposed twenty-two streets in three years and others were equally deplorable. It is sometimes forgotten that engineering schemes could not be constructed in a day, and this was even true of sewage than of water plans, for technical experience of water projects was much more extensive at this time. Civil engineering was still a rough-and-ready science, and Chadwick's theories were being hastily transferred from the drawing-board to the crowded towns. The new principles and techniques of draining and sewering were as yet not fully mastered. Schemes were obviously badly programmed and underestimated, and the overall impression one gains is of a protracted, shoddy, incompetent and sometimes downright dishonest series of operations. In blaming the Victorians for their tardiness in coping with sanitary problems, one must be reminded of the vast practical and technical difficulties involved.

  b. Other Authorities. Liverpool made desperate efforts to solve her sanitary problem. Newland's expensive sewerage scheme added a six-mile outlet and forty-six miles of sewers and main drains to Liverpool's fifty-three miles of drainage system in ten years. Only the completion of the Rivington Pike water project made water-flushed sanitation possible, and, with rooted objections from landlords like the Earl of Sefton, it was 1872 when 'the victory of the water closet was now assured'. Scavenging remained important, but the contractors were often inefficient, and the Inspector of Nuisance received a hundred complaints a week in 1847. Newland's plan was adopted after long deliberations in 1848, until which time, he claimed there had been 'no steady endeavour to carry on sanitary operations on sound principles as preventative measures; in place of this we see spasmodic efforts during periods of alarm'. Overcrowding and cellar-life were included in the programme. In Albert Street, for example, the 1,813 inhabitants had no more than 4·4 square yards apiece. 22,680 were removed from cellars and 'healthy habitations were simultaneously provided', although some Roman Catholic commentators suggested the Corporation blundered badly and caused overcrowding elsewhere by these evictions. The number of scavengers sprang from 65 to 333, 11,000 ventilated and drained houses were built, and 40,000 yards of street were paved by 1858. Despite these and other impressive efforts, in the thirty years after the 1846 Act the death rate remained around thirty-two in a thousand.

  Manchester's early endeavours concerned street cleaning and drainage, with the new egg-shaped stoneware and fireclay replacing the old brick sewers. Housing sanitation, as in Liverpool, waited on sufficient water. In the meantime, the night-soil men continued their efforts, although they tended to shift the ordure from where it was most convenient, as they were paid by the ton. By 1846 an army of 112 scavengers was hard at work cleaning privies and removing night-soil. Water-driven house-drainage was a later development. Salford's major sewage work was not commenced until 1863, and, in the same year, Ashton, pressed by the disasters of the Cotton Famine, was loaned £3,760 for a sewage scheme. Blackburn Council authorised drainage works in 1854. They were begun in 1856, and in 1860 the whole Borough was declared a single drainage area, with the main egg-shaped outlet sewer completed the following year. The pollution caused by sewage caused proceedings to be taken against the Council in 1865, and it was the eighteen-seventies before the Borough's problems were properly solved.

Oldham Council did little about arterial drainage. The Council assumed the function of removing manure to the South-West Lancashire countryside in 1853. Much effort was expended on road repair and construction. In spite of opposition from four Turnpike Trusts, twenty-four new streets were laid, and many others paved and drained. The Rochdale Improvement Act of 1853 prohibited drainage into the River Rock and provided for sewerage construction. Middens were supposed to be abolished but, in 1868, there were still 4,000. Only one Inspector was available to supervise the entire sanitation of the town, and, unlike some other towns, Rochdale did little to improve its roads until the time of the Cotton Famine when the unemployed were used. Even the removal of night-soil led to conflict over its ownership between the Commissioners and the large property-owners.

All in all, the emphasis was on road repair and clearance, presumably to ensure mobility and freedom for traffic, while house drainage, hindered by slowness in developing sufficient water-supplies, took second place. There seems to have been a desire to cleanse the surface thoroughfares and to dispose of night-soil from the town centres. As always, it was private property which held out longest, and it was normally after 1858—indeed, often well into the last quarter of the century—that the major towns of Lancashire approached the question of sanitation in a thorough manner.

Certainly the General Board of Health was anxious to promote the theme that Public Health was profit-making. Here one sees the obvious influence of Chadwick, with his austere equation of the Great Happiness of the Greatest Number with 'greatest national

product' or 'greatest national profit'. Communal ill-health prevented the maximisation of net social produce, and must be
drastically treated. The use of the Benthamite argument at a
humdrum provincial level is nowhere better illustrated than in the
work of the Inspectors investigating townships on behalf of the
General Board. Each Supplementary Report contained a financial
survey guaranteed to prove that the investment in a drainage
system would be an economical proposition. The argument proceeded in a didactic and facile manner, faintly reminiscent of the
mechanical gyrations of the master's Felicific Calculus. Rusholme
provides one such example. Over a period of six and a half years
forty people had died in excess of a normal mortality rate. There
were thirty preventable sicknesses for every one such preventable
death—a total of 1,200. Forty funerals at £5 plus 1,200 sicknesses,
allowing an expense of one pound on each, cost £1,400. Rawlinson
estimated that given a loss of five years on each life, £1,500 had
been lost in terms of production. The total loss was £2,900, or
£446 per year. £446 was the equivalent of 5 per cent interest
repayment on a capital loan of £8,920 'which could drain the whole
township'.

Financial character
    a. *Local Boards of Health.* Public administration ineluctably
becomes a question of money. The bill had to be footed, and those
on whom the taxation is levied need persuading that the optimum
balance between necessity and cheapness has been obtained.
Modern grumbles over public finance testify to this very human
attitude, and, in mid-nineteenth century Lancashire, the un-
familiarity of heavy public expenditure surely magnified the alarm
of the rate-payers. The idea of communal endeavour in social
fields was also a new one, and, where it seemed to contravene the
privacy of the Victorian gentleman, it raised some opposition. The
Public Health Act placed the financing agency, namely the rate-
payer, at the hub of the system. This was a typically Benthamite
gambit, for the interests of governed and governor were most
nearly allied, in that a representative group of rate-payers supervised the expenditure of their own rates. Asa Briggs has summarised
the position admirably: 'When Victorian legislation was passed
which tampered with the rights of private property, it was always
contentious and difficult to implement. . . . The most effective
argument for sanitary reform was that it would actually save

money.' A little later he speaks of the 'protracted local arguments' before rate-payers were satisfied 'that the long run was worth bothering about'.[1]

The financial aspect was emphasised by the loan-sanction clause in the Public Health Act ,which was Chadwick's main lever in promulgating his own theories. The General Board had the authority to sanction mortgages raised on local rates to supply funds. Chadwick obliged Local Boards to undertake reforms based on his 'arterial' schemes, and the Boards were then left with little choice but to use the band of engineers who agreed with Edwin Chadwick. These were mainly the Public Health Inspectors who were employed part-time in their official capacity and were thus free to work privately. Henry Austin, Rawlinson, Ranger, Cresy, Rammel and Lee were the most noted ones, while Chadwick blocked the work of his opponents—engineers like Rendel, Wicksteed and especially Thomas Hawkesley—elsewhere. Cheapness was 'the greatest single justification for the sanitary despotism of the Board', and despite the trenchant opposition of the Institute of Civil Engineers, tubular pipe manufacture sprang from 104 miles in 1848 to 2,600 miles in 1854. It was argued that, for instance, the new Waterworks planned at Lancaster and Ormskirk showed a tremendous saving on more outmoded schemes of providing water. Again it would seem profitable to examine the Board's financial character under the three headings already used.

Preston was by far the largest Board in Lancashire. It showed little more than a nominal interest in Public Health until 1853, when a considerable loan of £135,225 was raised to purchase the Preston Water Company. This represented a *per capita* expenditure of 3s. 4d., although, of course, rate-payers would also have had to provide water rates and additional rentals for improvements.

In the medium-sized areas, Newton Heath soon obtained permission to raise a loan of £11,000 and Over Darwen one of £3,000. Both these were for sewerage schemes and neither borrowed money nor did very much with regard to water supply. Over Darwen refused the Darwen Waterworks Company offer of £20 shares at £25, and it was 1859 before a general survey, costing £300, was decided upon. Over Darwen illustrates the working of the rating system. Seth Harwood, the Poor Rate Collector, was asked in 1855 to collect a General District Rate of 6d. in the pound, which was expected to realise £485. Six months later a one shilling rate was

[1] A. Briggs, *Victorian Cities* (1963), pp. 20–21.

called. Boards were able to levy two rates, one for general purposes and another—the Special District Rate—for specific needs. In November 1855 such a rate was levied for the construction of a main sewer. This sixpenny rate was followed by two more in December. One of these was a sixpenny Highway Rate and the other a sixpenny General District Rate. In 1855, therefore, there was a 3s. rate, with a calculated revenue of £2,910. With the loan of £3,000, this gave Over Darwen, in 1855, an income of almost £6,000. The rates alone should have raised a *per capita* sum of 3s. 9d., not unlike the cost quoted for Preston. The Collector was also responsible for obtaining fines in respect of nuisance offences. Finance was sometimes an important matter of controversy. In 1858 only a Chairman's casting vote carried a motion in favour of borrowing on the rates to pay for private improvements, and a month later it was rescinded, and it was resolved that 'bills for private improvements be forwarded to the parties'. Private improvements were a constant bone of contention, and in November 1858, legal proceedings were threatened on forty-one outstanding accounts amounting to £1,200.

The Ranger Report on St. Helens included valuable information about expenditure between 1845 and 1855. For water supply some £16,000 had been expended, and the Board empowered the St. Helens Commissioners to borrow a further £30,000. For sewering the Commission had spent £3,240 and it was given permission, in 1855, to raise loans of £10,000. £8,535 had been expended on paving streets and highways, and some £3,000 was estimated for future action on undedicated roads. Lighting had cost some £1,500 and improvements to the slaughter-house had cost £2,800. St. Helens had enjoyed an average annual expenditure of £3,300 in the ten years ending 1855. This was a *per capita* expenditure of approximately 2s. 5d., but plans for the future were obviously quite extensive. Over this period the rates usually amounted to 2s. 9d. in the pound.

The smaller towns present a varied financial picture. Rusholme quickly levied a Special District Rate of 8d. for a main sewer and a General Rate of 4d. as a yearly norm. As usual, there was difficulty over private improvements, which once split the Board in a seven to four vote. Crumpsall was equally swift to levy a rate of 9d. designed to raise £510, and this and later General Rates were followed by special rates raising considerable sums of £450 and £500. Like Rusholme, Crumpsall did not resort to loans, and the

General Board, investigating the complaints of rate-payers, advised
the Board to do so—perhaps with an eye to bringing into play the
loan-sanction lever. Crumpsall had considerable difficulty in pressing payments of rates. Fifty-eight were summoned in 1855, there
were twenty-one non-payments in 1856 and forty-four were
threatened with action in 1857. The Crumpsall Board had levied
a three-year special rate, and the test case of Joseph Entwistle
became a minor *cause célèbre*. The J.P.s dismissed the original
summons against him as the Board 'had not powers to make the
rate for three years'. This judgement was overruled by the Court
of the Queen's Bench. Two years later Entwistle was still in the
news, for the Queen's Bench had to compel a local magistrate to
issue a warrant of distress on him for £100 12s. 4d. Crumpsall also
busied itself with proceedings of a dubious legality, for they haled
miscreants before them and fined them. Men were fined 2s. 6d. or
5s. or 10s. for 'emptying an ashpit at an improper time' or because
they did 'boil or cause to be boiled a quantity of offal'. H. Bowcott
was fined several times for causing such nuisances, and the unlucky
Joseph Entwistle was fined 2s. 6d. for 'exposing manure at an
improper time'. Apart from court summonses, the Crumpsall
Board normally handled four or five cases of nuisance at its weekly
meetings. None of the other Boards examined attempted this. It
is, perhaps, an early and slight example of sub-legislative justice
and a tiny forerunner of Hewart's 'New Despotism'.

Occasionally rates soared above the 3s. mark, as in Crumpsall,
Kirkham, Lancaster and Wigan, but 1s. to 2s. 6d. appears to have
been the normal range. The rate is, of course, the most profitable
guide to the fiscal impact of the Local Boards on society. Around
1856–58 it might roughly be calculated that an annual sum of
£90,000 was the anticipated revenue from the rate-payers of
Lancashire's Local Boards, a sum of about 5s. per head of population. In terms of a set case, a Bolton rate-payer with a property
valued at £100 would have been charged £7 10s. in 1856. In
Crumpsall it might have been as high as £26. It is still said that
men pay taxes in sorrow and rates in anger. These sums were not
small, and they must be seen against the creeping extension of
other forms of taxation at this time, of which the Poor Rate is an
obvious example. The Victorian rate-payer, moreover, was not
attuned to massive public expenditure. The traditional annoyance
about local revenue was obviously aroused by these new items of
expenditure, especially as the costs often expanded over the years,

and conflict between the rate-payers and the authorities was frequently bitter and lengthy. An added irony was that, if owners
made improvements, the rateable values of their properties increased. One way and another the restrictions on local finance
were tight and cramping. Given this kind of political atmosphere,
given the long-term and often unseen aims of Public Health
endeavour, and given the dilatory and even chaotic activities of the
Local Boards—then the difficulties of rate-collection are easily
explained. Indeed, one can perceive a vicious circle forming.
Obstruction, by non-payment of rates and other means, left the
Local Boards unable to advance at a proper tempo and level of
competence. Such inefficiency and slowness doubtless aggravated
opposition, as rate-payers felt that value for money was not forthcoming. If, therefore, 1858 saw precious little betterment in social
conditions in Lancashire, then the financial aspect must be considered as an intrinsic feature of such slow progress.

b. Other authorities. The major characteristic of Public Health
finance in the cities and Boroughs of Lancashire was the large-
scale expenditure involved. Municipal government was a new
mode of administration, and the enormous expense involved horrified many rate-payers. Manchester's tremendous Longendale
scheme incurred borrowing from the Public Works Loans Commissioners of £650,000. The Rivington Pike project began with an
estimate of £200,000. This sprang to £450,000 and the eventual
cost was £1,345,969. Newland's sewering of Liverpool's streets
had cost £215,231 by 1858, and scavenging was still costing
£10,000 per annum. Liverpool also spent £537,000 on the purchase of the city's two water companies. Scavenging in Manchester
in 1849 produced a loss of £4,000, despite strenuous attempts to
meet the expenditure by the sale of sewage for agricultural
purposes.

As few plans for arterial drainage or public water supply were
in operation by 1858 in towns outside the Local Boards of Health,
the financial aspect requires little explanation. The question goes
by default, for the main projects were developed in the post 1858
period. Perhaps the colossal sums outlined above are in themselves
a pointer. The towns of Lancashire were growing rapidly and the
urgency to provide public services and utilities was growing proportionately. Faced with the expense of administering a variety of
facilities, such as gas-lighting, baths and wash-houses, police
forces, cemeteries and parks and a dozen others, there was bound

to be caution in indulging in possibly exorbitant schemes. It was after 1860 that Lancashire's larger textile and industrial centres were to come of age, and come to terms with the realities of modern municipal practice.

iii. Summary

It cannot be pretended that the first phase of Public Health reform was a large-scale success, least of all in Lancashire. Sir George Newman's summary is an admirable one. 'Speaking generally, the 1843 Commission found the existence of a serious national evil of sanitation and ill-health, and recommended legislative remedy, whereas the 1869 Commission found that the remedy had proved ineffective, and recommended that the present fragmentary and confused sanitary legislation should be consolidated.'[1] The adoptive nature of the legislation was described in 1858 as 'a chaos as regards authorities, a chaos as regard rates, and a worse chaos than all as regards areas'. In the key area of Lancashire the administrative achievements of Local Boards, Borough Councils and Improvement Commissions had failed to measure up to the schedules laid down by governmental legislation. If 'sanitary neglect is a mistaken parsimony', then Lancashire stood part condemned of uneconomic activities, for few major advances had been made. Of the larger towns, Manchester, Liverpool, Oldham and Ashton ran public waterworks, and water sewerage was still a rarity everywhere. The rapidly growing Barrow was perhaps the worst example, for it had no Public Health jurisdiction until the 1872 Public Health Act. Smaller townships had fared no better. Taking random examples, one finds that Crumpsall, far from having a sewage scheme completed in 1858, has only negotiated a contract with Thomas Walkden for ashpit and night-soil clearance by the end of that year; that Poulton's first bye-laws on privies, cesspools and ash pits were dated 1858; that Bradford (Manchester) decided in 1864, 'to proceed with the sewering, paving, flagging etc. of Bradford Road South and other improvements within the district' but that would not 'interfere with any arrangements' between property owners and the Patent Pondrette Manure Company; and that it was reported to the Barton Rural Sanitary Authority (which replaced the Local Board) that, in 1876, 'with some very few and trifling exceptions, no sewers whatever exist in the district, and

[1] G. Newman, *The Rise of Preventive Medicine* (1953), pp. 258–59.

where there are street sewers very few of the house drains are led
into them', that 'the whole area of the district is very ill-provided
with water', that 'no systematic removal of refuse' exists, and that
there are 'many cottages totally unfitted for human habitation'.
Then one must recall that hundreds of townships in the county
did not even enjoy the benefits of such Local Boards as
these.

The upshot was, of course, but little improvement in the health
of the populace. The national death rate was roughly 21 per
thousand in 1839. In Lancashire the mortality rate was 29·4 per
thousand in 1839 and 25·4 in 1861. Stated differently, one in every
forty-six Lancastrians died in 1839; one in every fifty-two in 1861,
hardly a significant improvement. Disease remained rampant.
Varied fevers continued to take their toll, especially in Manchester, Salford and Chorlton areas, and there was a major outbreak of Cholera in 1866 which killed 2,600, or one in a thousand,
in Lancashire, including the staggering figure of 2,122 in Liverpool. Typhus, prominent as 'Irish Fever' in the late forties, again
sprang into notice as 'Famine Fever' during the Lancashire
Cotton Famine of 1862–65. Manchester, Preston, Accrington,
Chorley, Salford and Blackburn were badly hit. Bronchitis,
Diphtheria, Tuberculosis and other Pulmonary complaints became
rife enough in the textile districts to warrant special enquiries in
1861. In Manchester alone in the years 1857–60, 10,763 died of
Typhus, Scarlet Fever and Smallpox. Furthermore, both in death
and disease, the figures for the North-West were double the
national average with regard to infants.

The chief reasons for failure were threefold. Firstly, it is
unjust, perhaps, to expect spectacular results in a decade. In a
sense the problem was more novel than the problems of crime or
poverty. With the criminal or the pauper, the circumstances had
changed, and there was a need to reorientate to such circumstances
in terms of administrative techniques, different types of officials
and new and enlarged buildings. The problem of urban health
made its effect felt on everyone, not merely on the poor or the
unlawful groups in society. The answer to the difficulty implied a
ubiquitous intervention into the private life of each individual,
and this was guaranteed to stir up objection. The answer also
required civil engineering on a new grand and elaborate scale, and
it is scarcely surprising that this, too, was slow to evolve. The disturbing features of communal health were not, moreover, static.

A quick glance at Lancashire's population increase by 1861 is sufficient testimony to this. In 1841 the population was 1,667,000 and in 1861 it was 2,240,440—a rise of 762,440 in the twenty years during which the first vacillating steps towards sound Public Health were attempted. This increase of over 50 per cent, with its automatic pressure on the water and sewage facilities available, suggests that possible credit is due to Lancashire for keeping pace with its troubles. At least 1861 did see some forward-looking schemes of water-supply and sewering, and the death-rate was slightly lower. Perhaps the observer should, in retrospect, praise the municipal authorities for making any kind of start at all. The most arduous administrative task is the conception of a scheme of governance, and, if no more was accomplished, the Public Health reformers of 1844 to 1858 laid substantial precedents for the future. Certainly the official structure of today may be traced back into this mid-Victorian period. The Public Health Acts of 1872 and 1875 which made for a compulsory and consolidated approach to Public Health, used the idea of the small area committee in shaping the country into Urban and Rural Sanitary Districts. The Urban Districts were, in fact, the old Local Boards, Borough Councils and Improvement Commissions. In 1888 the County Councils undertook overall supervision of Public Health (Edward Sergeant was Lancashire's first County Medical Officer) and, in 1894, Urban and Rural District Councils were established, alongside the existing Boroughs, and based primarily on the old divisions. It is interesting, for example, to trace the administrative history of a township like Ormskirk from Local Board of Health in 1850, via Urban Sanitary District to Urban District Council. Public Health, necessarily so because of its local import, has helped enormously in the shaping of English municipal government. It is equally intriguing to trace the extension of the central authority from Central Board of Health, via Privy Council and Local Government Board, to the recent Ministry of Health. The familiar bipartite system of government—the central agency legislating, sanctioning, advising and inspecting; the local agency executing and implement- ing—is the product of 1848. Throughout the Public Health sphere there are several features which date from this time, among them the full-time use of specialists, particularly medical officers, sur- veyors and the like; the control by elected committees; and the acceptance of the theme that such utilities as water and sewage are in the public rather than the private province.

Secondly, an examination of the work of Public Health authorities before 1858 suggests that they were not well administered; that they were under some duress from opponents both on and off the Boards or Commissions; and that the financial character of these bodies was awkward and inhibiting. Couple with these factors the sheer practical difficulties which were involved in building programmes, and, again, no surprise need be expressed at the hesitant, sometimes negligible, progress made. It is rightly thought that pure *laissez-faire* did not rule nineteenth-century government as completely as was once thought, and that the move towards the Collectivist State was aided by a pragmatic 'administrative momentum' regardless of the prevailing cult of individualism. Public Health is quoted as an instance of this movement, but, in a mild way, a local study of public administration may help to redress the balance of the argument. It might be concluded that local administration lagged behind the remedial action suggested by the state, and that the national furore about health lost much of its vitality when worked out at a day-to-day level. Legislation sometimes flatters to deceive, and it is wise to observe how the recipient is faring. It must be admitted that, in Lancashire, ten or so years of both local and national Acts did little more than begin to solve the problems of Public Health. The *status quo* was not unduly disturbed, nor was the privacy of the citizen tampered with overmuch. *Laissez-faire* looked to be besieged, but on closer inspection, the 'administrative momentum' was so laborious and shallow that the old order changed but slightly.

Thirdly, Public Health knowledge was inadequate and the civic spirit untuned to rapid progress in the health field until after 1870. It was then that several breakthroughs occurred, which, by reacting one upon the other, caused a major advance in communal health. It was in the eighteen-seventies that the first high wave of Collectivism rose, which was reflected in the heavy legislative programme of Gladstone's First Ministry and in the early social reforms of Disraeli's subsequent administration. An acceptance of positive state action was essential to the furtherance of Public Health reform. The preventative aspect—lay on water and remove filth—was indispensable in all conscience, but it was slightly negative. Other factors, requiring more definite interference, were also critical. One of these was housing. Farr's vital statistics pointed that bad moral of overcrowding. Liverpool and Manchester had mortality rates of thirty-nine and thirty-two, and anything over thirty meant 'highly destructive' conditions. He was able to correlate the numbers of deceased with the numbers per square mile, demonstrating that, in the country with less than 200 per square mile, the death rate almost reached the so-called natural rate of seventeen, but that it rose proportionately until it more than doubled in Liverpool with 66,000 per square mile—a mean proximity of seven yards. In 1870, he averred, 'the health of the whole population of the country has remained stationary' for the past twenty years. Housing in Lancashire had barely kept up with its augmented population. In 1831 there were 228,130 houses, with an average of six in each, whereas the average in 1861 was 5·5, spread over 2½ millions of people. Men like Duncan of Liverpool had long pointed out the evils of overcrowding, but it was only after 1868 that the Torrens Act and the Richard Cross Acts came into being. They made the initial breach in the sacrosanct rights of property and a whole welter of Acts relating to housing were to follow. Other features, such as nutrition and conditions of work, were soon to be met by governmental action, and, of course, the eventual rise in the material standards of life were also to make their mark on the health of the nation. The whole paraphernalia of Public Health supervision, of course, revolved around the Slater-Bruce Act of 1875. 'This model enactment' was comprehensive beyond precedent, and, as Frazer has said, 'all the cities and towns in this country have become places fit to live in under provisions contained somewhere in this Public Health Act'.[1]

Another type of bottleneck was negotiated during the latter half of the century with Pasteur's and Koch's discovery of the Germ Theory of Disease. It must not be forgotten that the Environmentalists had done the right things for the wrong reasons. Sometimes—as when, in an effort to dispose of filth swiftly, the local water supply was utilised—there were obvious dangers. The true connection of filth and disease having been revealed, Public Health reformers were infinitely better armed, and communal and private standards of hygiene could be emphasised. Still in the sphere of medicine, there were some forward strides in the education of doctors between 1830 and 1858, culminating in the 1858 Medical Act which established the General Council for Medical Education and Registration. This enactment, stimulated by the demands of a middle class 'health consciousness', was obviously

[1] W. M. Frazer, *A History of English Public Health 1834–39* (1950), p. 224.

to pay huge dividends as the century wound on, coupled as it was
with the crucial discoveries in medical science. The reforms
in administrative and medical techniques were matched by
improvements in the technology of civil engineering and domestic building. By the end of the century gigantic schemes were being accomplished with a smoothness and efficiency quite foreign
to John Isherwood's deceitful and fumbling efforts at sewering
Over Darwen.

John Newlands, Liverpool's Borough Engineer, had lamented
the paradox of all social administration that 'preventive measures
are obnoxious to obloquy, for the more successful they are, the
less apparent is the need for them'. Most commentators are agreed
that it was the last quarter of the century when this balance of needs
and remedies was at its most harmonious, and that the 1875 Act
was the great advance in sanitary administration. In comparison
the 1848–58 phase, in Lancashire, as in the nation at large, is no
more than a hint or, more justly, a harbinger of what is to come.

IV. The New Police Forces

i. Their introduction

General propositions

Charles Reith has averred that 'force is always a basic ingredient of all means of securing effective observance of laws' and that, broadly speaking, such force is implemented either by 'kin-police' or by 'ruler-appointed police'.[1] In theory, England had tended toward the former of these approaches. The collective responsibility of the Anglo-Saxon township and hundred had become vested in the offices of Constable and Head Constable. These rôles had remained localised, and they were rooted in the Common Law. The Constable, as 'executive agent of the vill or township', survived into the nineteenth century, along with the principle that police powers are mostly grounded in the Common Law and differ little from those of ordinary citizens. From late medieval times, however, and, more emphatically, from the early days of nation-statehood, Justices of the Peace had played an important part. Constables became the mere subordinates of local agents of the crown, and 'to the second quarter of the nineteenth century, the Justice of the Peace was the superior, the Constable, the inferior, conservator of the peace'.[2] Nominees had long been deputed to act as paid constables, normally with satisfactory results, and the use of military force was not by any means a nineteenth-century phenomenon. An idyllic view of our Anglo-Saxon forebears perhaps hides a grimmer reality, in which, as in the post-Conquest era, the feudal lord played a substantial part in the maintenance of order. Given the harsh adherence to feudal law and the later use of the militia, as well as the predominant rôle of the squirearchy, it might tentatively be suggested that England had a lengthier tradition of 'ruler-appointed police' than at first sight appears.

[1] C. Reith, *The Blind Eye of History* (1952), pp. 17–20.
[2] *The Report of the Royal Commission on Police, 1962*, paras. 25–34, pp. 9–12. Also, J. Hart, *The British Police* (1951), pp. 22–6.

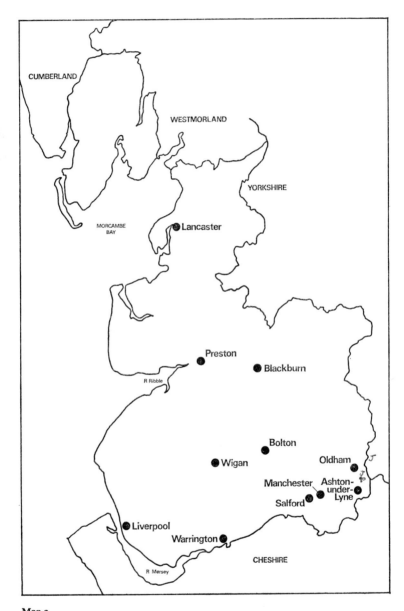

Map 3.

The County of Lancaster showing the administrative areas of the Borough Police Force formed under clauses of the Municipal Corporations Act, 1835 (1836–56). All areas but those shown were part of the Lancashire County Constabulary area formed under the County Constabulary Act, 1839.

The Royal Commission on Police of 1962 quoted its predecessor of 1929 in defining a policeman as 'a person paid to perform, as a matter of duty, acts which if he were so minded he might have done voluntarily'. In practice, however, few would doubt that no more than a handful would ever be so minded, and that the dictum is little more than a legal fantasy. It is, perhaps, in this uneasy compromise of kin-and-ruler-appointed police that the great problem of English policing has its origins; namely, the difficulty of reconciling effective action with individual freedom of action. The 1822 Police Committee had, for example, seen the police idea as curtailment of individual liberty. Thus English police history veers between the principle that individuals are responsible for preserving the peace, and the fact that when rioting occurred the authorities had no option but to put it down.

This delicate balance was completely unhinged by the social changes of the Industrial Revolution period. The demographic explosion in Lancashire doubled the county's population from 673,486 in 1801 to 1,375,600 in 1831. By 1851 Lancashire was, after London, England's most crowded area, with a density of 1,003 per square mile, with Middlesex at 546 the second most closely packed county. What has been termed the 'know everyone' system disintegrated. The sheer number of people robbed the township of its ancient advantage, namely, the Aristotelian concept of the unit small enough for one man to be acquainted with practically all his neighbours. The J.P.s and Constables, sometimes on a voluntary basis and with their fellows' co-operation, had once managed their watch and ward, but now more people required a bigger and more effective police force. The crowded towns provided the same types of crime, which had caused considerable trouble in the eighteenth century, on a proportionately larger scale, and criminal disorder pressed hardly on outmoded and ill-equipped authorities. Expanding commerce produced its own set of possible thefts; frequently dire want was a major factor; the drink and prostitution traffics were fostered by expanding town-life; criminal tendencies seem to have been stimulated by the often degrading social milieu; and there was the new danger of proletarian mass-action, with its consequent threat to property. By the eighteen-thirties, the situation was apparently out of hand. *The Constabulary Report* of 1839 felt that about 40,000 persons were 'living wholly by depredation', apart from countless others

who supplanted more honest callings by occasional crime. The
problem was a real and pressing one.

As with pauperdom and ill-health, the chief solution emanated
from Benthamite quarters, and, inevitably, from the inexhaustible
pen of Edwin Chadwick. During the twenties, Chadwick had
made penology and police his own special subjects. In 1829 he
published his famous article in the *Westminster Review* on police
methods which so impressed Senior, Hill and Francis Place as
well as Bentham. Chadwick produced the classical Benthamite
definition of Police work, and he wrote the sections on the Minis-
tries of Police and Health for Bentham's *Constitutional Code*.
Indeed, with Bentham's own interest in law and with so many
lawyers—including Chadwick—in his entourage, it would be
surprising if legal, and consequently police, reform had not been
high on the Benthamite list of priorities.

One of the most lucid and most publicised expositions of
Chadwick's viewpoint was the *Constabulary Report* of 1839, for
which he had spent three years conducting the enquiry. Charles
Rowan and C. S. Shaw Lefevre joined Chadwick in this enquiry,
which was obviously the model for the vast public health enquiries
of the eighteen-forties. Much of the evidence was gleaned from the
Poor Law Unions, and, as usual, Chadwick painted a horrific,
nightmarish picture of the problem, with up to 120,000 engaged in
some form of criminal endeavour and a prison population rising to
20,000. As with the Poor Law and with Public Health, Chadwick
advanced a classic case, based on the artificial harmony of interests.
Three principal steps are discernible in his argument.

Firstly, the wretched state of law enforcement, especially in
view of radical social changes, rendered the criminal life a possibly
prosperous one. Simply, crime paid. The 'habitual depredator'
lived 'much higher' than the law-abiding labourer and thus
honesty was 'less eligible' than criminality. Chadwick had made
this point previously with even more firmness. He had written
that criminals 'see an uninterrupted course of the success they
have already experienced' and that crime had to have pain, not
pleasure, as its consequence. He also attacked the prisons, which,
softened by the likes of Fry and Howard, were 'more eligible'
than some ordinary spheres of livelihood and were also 'thieves'
colleges'. Crime was social waste and it had a triple edge. The
criminal unjustly participated in the gross national product. The
citizen, under constant threat of robbery and violence, was im-

peded in his pursuit of the halcyon goal of self-interest, and thus in his proper subscription to the national output. And the national wealth was further deprived of an annual sum of £2,000,000 by a fruitless, uneconomic and antiquated system of law enforcement. As with poverty and disease, the moral aspect was a secondary one.

Secondly, Chadwick having observed that crime thwarted the interplay of *laissez-faire*, outlined a scheme of tutelary action. If such obstacles existed, they must be removed by government activity, thereby keeping clear the arena. People must, in short, be tutored towards the pursuit of happiness. Hence the ideal of a policeman to each 1,769 people or 4,403 acres, in order to prevent the commission of crimes. Just as the New Poor Law was designed to prevent an unnatural labour market; just as Public Health reforms were to be designed to prevent unnatural rates of death and disease; so was the New Police designed to prevent an unnatural quantity of crime. As Chadwick wrote himself, 'the first great object of a police, that to which every practical adoption should conduce, is to prevent the commission of crime'. A large and well-organised body of men, thought Chadwick, could render the infraction of personal and property rights a difficult task. Given the grave dangers to property from robbers and rioters, there were many rate-payers, land-owners and businessmen ready to lend a mundane backing to the Preventive theory.

Thirdly, a typically rational attitude was developed concerning the organisation of such a police. The Commission urged the abandonment of 'management by a numerous body of uninformed and virtually irresponsible persons' and warned, with prophetic accuracy, of the 'extreme inadequacy of any merely permissive measures'. Fire, nuisance, accident and traffic services were also 'renderable' by the police, and, all in all, a comprehensive force was planned. Chadwick had always wanted a national police agency, with geographically based divisions. The police were to be 'a centralised national establishment armed with formidable powers of intervention and supervision, and directed from an executive department', for Bentham had been 'sanguine that under his system of centralised, permanent control, criminal activities on any material scale would soon cease'.[1] The Metropolitan Police, suggested Chadwick, could act as the focus for 'central control with local management', by its use for organising, training

[1] L. Radzinowicz, *A History of English Criminal Law* (1956), iii, pp. 446–74.

and selecting the new forces. This extension of the trained
Metropolitan Police would provide a national brigade of policemen, with magisterial control locally. Strangely, Chadwick objected to the Boards of Guardians having supervision, but this,
of course, was because he was delighted with the success of the
Metropolitan force. It was argued that such a system would lead
to considerable savings, for the 'inefficient state of the civil force ...
is in reality the most expensive' mode of law enforcement—the
Blackburn Riots of 1826, for instance, cost £15,000. The national
force of some 8,000 would cost £450,000 per year, and possibly
less. The French mode of 'surveillance', incorporated in the 1810
Penal Code, was examined by the Constabulary Commission, and
many forms regarding police-work were also dispatched to the
Commission from France. These concerned the collation of
statistics and the keeping of criminal records, and they were not
unlike some of the *pro formas* later to be used by the Home Office.
Chadwick and the other Commissioners mocked the idea that
effective police-work was anathema to liberty. Citizens, feeling
their liberty compromised by the police, were not co-operative,
and thus the police were 'paralysed by the public'. Without co-
operation, 'a police or constabulary force cannot perform properly
even its ordinary duties', let alone infringe liberty.

Many other solutions were urged. The *Constabulary Report*
dismissed several existing practices—preliminary enquiry, pursuit
by private persons, private as well as township watches and so on;
it relied almost solely on the New Police. Other parties, however,
pressed for differing methods. There was some tradition of Police
reform. After the Gordon Riots, the novelist, Henry Fielding, had
initiated some magisterial reform under the Middlesex Justices
Act of 1792. This introduced stipendiary magistracy and the
grouping of constables, and these ideas were implemented by the
Manchester justices in 1795 and the Lancaster justices in 1805.
The J.P.s remained anxious to control the system completely, and
urged 'the expansion of the civil force around the magisterial
office'. Lancashire magistrates had told the Constabulary Commission that no alteration was needed. Again, a Glasgow magistrate, Patrick Colquhoun, outlined a plan based on prevention in
A General View of the National Police System and *A Treatise on
the Police of the Metropolis*. This was in the era of 1796 to 1806,
and the time was scarcely ripe for radical reform, with the French
wars raging.

A strong school of thought believed that private enterprise was by far the soundest approach. Tradition, thrift, love of freedom and the apparently superior efficacy of private initiative were reasons for adhering to such a system, and common informers and thief-takers were regarded as major weapons in the fight against crime. There was a superficial Benthamite ring to this attitude, in that the bounty-hunter, like the thief, was motivated by self-interest. Saunders Welch had, in the late eighteenth century, promulgated the idea of groups of vigilante householders, and by 1839, there were hundreds of voluntary associations, for patrol and prosecution purposes, dotted about the country. From the time of Colquhoun, many enlightened men, including several law reformers of the Romilly or Mackintosh ilk, feared for freedom; hence the failure of Peel's 1822 Police Committee in days propitious to legal reform. Simply, they judged that criminal law barbarism was the only obstacle to improved crime rates, and this view caused a long delay in police reform. The large-scale liberal reforms associated with Peel's tenure at the Home Office were therefore seen, not without plausibility, as the key to the situation.

A variety of other substitutes for the ramshackle old system was suggested. They included the formation of parochial bands of policemen; the complete takeover of police functions by insurance companies, rather after the fashion of fire protection at that time; and the doubling of police salary scales in order to secure better quality recruits. It is perhaps too easily forgotten that the adaptation of military personnel to a *gendarmerie* on the continental pattern might possibly have occurred. A Captain F. Hamilton had devised a scheme for using all pensioned ex-soldiers to form a rural police, in order to save money and to provide employment for retired servicemen. A long letter, dated 30 November 1836, was sent to Lord John Russell, and he forwarded it to the Commission for its perusal. The military weapon was not only an extreme but often an unserviceable one, and England did not have a large-scale standing army like some of her neighbours. None the less, the militia had frequently rescued the civilian populaces from difficult situations, and the extension of the railways and the electric telegraph was to make the job of military surveillance a much simpler one.

In any event, there is some controversy about the parenthood of the preventative principle, as opposed to all other schemes, which were based on awaiting the manifestation of crime. The work of Fielding and Colquhoun has already been noted, but Charles Reith argues that the actual adoption of the preventative ideal was not due to Chadwick. At the time Colquhoun was pressing his views, Sir John Moore and Colonel McKenzie of the 52nd Light Infantry were advocating prevention, as opposed to severe punition, in military discipline. The idea was 'saved from oblivion by a young officer, Charles Rowan, and eventually adopted by the nation'. Further influenced by Charles Napier, author of *The History of the War in the Peninsula*, Rowan eventually became First Commissioner of the Metropolitan Police, and, with Richard Mayne, organised that force. His General Instructions were akin to Moore's Military and Moral Training Manuals. They state emphatically that 'the principal object to be attained is the prevention of crime' and the hierarchy of divisions, sections and beats is an exact replica of Moore's regimental police schedule. Reith challenges Chadwick's 'remarkable effrontery' in his claiming to be the inventor of preventative police; he concludes that his work with police was 'one of his most outstanding failures'; and he claims Rowan's part in the Constabulary Commission has been underplayed.[1]

On balance, however, one must accept the orthodox view regarding the Benthamite influence in general and that of Chadwick in particular. Chadwick had, it will be recalled, established the Utilitarian policy on police by 1829, and it had been received with delight by his confrères. The atmosphere in which Peel undertook the domestic reforms of the twenties was certainly helped by Benthamite lobbying. On Reith's own admission, the preventative principle, as applied by the Metropolitan Police, was already waning by 1842, before the provincial forces were properly underway. Many provincial forces were to lean heavily on the Metropolitan example, but it is of interest to note that it is practice—uniforms, discipline, drill, beats, officer-men relations—rather than the principle which was most heeded. Police historians have tended, not without justification, to concentrate their efforts on the Metropolitan Police, but it was not the only police force in the mid-nineteenth century. Rowan may well have instigated its organisation, but the provincial forces owe much more to Chadwick's administrative theory, preached, as it was, in the Borough Councils and County Magistracies.

[1] C. Reith, *A New Study of Police History* (1956), pp. 24–28, 116–18, 129–37, 199–214 and 221–49.

Police theory must not be seen in a vacuum. It was inextricably linked with other social problems of the day. Chadwick was anxious to use the police to support the New Poor Law. Vagrancy itself was a cause of crime, with migratory bands of thieves and beggars roaming abroad. The Poor Law reformers, like the Public Health reformers, were well aware of the collateral causes of crime in conditions of social distress. Poor Law, Public Health and Police—each sprang from the other and created a social inter-action. Invariably, the same men—Guardians, Local Board members, Watch Committee-men—were instrumental in striving for reform. Invariably the Utilitarian theme of rational administra-tion and economic management carried the day. This is not to deny the work of Rowan, either as Metropolitan Police Commissioner or as a member of the Constabulary Commission. But Chadwick stood at the centre of a vast interwoven mesh of social administra-tion, and, in this sense, it is difficult to reduce his stature. Histori-ans are wont to dilute the strength of Benthamism in nineteenth-century administration. It is claimed, with some truth, that *ad hoc* administrative action was more important than administrative theory. None the less, 'administrative momentum' must have shape, and the formula which was largely accepted—and it is not always remembered that there were other formulae available—was substantially Benthamite. The fury of the opposition was certainly directed to that quarter. When firm plans were mooted, the objections came from all the experienced quarters. Many Tories and some Whigs were fearful of state encroachment, Manchesterism scorned any meddling with *laissez-faire* or the independence of local government; the popular press stirred up a fiery opposition; and many J.P.s and Corporations were un-happy. Predictably, the lower classes saw the 'blue-butchers' as yet another tool of oppression. The workers of Bury, who, in 1839, opposed the arrival of 'a brutal, bloody, bullying and unconstitu-tional force' of twenty London police, showed native shrewdness, for Chadwick did hope the police would supplement the Poor Law Unions and he did disapprove strongly of working-class organisa-tions. It is significant that Chadwick encouraged the use of cutlass or truncheon instead of musket; not because of the humane, civilised reason usually accepted, but because a hand was left free for apprehending, and the power to arrest made the police a superior agency to the military. Chadwick's working-class readers must have observed with amusement the irony of his emphasis on 'the need of an efficient police for the protection of the greater interests of labourers against violence' during trade disputes. The gulf between Chadwick's bourgeois rate-paying support and the disgruntled proletariat was wide indeed.

The weight of the opposition was, as with Public Health, heavy enough to weaken the doctrinaire vigour of the New Police theory. Nevertheless, Lancashire was soon policed throughout, in direct contrast to the uneven character of the county's efforts to establish Public Health authorities. In this section the police forces of Lancashire will be examined, so that some assessment of their reformed character can be attempted. Before such an investigation, however, it will be necessary to review the situation before reform and also to inspect the process of reform itself.

Law and Order before reform
Before attempting to describe the establishment of the New Police in Lancashire, the conditions in the county prior to reform must be outlined. Government papers and records maintained locally are full enough for such an exercise, and it is possible to examine the extent of crime and the policing system used to combat it.

The key to such an examination is the *Constabulary Report* of 1839, which, aside from its general criticisms and recommendations, touched on particular areas, such as Lancashire, in some detail. Liverpool Watch Committee reported that 4,711 'depredators' lived in Liverpool, with 2,071 houses as their resorts. Dowling of the Liverpool Police and others gave evidence concerning canal robberies—a useful illustration of new types of crime—and objection was raised against the plan of separate police forces, for canals, railways and so on, as such self-protection left too many interests unguarded. Neglect of criminal precaution was noted in Lancashire and Cheshire, especially in Bolton where murder seemed a little too frequent. Robert Orrell, testifying on behalf of manufacturers in Lancashire, spoke of their lack of security and their fear of violence. The report contained surprises for those bred in the Dick Turpin and 'Jamaica Inn' tradition. Thomas Bart, a straw-hat salesman, said that 'where travellers feel the least comfortable in travelling are the neighbourhoods of the Northern manufacturing towns, as in the vicinity of Manchester, where some ferocious highway robberies have been committed'. He particularly criticised 'the neighbourhoods of Bury, Preston and Rochdale', whilst the Blackstone Edge and Todmorden Vale roads were never used, for the people thereabouts were 'barbarous to an unusual degree'. The now pleasing suburban reaches of the Wirral formed England's most popular wrecking area. Liverpool was the centre for this horrid and gruesome trade, with female wreckers biting off the fingers and ears of sailors whose rings they could not easily move. Typically, the Cheshire J.Ps were annoyed by the Liverpool police wishing to encroach over the bounds of their jurisdiction. Deputy Constable J. S. Thomas and Superintendent Davies of the Manchester Watch were among those who bore witness to the problems created by the 'new Population' of 100,000 Irish in Lancashire. There was a special need 'for public security', it was felt, 'in these excited districts'. It was the business of excise collection which proved 'peculiarly dangerous' in Manchester, because, according to Mr. Thomas, the customs officers were 'beat off notwithstanding the sabres with showers of stones' by the Irish.

Some idea of the extent of crime may be deduced from the crime figures. From 1805, when statistics were first recorded, there had been an increase in commitments. In the five-year period 1827–31, the average number of commitments in Lancashire was 2,215. The population of the county at the 1831 census was 1,335,600, thus giving a ratio of one commitment per 600. The national average was 17,000, a ratio of one to 700. Such figures suggest that, not only did Lancashire have a considerable crime rate, but that it was higher than the national one. Other evidence supports the view that Lancashire had a wide extent and range of crime. Lancashire had five main gaols—Her Majesty's Gaol at Lancaster, Houses of Correction at Salford, Kirkdale and Preston (all four under the supervision of the County Magistracy) and the Liverpool House of Correction, controlled by the Liverpool Council. These normally held a total of some 1,500 inmates at any one time.

The Constabulary Commission asked for questionnaires to be answered by prisoners. Thirty-three of these were filled up by Lancashire prisoners, with Mr. Bachelor, Governor of Liverpool Prison, forwarding twenty-three of these long *pro formas*. Each contained no less than seventy-one questions. One example— that of John Edwards, fifteen years of age, convicted for taking a drawer containing money out of a shop—may illustrate the range of the survey. He had worked two years as a copper plate fitter and six months at a druggist's; he was illegitimate, but lived with his parents. His father, an auctioneer and appraiser, was an 'honest, industrious and sober man', but, two years earlier, his mother had left to live with another man. He had attended church regularly with his father and 'great care was taken' of him, although, having been 'induced' by other boys to run away, he had been fastened to a bedpost and flogged. The boy could read and write, but had not read the Bible nor attended a place of worship for eighteen months. Questions on his occupations and his habits (he was an attender at Night School) followed, and then there were a series on his convictions—'bad companions' had apparently proved his downfall. Twenty-seven questions delved into the character of his depredations. He had been apprehended six times and convicted five times. He had committed some forty crimes; he had used pawnbrokers as fences; and 4s. was his best weekly haul. The questions attempted to ferret out the circumstances of crime, and how the present system abetted them. Each examinee was asked to what extent he derived 'encouragement in your criminal causes from the remissness of the police, or constables' and whether 'fear of constables' influenced them or not. Many of the questions were, of course, leading ones, and the answers much too stereotyped, but they do help paint the Victorian picture of crime. It was partly because of such investigations that the Commission was able to conclude that crime was not primarily caused by 'unavoidable want or destitution' but by the ease of living off crime 'with a less degree of labour than by regular industry'. Bachelor himself forwarded a memorandum on juvenile delinquents, in which he blamed the 'facilities existing for depredation' and the 'depravity of their parents'.

In the year previous to the *Constabulary Report*, the Criminal Registers show that 2,568 Lancastrians were committed for trial for indictable offences. Only 292 charges were not for crimes of gain— 34 charges of riot, 5 of murder, 35 of manslaughter, 130 of assault, 63 of keeping Disorderly or Bawdy Houses, and 24 miscellaneous, including 8 bigamies. Remarkably, only 5 of the 63 disorderly house charges were upheld. This left the colossal total of 2,276 charged with larceny or connected crimes—or 89 per cent of the total. 522 were not convicted. Of the remaining 2,000, no less than 403 were transported, 44 for life, 1,643 were given short terms of imprisonment, 17 were fined and 35 whipped, while remarkably enough, only four were sentenced to death and but one of these actually executed. Sadly enough, 44 of the number were twelve years of age or under. Three of these were ten-year-olds, and one received a week's gaol and a whipping. Two of nine were imprisoned for a week and four months. Another of eight years served a week in prison, and, most incredible of all, a child of seven was imprisoned for two months. Yet none of the thirty-four cases of riot led to a savage sentence. Acquittals, fines or very short terms of imprisonment were deemed sufficient. What might be termed allied offences were also dealt with leniently. The twenty-four cases of assault on peace officers and three cases of damage to mines were not treated as severely as the hundreds of thefts brought before the judges. This applies even when the riot was specifically 'to raise wages'.

Perhaps a fuller guide to law and order can be found in the lists of convicts in national prisons from which the names and data of those convicted in Lancashire may be extracted. In the Quarter ending 31 March 1831, 233 such attested convicts were held in one or other of the eight convict hulks. This stop-gap substitute for transportation was necessary when the American Colonies were lost, but was continued well into the nineteenth century. Four were in the 'Leviathan' and five in the 'York', both at Portsmouth. 118 were incarcerated in the 'Fortitude', off Chatham. Also at Chatham, in the 'Euryalus', were 30 juveniles. At Woolwich there were 34 in the 'Justitia' and 31 in the 'Gannymede'. Three ships lay off St. Georges, Bermuda. Lancashire had but one representative on the 'Antelope', two on the 'Cormandel' and eight on the 'Dromedary'. During the quarter in question, 80 were transported to New South Wales, two were pardoned and two—John Morgan, aged nineteen, and Henry Pike, aged twenty-one—died. Seven were serving life sentences, whereas the remainder were sentenced to terms of seven, ten, fourteen or fifteen years. Practically all the offences were for forms of larceny. The savagery of the sentences may be judged from the nature of some of the robberies. Thefts, resulting in such long and dreadful punishments, included a watch; 20 pounds of brass; 8 yards of cloth; bread and bacon; a pair of boots; 2 hundredweight of coals; 2 pairs of shoes; a leg of mutton; 4s. 5d.; 2 pairs of stockings; 1 handkerchief; 2 lamps; 3 sacks; an apron; a hen and cock; a cheese; 3 spoons; and a knife. The logic was terrifyingly feeble. Frederick Williamson was sentenced at Liverpool to seven years for assault; William Maudsley was sentenced at Kirkdale to ten years for wounding two asses. Probably a close examination of the Hulk reserved for juveniles is required to drive home the harshness of early Victorian justice.

Thirty Lancashire lads were on the 'Euryalus'. Two—fifteen-year-old Matthew Carlisle and twelve-year-old William Naylor—were doomed to life imprisonment, for house-breaking and stealing a cow respectively. Patrick Conway, aged thirteen, was serving fourteen years for stealing a brass bowl. Five were doing ten-year terms, two of whom—John Murray and William Locklan—were twelve-year-old boys, convicted of stealing a handkerchief apiece. The other twenty-eight had seven-year sentences, and sixteen of them were fourteen or under. A pair of stays; a pair of clogs; a thimble, thread and tape; some sugar; a shirt; a piece of beef; twelve shillings—each such stolen item was sufficient to chain these children below the decks of the 'Euryalus' for the whole of their adolescence. Somehow Christopher Hall's case seems most pathetic of all. Aged twelve, he was convicted for seven years at Preston for stealing a currant pie. The legal reforms of the twenties, commonly associated with Peel, are often purported to usher in a new era of penal leniency. Certainly the death penalty had all but vanished—but stringent prison sentences in vile conditions and transportation remained very much the mainstay of the judicial system.

Another factor in the situation was the danger of mob-action for social or political reasons. In the new crowded urban areas, proletarian unrest was, of course, apparent before Chartism became prominent. During the St. Helens coal-strike of 1831, special constables were 'not of the slightest utility' and the 10th Hussars had to be sent to maintain order. In the thirties agitation directed at the Poor Law or in favour of Factory Reform grew. Disappointment with the Reform Act and the fate of the Dorchester Labourers turned Trade Unionists and others to political measures. Slumps and bad harvest in 1836 and 1837 worsened the position, and, in May 1838, the Charter was presented. From Spring 1837 to January 1840 was the first phase of Chartist activity. Historians have noted 'the remarkable synchronisation of these outbreaks', although it is accepted that 'spontaneous tumult' in various places was the real danger. By the beginning of 1840 the 'tumultuous upheaval' had subsided, but certainly the threat of mass action was a frightening one to the middle and upper classes in the country.

As suggested in the *Constabulary Report*, the Irish immigrants were yet another feature of the criminal scene. The Preston Council discussed the matter in 1839. Samuel Bannister, the Chief Constable, 'urged the propriety of doubling the police force' because of disturbances caused by railwaymen. Mr. Catterall argued that this was unnecessary, and that 'a supply of military', as in Blackburn, Wigan, Bolton, Burnley and Stockport, was the answer. Councillor J. Smith said that the disturbances were regular enough to warrant increased police, while his colleague, Councillor Black-hurst, felt that 'the Council need not be afraid of a few Irishmen', and that it was 'no disgrace to carry a firelock'. Alderman Haydock, the Chairman of the Watch Committee, successfully moved a motion to augment the police force. The major disturbance referred to in this debate had occurred in North Road, when some thirty intoxicated Irish navigators had attacked a band of con-stables and injured four of them. With Preston often associated with Chartist violence, it is interesting to note that the Irish seem to have been feared more at this time. James Park said that for every Chartist there were twenty peaceful workers. It is evident that most of the features mentioned in the *Constabulary Report* were well illustrated in Lancashire. There was a broad range of disorder and illegality from the excess of petty thieving, common to the crowded and degrading towns of Lancashire, to barbarous activities such as wrecking and highway robbery. There were com-mercial crimes, like canal robberies. Some thirty or more of those convicts serving sentences in 1838 after committal in Lancashire had been guilty of large-scale thefts connected with textiles, bales of cotton, canvas, cambric, muslin, fustian, calico, lindsey and so on. There were bawdy house offences, which were so difficult to uphold, possibly because landlordism, with its magisterial con-nections, was involved. These were often, of course, the same as the lodging-houses hated by the Public Health reformers. Liver-pool, for instance, had 711 brothels in 1838. Then there were the huge problems posed by riot and disturbance, either by Irish railwaymen in drink or weavers and coal miners on strike. Finally, arising from its base of political and social discontent, was the Chartist phenomenon of apparently concerted mass-action. It has been seen that, on capture, the miscreant could expect little mercy at the hands of the judicial system. How, in fact, did this judicial system operate?

Parliament was obviously the fount of the legal hierarchy, but Parliament was often apathetic and reluctant to legislate. Troubles in Lancashire were rarely discussed and there was an anxiety not to meddle with existing modes of legal management. The Home Office, together with the government's law officers, offered advice and attempted co-ordination and, through loans of Metropolitan Policemen and Enrolled Pensioners, provided reserves of strength when the provinces were sorely tried. In the Counties the Lord Lieutenant—at this time, the Earl of Derby for Lancashire—presided over the magistrates and the county yeomanry. Safe in Knowsley Hall, with a troop of servants for bodyguard, it is unlikely that the Earl of Derby, like others of the landed gentry, was directly bothered by disturbances in the town centres. Leadership was thus often lacking, although John Foster, Stipendiary Chairman of the Salford Quarter Sessions, organised the J.P.s in the Manchester area into a formidable combine in 1839. Through the Quarter Sessions, the magistrates administered the constabulary and the yeomanry, and such meetings displayed, according to Mather, 'all the parsimony, all the prejudice, all the incompetence of the individual magistrates of whom they were composed'. The area supervised by the County J.P.s was everywhere outside the corporate towns, but their only police were the High Constables of the Hundred, and the Petty Constables of the Parishes and Townships. The Lancashire magistrates, however, reported to the Constabulary Commission that there were 660 peace officers in the county area. These were frequently nominal offices, and, in practical terms, the active rural police were illiterate and of poor quality.

The towns were perhaps faring a little better than the rurality of Lancashire. Boroughs were obliged to organise police forces under the terms of the 1835 Municipal Corporations Act. It is, however, safe to use 1838 as an approximate line between unreformed and reformed police-work, for, before that date, only Wigan, Liverpool and Preston had pressed this advantage and with very mixed results. Manchester had two bands of policemen—thirty day-police, controlled by the Constables of the Township, and a night watch of 150, supervised by the Watch Committee established by the 1829 Police Act. A move in 1836 to combine the two was defeated, and, when the Borough Police was later formed, Manchester was to find itself with three police bodies of over 600 men. On its formation in 1836, the Liverpool Watch Committee appointed a sub-committee to report on the state of police in the Borough. The day police was one superintendent, 44 constables and 17 supernumeraries. This cost £8,000 per year, and there was 'no permanent street patrol'. The nightly watch cost £9,200. It had a superintendent, 16 captains, 130 watchmen and 19 others, a total

of 166. 45 watchmen were unfit and 25 had 'very doubtful qualifications'. In 1810 Preston had three policemen costing a weekly £3,
and a night-watch. Thomas Walton became Preston's first Superintendent (later first Chief Constable) in 1815, assisted by an
Inspector and five P.C.s. Ashton Court Leet normally appointed
some six constables and a score of assistants, and then, under the
1827 Improvement Act, some provision was made for salaried
constables in the township itself. These hardly interfered with the
Court Leet appointments, and in 1837 the Court Leet had 11
officers in its township division and 22 in the three outlying
divisions.

Rochdale was served by a tiny group of ageing watchmen and was
one of the towns in Lancashire where a vigilante group had been
formed—the Rochdale Association for the Prosecution of Felons
in 1797. A Police Commission was formed under the 1825 Improvement Act, and Thomas Butterworth captained a dozen night
watchmen. In 1830 Charles Johnson, who was also Rate Collector
and Inspector of Nuisance, took over. After a chequered career as
Chief Constable he was dismissed in 1837. Samuel Milnes replaced
him, but was also dismissed within three months. James Butterworth was the next appointment. The Court Leet was, as in
Ashton, Bolton and Manchester, responsible for the day watch.
From 1792 the Salford Police Commissioners had engaged a
number of watchmen, varying from 12 to 20 according to the
Town's financial state, and, at one period, the Watch was totally
disbanded. In 1834 there was a total of 22. Until 1837 Warrington
had only a few watchmen supported by private subscription. In
1838 the four parish Constables appointed a Constable, James
Jones, and four assistants to patrol the town night and day, and
this scheme continued until incorporation in 1847. From their
establishment in 1827, the Oldham Commissioners controlled a
pioneer wage-earning force, which never exceeded 10 constables,
and the Wigan Court Leet ran a scheme of watching manned, in
1831, by two Bailiffs and 14 Gatewaiters. It is impossible to
estimate the total numbers involved in police-work in Lancashire
in the eighteen-thirties. The numbers varied considerably; there
were part-time and even nominal posts. In Lancashire's dozen or
so large towns, it appears there were probably over 600 men
engaged, however fitfully, in police work. If, in the rural areas, the
magistrates' estimate be accepted one might hazard the very rough
guess that Lancashire was policed by some thousand men. This

K

was, of course, supplemented on occasion, not only by troops, yeomanry and Metropolitan police on loan, but by large levies of Special Constables.

This completes a picture of complexity amounting almost to obscurity. A complex of crime and disorder faced a complex of efforts to match it. In the nature of things this favoured the former. The lawless had adapted themselves to industrialism with alacrity, while mass action was made much simpler by growing conurbations. The authorities attempted to meet the problem with outmoded agencies, which were slipshod, inefficient and, above all, disunited. Although punition was brutal and severe, the balance in the centuries old struggle between law and crime favoured the criminal. The forces of law were in such disarray that they could combat no section of illegality successfully, whether it was sneak thieving or rioting. It was in these discouraging conditions that Lancashire prepared itself for police reform.

Their establishment 1836–1856
Historians have perhaps been a little over-anxious to lay all police reform at the Chartist door. It has been argued that the 1839 Police Act was the result of Chartist unrest and the desire of the military authorities to relieve the strain thrust upon them—'it was to take the threat of a revolution to overcome the almost universal English distrust of a regular rural police'.[1] There is no doubt that the new policemen were expected to prevent rioting as the Metropolitan police had done in 1832, and Chadwick did not hide his view that industrial discontent might succumb to a reformed police. But the Chartist threat was only one of several motivations. Firstly, the theory is palpably unfair to the 1839 Police Commission which considered 'riotous assemblage' quite properly as but one piece in the pattern. The sheer havoc played by robbery in the country was uppermost in the minds of the Commissioners who, it should be recalled, had begun their deliberations in 1836 and ended them before any major Chartist outbreaks. Many of the elements observed in Lancashire—new categories of crime, new causes of crime, new opportunities for crime—were noted by the *Constabulary Report* as well as more specific issues such as Irish immigration. The case, as presented and in part accepted, for a reformed police was not Chartist centred. Secondly, the drastic recommendation of a national brigade as 'an extension of the

[1] A. R. Schoyen, *The Chartist Challenge* (1958), p. 82.

trained Metropolitan police', with its rigid central governance and
its shuttle service of personnel to avoid local attachments and bias,
was not implemented. The opposition of the popular press, of the
ultra-radicals and of many J.P.s and the apathy of much of the
landed gentry made the 1839 County Constabulary Act a relatively
innocuous one. It merely proffered a rather timid permission to
magistrates to form county forces if they so desired, with the
opportunity for some consultation with the Home Office. This was
hardly the thorough-going act of a state terrorised by Chartism,
and, although Chartist threats continued through most of the next
decade only twenty-two counties had adopted the Act in full by
1853. The Bill was certainly mooted because of Chartist threats,
but it was a weak and faulty piece of legislation, subject to delays
and requiring amendment in the following session.

The Boroughs, where, conceivably, most Chartist unrest might
be expected, were catered for already by the Municipal Corporations Act of 1835, which allowed incorporation towns to form a
Watch Committee and a police force. The larger Lancashire
towns, it will be seen, made brisk attempts either to implement the
1835 Act, or, if not of Borough status, to become incorporated that
they might. Perhaps the Chartist fear has been exaggerated.
Chartist endeavours in Lancashire were, judging from the Home
Office papers, closely associated with Manchester or towns such as
Rochdale, Bolton and Oldham, abutting on that city, and the
astonishing absence of much Chartist activity on Merseyside, with
its strong tradition of political militancy, has not been given
sufficient recognition by historians of Chartism. The dramatic
quality of Chartism has possibly inspired its narrators to assign
undue influence to it. Perhaps, indeed, the 'public order' aspect of
Chartism has been itself overdramatised. There is no doubt that
it was alarming, but it was neither a perpetual nor ubiquitous
movement, and its contemporaries may well have thought that
special and temporary action—special constables or the militia, for
example—was the answer. Constant theft and fear of theft, dull for
the social historians, but niggling and irritating to the shopkeepers
and tradesmen of Victorian Lancashire, was doubtless a more
pressing factor in police reform.

Another general theory explaining provincial police reform has
been advanced, especially as it affected the Boroughs. Apart from
population growth and the eagerness for municipal reform generally it has been suggested that there was a wholesale departure of

criminals from London because of the efficiency of the Metropolitan Police. This, it is argued, forced reform on the country at
large. This view has been strenuously challenged by the police
historian, Judith Hart. She claims that the statistics are both faulty
and inconclusive; that only about half the Boroughs took advantage
of the 1835 Act, and, unlike London, suburbs were not provided
for; and that previous Metropolitan police help—supposedly a
fillip to reform by dint of example—had been exaggerated. She
further points out that the County forces had to be established,
not to emulate the Borough forces and deal with criminals driven
out by the new police, but because the towns remained deficiently
guarded and a general county-wide problem existed, aggravated by
Chartism. This analysis seems admirable, except perhaps that the
emphasis on Chartist discontent is again urged with a little too
much vigour.

Turning specifically to the organisation of police forces in Lancashire, one finds no single motive nor common circumstance. By
1856 twelve police agencies had been formed (see Table III). The
County force was started in 1839 immediately following the 1839
County Constabulary Act. The Borough forces were Lancaster,
Warrington, Wigan, Liverpool, Bolton, Manchester, Salford,
Preston, Ashton-under-Lyne, Oldham and Blackburn. The time-
element alone is crucial, for the dates of commencement for these
twelve bodies range from Lancaster in 1824 to Blackburn in 1852;
that is, both before and after the Chartist era. Indeed it is necessary
to examine the different groups of police organisations in order to
explain the reasons and motives for their formation.

The County force was mooted in 1839, when the Chartists had,
of course, been active. But it was mooted in October, when the
violence had quietened and when many North-Western Chartist
officers were safely jailed. On 14 October the J.P.s of North Lonsdale and South Lonsdale decided at their Quarter Sessions that a
Constabulary was needed, and a group of five J.P.s met with two
J.P.s from each district to discuss the possibility. Legal advice had
to be obtained from the Attorney General. He ruled that police up
to the ratio of one to a thousand inhabitants was permissible to be
paid for out of the county rate. Boroughs and towns of over 10,000
were to be exempt, provided they policed themselves efficiently.
This apparently satisfied Liverpool's anxieties, for the Watch
Committee thought the Act 'an infringement on the principle of
local government'. Joseph Walmsley, the Mayor, in a letter to the

Home Secretary the Marquis of Normanby, claimed, somewhat overenthusiastically, that Liverpool was 'certainly one of the most peaceable in Her Majesty's dominions'.

It was resolved on 6 November, to install a County Police. A letter from the Home Office acknowledged receipt of the J.P.'s representation, and transmitted to the Clerk of the Peace for Lancaster the necessary rules for establishing a police force. Lancashire was one of the earliest Counties to take advantage of the Act, and, along with a handful of other Counties, received a number of circulars about rules and instructions for Constables

Table III: **Lancashire Police Forces 1836–1856***

Force	Date of Inauguration	Population	Initial Establishment	Strength in 1856
County Force	1839	995,000	502	614
Lancaster	1824	10,000	9	10
Wigan	1836	21,000	6	23
Liverpool	1836	206,000	290	886
Preston	1836	36,000	7	40
Manchester	1842	243,000	398	554
Bolton	1842	50,000	22	26
Salford	1844	53,000	31	95
Warrington	1847	23,000	5	9
Ashton	1848	31,000	13	23
Oldham	1849	53,000	12	22
Blackburn	1852	47,000	12	29

* The figures of initial strength are drawn from Watch Committee and County Constabulary Committee Minutes, while the later figures have been extracted from *The Reports of the Inspectors of Constabulary, No. 2, Northern District*, 1857. Population figures relate to the inaugural dates.

and the appointment and qualifications of Chief Constables and other officers. These negotiations fail to mention insurrectionary dangers or any other specific points. Lancashire adopted the 1839 Act, and seemingly followed the composite line of the *Constabulary Report*. It adopted the Act as a general piece of legislation and, as in the other Counties, the rules formulated for Suffolk were accepted *in toto*. It would appear that the County established a police force on general grounds, attracted by the passage of the 1839 Act, rather than because of the specific threat of Chartism. A Chief Constable was appointed in December and the appointment was approved by the Home Office. He was Captain John Woodford late of the Rifle Brigade and Adjutant of the Duke of Lancashire's Own Militia. He immediately visited London, that he might base his administration on Colonel Rowan's pattern. This seems to hint at a county magistracy alive to the many dangers of crime in an overpopulated region and ready to turn for aid to the other densely peopled spot in the United Kingdom. Add to this that the initial move came from the J.P.s of Lonsdale—scarcely a hotbed of Chartist insurrection—and that most of the Chartist centres were at first expressly exempted from the jurisdiction of the county force, and the Chartist bogey is considerably diminished.

The eleven Boroughs followed no steady pattern. The ancient town of Lancaster established its Borough Police in 1824, under the Improvement Act of that year, and the relevant Minutes run through from 1824 without any procedural alteration. The 1835 Municipal Corporations Act was the motivating factor for reforms in Wigan and Liverpool, and, in January 1836, immediately the Act was in force, both Councils appointed large Watch Committees of over twenty to set up 'a body of preventive police'. The Liverpool police was founded on strict Chadwickian lines, for it was felt that 'the establishment of an efficient preventive police' would 'by diminishing crime, prove a saving in contingent expenses'. Great improvements were expected 'with little addition to the sum now expended upon a system which has been found to be totally inadequate'. They both predated the Chartist challenge.

Manchester and Bolton form another little group. Here police reform became involved with the struggle between incorporators and anti-incorporators. Manchester was incorporated in 1838, and the new Council raised a force of 343. The Police Commissioners refused to dissolve their night-police and the Court Leet its day-police. There were considerable difficulties in raising the £20,000 police rate, and both Chartists and Anti-Corn Law Leaguers were causing trouble. The consequence of incorporation was the concurrent operation in 1839 of three forces. The government was so disturbed that a Manchester Police Bill was hurriedly passed, and a Chief Commissioner of Police was appointed for two years over 'a specially organised police force'. Sir Charles Shaw was appointed to resolve this farcical situation, and he recruited a force from all three bodies at an annual cost of £16,500. On Manchester's protestations, the government decided not to extend Shaw's office, and, in October 1842, the Borough police took over again. A similar situation arose in Bolton. After incorporation in 1838, the Bolton Watch Committee were anxious to form a force of twelve men. The Greater Bolton and Little Bolton Courts Leet claimed to be still the legal authority and they threatened legal action against any new constable acting in the name of the Borough. They retained control of the lock-ups, forcing the Council to use gaols at Preston, Kirkdale, Lancaster and Salford. There was considerable non-payment of rates, and the Council's financial state became chaotic. Over two years the council collected only £443 out of an aggregate levy of £5,971. A sizeable Chartist riot in 1839, which led to the burning of Little Bolton Town Hall, aggravated the situation. Thus Bolton requested the government to include them in the Manchester Police Bill, and Lieutenant-Colonel Angelo was made Commissioner. He quickly resigned his post for he felt the smallness of the force to be insulting and 'a complete robbery on the inhabitants of Bolton'. Shaw was given command, with the aid of Superintendent James Boyd. After the validity of the Charter had been confirmed, the Borough took over control on 1 October 1842.

Salford and Preston make up a third duo, this time of Boroughs forced into reform by the threat of the County Constabulary. Salford denied itself incorporation, fearful that such a step would add to the rates. The County Police Act, however, forced its hand, and, to retain its independence, the town petitioned for incorporation. This was granted in 1844, and a police force was then established. Preston had had a small paid force since 1810, and its Watch Committee, formed under the 1835 Act, pleaded 'to be exempted from liability' to the County Constabulary Act. In 1840 a County Constabulary Amendment Bill was passed to bring recalcitrant Boroughs into line. Preston had no separate court of Quarter Sessions—which could have been one exemptive qualification—but it had a Local Act and a population of over 10,000. Preston objected to the County Constabulary as being 'inconsistent with the principle of self-regulation'. It was 'an arbitrary rule' for 'fewer constables can effectually watch and preserve the peace' in a concentrated population which was 'orderly and quiet not disorderly and easily excited'. The Preston Watch Committee had actually been formed in 1836, and, on Home Office recommendation, had increased its force a little. Now pressure was on Preston to raise its force to a score or more. Both Salford and Preston negotiated police matters with a grudging eye on financial pros and cons, and with little concern for Chartism, or indeed, crime of any kind.

The other four forces were straightforward cases of growing

towns becoming incorporated and automatically setting up independent police arrangements. Warrington became a Borough in
1847, and the first Watch Committee meeting was held on 15 July
1847. Ashton was incorporated in the same year, and the Borough
force was established on 9 February 1848, after the formation of
the first Watch Committee. A year later the Oldham force was
formed, and its Charter had been precipitated by a policing
problem. Attempts at incorporation had been abortive in 1833, but
the Rural Police Act would have made the Oldham rate-payers
responsible for twenty-one P.C.s. Political and financial resent-
ment flared, and, after some eight years' conflict, incorporation
was accepted. A police force of a dozen was instituted, and, as in
Preston and Salford, the action was, in fact, a move to prevent,
rather than to extend, police-work in the town. Finally, on 1 March
1852, Blackburn's new Borough Council established its own police
department, a year after incorporation. Possibly the County Constabulary was once more the nigger in the woodpile. On 6 January
1841, a public meeting in Blackburn appealed for its abolition on
the grounds of its 'enormous expense'. The yearly police expenses
then amounted to £870, and it is interesting to note that the first
annual expenditure of the Borough force, twelve years later, was
only £728. Each of these developments was a purely administrative
step, albeit with some political overtones, and it is difficult to con-
nect them with the legal or social condition of the nation at large.

There is then no single explanation of the development of Lancashire's police forces in this period. Working class unrest, the
Irish problem, crowded towns and new classes of crime are all part
of the question, but they fail to cover it completely. If any con-
sistency can be observed, it must be the prior consideration given
to the basic principles of local government. Finance constantly
entered the reckoning, as Councils and rate-payers fought shy of
increased expenditure. On the other hand there was the rate-
payer's natural wish to ensure security for the community to which
he belonged, as well as the growing pride in municipal institutions
which some commentators have noted. Authorities then, as today,
were primarily concerned with that precarious juggling of prestige,
efficiency and economy which is the hall-mark of local rule. In 1856
a County and Borough Police Act was passed which made policing
compulsory and liable, under certain conditions, to inspection. By
this time, Lancashire had its County Force, with another eleven
departments principally located in the south of the County. Some

large towns, like Rochdale, Burnley and Bury, still remained unincorporated and thus without separate police systems. Unlike the haphazard character of Public Health organisation, however, the whole of Lancashire had theoretical police coverage, even if the Boroughs were not answerable to the Home Office in the way the County was. The early legislation permitted small Boroughs to maintain tiny bands of police, which might well have been consolidated less wastefully within the larger County force. Only Clitheroe of the Lancashire Boroughs, failed to form its own force, preferring, with some sense, to allow its small population to be policed by the County. Twelve forces, nevertheless, existed, and the following sub-sections attempt some analysis of their function and character.

ii. Their structure

Control
It would seem best to inspect the structure of the new Police Forces by raising four important questions. Firstly, how and by whom were they controlled? Secondly, what type of person made up their complement? Thirdly, how were their finances organised? Fourthly, to what extent was the preventive principle successful?

In answer to the first question it may be stated baldly that police administration fell into a dualism of central and local control familiar to many English governmental agencies. Chadwick's wish for a national system was unfulfilled and remains unfulfilled. The compromise was maintained of the constable who derived power from the Common Law and yet being subservient to the sovereign's officers, to wit, the magistrates. 'External control' of an 'impartial force' was the Victorian answer. And yet, or so the Royal Commission of 1962 claimed, 'the creation in the last century of statutory police forces throughout Great Britain marked a major breach with the past', in that constables were co-ordinated into groups under local democratic supervision, and in that, especially through finance, effective control often came to rest with the new local councils. 'Not surprisingly', it concluded, 'the resulting pattern of administration was somewhat confused.' At the same time the Commission emphasised that police powers were still 'rooted in the Common Law' and that the persistence of local tradition explained 'so many separate police forces, each identifies with its own particular locality'. A. L. Goodhart, however,

appended a dissenting memorandum, suggesting that sentiment-
ality perhaps clouded men's eyes to the real break with the past.
The modern police constable, he argued, was not the descendant
of the parish constable, but was born of the new post–1829 mores.
In effect, he said, the 1835 Act made the police completely 'subject
to the orders of the Chief or Head Constable', who was, in practice,
uncontrolled.

How far was the new administration in Lancashire a sharp
breach with the past, at least until 1856? The County force was
administered by a joint committee of J.P.s and local representatives. The J.P.s both in the county at large, and in the urban areas,
were, of course, the same men who had operated the older régime.
The County Constabulary was, in a sense, a consolidation of constables supervised by the magistrates in concert. The enthusiasm
of County Magistracy was, moreover, quickly dimmed. The South
Lonsdale J.P.s who had floated the plans for a County force, were
soon anxious to form a separate Police District, as the expense out-
laid and the protection received were disproportionate. Prescot
Guardians petitioned for abolition in April 1841, and, the following
summer, the Annual Sessions voted 71 to 28 to discontinue the
force. In September 101 J.P.s voted for abolition, and another
ballot six months later resulted in an 81 to 56 poll in favour of the
abolitionists. The County Police Act, however, required three
quarters' approval either for acceptance or retention, and thus the
County force luckily survived its opening years. The upshot was a
massive reduction in the force from 502 to 355. The larger towns
were equally critical. A public meeting of rate-payers in Blackburn
in 1841 appealed for abolition 'Under the present system (wrote
the chronicler) the Police expenses of the township of Blackburn
amounted to about £870 a year (Shame) while under the old
system, when Mr. John Kay or Mr. Pervis were constables, the
same work was done for £100.' A prisoner escorted to Preston in a
carriage was considered extravagant, and, it was scornfully announced, that the County police 'must ride about in their gigs and
their stuffment, forsooth.'

The matter became extremely serious when, in 1850, the Milner-
Gibson Select Committee met to discuss a Lancashire County
Rates and Expenditure Bill. This was prompted by the Rochdale
Guardians. William Roberts, one of that body, spoke of increased
expenditure 'becoming very burdensome to the rate-payers'. It
was, he contended, difficult to keep check of the J.P.s who ruled

the County when, as in Rochdale, they steadfastly refused to attend
the Boards of Guardians. The Guardians wished for a Financial
and Administrative Board, drawn up constitutionally with two
representatives from each Union Board, to supersede the J.P.s in
their Annual Sessions as the financial controllers of the County.
The Committee opposed the Bill on the grounds that the Boards
would cause 'a serious risk of injury and impediment to the public
service, without any equivalent advantage', and it was not until the
1888 County Councils Act that the government of the Counties
became more widely democratic. One change in the County
administration must be noted. In 1840 an Act 'to amend the Act
for the Establishment of County and District Constables' was
passed, and this replaced the County Rate with a Police Rate,
permitted the construction of new premises, sharpened the financial
mechanics of the system, allowed division into police districts, and
ordered 'that all such local Constables shall be subject to the
authority of the Chief Constable and to such regulations as shall be
made. . . .' It was on the basis of this sensible Amending Act that
the County Authorities resolved to build some station-houses,
which had hitherto been impossible, and to equate Police Districts
with Petty Sessional Divisions. It also brought pressure on
Boroughs, such as Preston, to meet the authorised standards of
policing.

As for the Borough Councils and their Watch Committees, there
was obviously a certain amount of continuity of personnel with the
past. The incorporators in many Boroughs were members of the
existing Council or Commission who were ambitious to see their
powers extended or clarified. In Manchester and Bolton there was,
for some time, violent objection against incorporation, and certainly
the government of Manchester after 1842 was very much improved. In Oldham, too, there had been heated opposition to
incorporation, but the transfer from Police Commission to Council
eventually went smoothly enough. John Platt was the leading
'Charterist', as incorporators in Oldham and elsewhere were known.
He eagerly pointed out the embargo on capital expenditure
imposed by the 1826 Improvement Act, which forbade an expense
of more than £200 on a single item.

In Liverpool and Wigan the Municipal Incorporation Act of
1835 was implemented by the existing Councils, although, as in
Manchester, there is little doubt that a considerable improvement occurred in Liverpool's municipal governance. Liverpool

Watch Committee was twenty-four strong but a sub-committee
was immediately appointed to organise the new police department. This seemed to operate fluently enough, and was surely
sounder than the old system of two bailiffs helping the mayor.
There had been some opposition in Liverpool, and, in later
years, there was conflict between local authorities and magistrates. In 1851 the Liverpool J.P.s accused the police of incompetence, in connection with a case concerning a publican
named Jonghin. Three policemen—Butler, Slee and Kelly—were
acquitted of illegal action, but it was suggested that little liaison
existed between the Outdoor Department and the Detective
Department with regard to robberies. The police authorities, in
turn, criticised the J.P.s for the abuse of their licensing system,
with transfer of licences a common abuse. Liverpool had licensed
premises for every 265 of its inhabitants.

Wigan Watch Committee had J. S. Heron as its Chairman,
together with twenty-one other members. Its administration seems
to have been less smooth. Discussions were vehement enough to
lead to a strict order from the chair that 'any member of the
Committee when delivering his sentiments do so upon his legs,
and address himself to the chair'. There were frequent angry
exchanges. When the Chief Constable was discharged in October
1840 the voting was 10 to 9 after a bitter contest. The minority
registered a long protest in the Minutes, which was 'expunged'
two months later.

Preston's Watch Committee consisted of the Mayor, Aldermen
Haydock and Monk and four Councillors. It was inaugurated at
the time of the 1835 Act, but only the pressure of an expensive
County troop of police forced Preston to act on police reform.
Similarly with Salford, who, in effect, sued for incorporation to
avoid reform. Little, perhaps, could be expected of authorities
acting so grudgingly although the Salford Watch Committee were
anxious that its force was not 'of so satisfactory a character' and
tried to improve it. In the three remaining towns there appears to
have been little or no awkwardness. Ashton Improvement Commissioners ceased in February 1848, and the new Corporation took
over without difficulty. Warrington was incorporated mainly for
Public Health reasons, and, although the Police Commissioners
did not vanish until 1854, the control of the police fell to the new
Watch Committee from 1847 onwards. Again, there was no
strenuous objection. Blackburn wished for incorporation and its

problems 'were rapidly assuming formidable proportions, alto-
gether beyond the scope of the Commissioners'. The transfer was
smooth and peaceful, with John Hargreaves acting as clerk to both
Commission and Council and William Hoole, the Commission's
chairman, acting as Returning Officer for the Borough's first
elections.

Viewed in this light, the administrative changes involved in
police reform look less than spectacular. Normally the new
administration was exactly the old administration extended and
refurbished. Even as in Bolton or Manchester—where opposition
was acute, it was usually a section of the old régime who were
struggling to expand its scope. New men were not necessarily
forthcoming because of the passage of the 1835 Act. Manchester
and Liverpool were, obviously, large enough to take rich advantage
of the schemes, and to amend their organisation beneficially. In
none of Lancashire's eleven large towns were the magistrates in
full control of law enforcement before the 1835 Act was implemented. It must also be recalled that the Act was a conservative
one, and Commissions could retain special powers. Voting rights
were restricted, and Liverpool, for example, mustered only 6,000
electors under the new provisions—many Improvement Commissions had constitutions which were not much less democratic. The
basis of supervision—the holding of substantial property—remained untouched. The range of populations catered for veered
from 20,000 to nearly 400,000, while the complements ranged from
five to nearly 400. Add to this the criticism that Watch Committees
were too close to the police (leniency towards publicans is an
example often quoted) and that perhaps the police, drawn from
small catchment areas, were too close to the people, and the early
record of police administration begins to seem slightly tarnished.
The doctrinaire police reformers could not then have been over-
joyed at the organisation and controlling powers of the new forces.
The geopolitical pattern was established by the County and
Borough authorities themselves. As with Public Health and, to
some extent, the Poor Law, local self-determination had retained
its hold, and age-old boundaries and sometimes systems were
perpetuated.

Central control was too flimsy to counter such local independence. In the case of the Boroughs the only contact with the state
before 1856 when inspection was introduced, was the quarterly
return. Several Boroughs never acceded to even that request.

Probably one attraction of organising a Borough force was, in fact, the escape from any Home Office jurisdiction, for under the County Police Act of 1839, the state retained some control over the shire forces. It has been possible to read all the correspondence which passed from the Home Office to the Lancashire force during the period under investigation. Between 19 November 1839, when the inaugural letter was dated, to 21 July 1856, when the New Act came into force, only 118 letters were posted to the Lancashire authorities, and the county was never visited by a Home Office official; indeed, there was no officer to perform such a task. This paltry connection amounts to about six letters a year. There was only one in 1843; four in 1845; two in 1849 and 1850, and 1851; and three in 1855. The substance of this thin batch of communications is even more disillusioning. Fifteen are circulars to all forces, relating to rules, plans for station houses, reinstatement elsewhere of ex-policemen, court costs for false charges, age limits, reminders of quarterly reports not forwarded, and so on. No less than 49— almost a half—concern augmentations and reductions in staff or, in one or two instances, alterations in divisional boundaries, and these are all automatic stereotype acknowledgements.

An interesting set of two dozen letters refers to the building of Station Houses. The circular about plans for these buildings was made available in April 1841, but it was not until the early spring of 1844 that Major Jebb, the Inspector of Prisons, approved the first installation of the force. Such dilatoriness in building new premises suggests either miserly and inefficient organisation, if the county was as deficient in police as is normally thought, or the use of old buildings, which indicates the existence of a previous police service. The new county force mustered 500 men to begin with, and these presumably had to be housed. A transfer of a building's function, moreover, was impossible without Home Office consent. The hypothesis of the county force being a consolidation of existing resources seems to find some backing in the apparent adequacy of existing police offices and gaols.

The first new Constable Station was at Kirkdale, where, in his recommendations, Jebb revealed his obsession with the earthenware as opposed to the cast-iron soil-pan. In the November of 1844, near neighbours of Kirkdale—Wavertree and Woolton—had plans approved. Jebb again suggested recommendations, 'if they can conveniently be carried into effect'. In seventeen years only twenty-four small schemes were presented, and, by 1856, the complement was over 600. If the Police authorities were further delayed by contractors then progress must have been rather slow, as it was with many Public Health enterprises. It is perhaps of interest to note a discernable pattern in the building programme, beginning with a cluster of eight around Liverpool, a group of six around Wigan, and a bunch of five in the Fylde.

Nineteen further letters portray vividly the relative powerless- ness of the Home Office, or at best, its extreme reluctance to intervene. Some are fairly straightforward, with the Home Office, for example, complying with the appointment as constables of Robert Hood, Joseph Booth and James Wilde despite their being over age. Complaints levelled against the County force were countered in the same negative fashion. The Home Secretary had 'no power to interfere' in the case of a Bury policeman, John Rogers, who complained of his treatment. The Prescot Guardians, eager for an end to the force, were told that the Home Secretary could not 'reduce or abolish'. R. Sumner lodged a general complaint, but the Home Secretary, he was told, 'cannot interfere in such a case'. Leonard Williams of Lancaster objected to a reduction in the police force, but the Home Office was forced to admit its helplessness. The central department could not even give permission to Superintendents to act as Inspectors of Weights and Measures, while, unkindest cut of all, it had to give retrospective approval to the use of swords by Wigan police some weeks earlier. The remaining eleven letters are a miscellaneous collection. Only two hint at the Home Office taking positive action, and these were of petty import. In 1839 a Mr. Sharples' qualifications were considered inadequate for him to join the force, and, in March 1840, two men, John Morden, and John Woodhall, were refused on the grounds of illiteracy. The contact between state and county was, in effect, almost a constant denial of the link.

All in all, the administrative changes were not dramatic. Basically the existing County authorities had consolidated their existing resources and built upon them, and the larger towns had furnished existing modes of government with more powers. This is not to say that the administration was inefficient but that it was not brand-new. No fundamental change had occurred, and the state played but a feeble part. In some ways continuity of administration can have advantages, for the sharp break with past habits can be disastrous. On the other hand, the existing authorities, in terms not only of men, but of boundaries, had not been satisfactory, and it was unlikely that they could cope happily with the grave problem of crime. When police personnel are discussed, the poor quality of much police work in Lancashire will be evident, and, indirectly, the County Magistracy and the appropriate Watch Committees must accept a sizeable portion of the blame. In general, therefore, the control of Lancashire's twelve police departments was neither original in inception nor inspiring in character.

Personnel

Expertise was the Utilitarian panacea for many ills, and crime was no exception. If paid, competent officers in sufficient numbers were mustered to replace the outmoded amateurs of the past, then would crime figures fall reassuringly. The new system had to stand or fall by the effectiveness of its officers, for it relied completely on the humdrum contact of police constable and man-in-the-street. The irregular and haphazard essays of unpaid voluntary Parish Constables, pathetic old watchmen and occasional day police had proved valueless. A trained, uniformed and professional brigade must be substituted, ran the argument, of a quantity and a quality which would effectually deter the would-be law-breaker by its actual physical presence and impression of zeal. Like the Relieving Officer in the New Poor Law, the Police Constable was the key to the system. Just as the Relieving Officer's burden was heavier because of the Guardians' ineffectiveness, so was the Police Constable's responsibility made greater by the weakness in the administrative machine. The County J.P.s had their County Constabulary Committee Meetings, which, like the Watch Committees, met, as a rule, monthly. The police executives were thus part-timers meeting occasionally, while crime, by its very nature, was random and unexpected in its incidence. Each outbreak of crime led, in a sense, to a police officer faced with a sudden emergency. The numbers and ability of Lancashire's first new policemen are then a critical issue. The Constabulary Report estimated that, outside London, 8,119 police were required. The Commissioners suggested either one P.C. to 1,769 people or to 4,403 acres. It will be recollected that Lancashire had something approaching 1,000 officers before reform so it was hardly a case of starting from scratch. Using the figures of the 1831 Census as base, this implies that Lancashire had a police officer to every 1,335 citizens or to every 1,203 acres—ratios both well within Chadwick's calculations.

The County's ambitious initial establishment of 502 was not at

first reached; 428 was the mark attained, when J.P.'s decided, in
the face of much opposition, to reduce the establishment by 147 in
May of 1842. Rather than have two Chief Constables, as the Act
allowed, Lancashire obtained permission to have two Assistant
Chief Constables. Captains Robert MacDonald and Edward Willis
were appointed, but the former lost rank in the 1842 economy
purge. Superintendents were normally in charge of a Police
District identical to a Petty Sessional Division. Inspectors and
Sergeants were not scheduled in the 1839 Act, but, following his
discussions about rank with Captain Hay of the Metropolitan
Police, Woodford proposed a graduated scheme of Inspectors,
Sergeants, 1st Class, 2nd Class and 3rd Class Constables, along the
Metropolitan pattern, as what he called 'a stimulus of exertion'.
After 1842, the force grew rapidly. It was, according to Woodford,
'favourably received by the respectable and orderly portion of the
community', and, again according to Woodford, it rose in numbers
under the pressure of the rate-payers. Although the force grew
rapidly, one must balance the increase against the rise in population. In 1848 there was one police officer to 1,700 persons within
the county area; in 1857 it was one to 1,550. This was no sensational increase, therefore, but rather a keeping of pace with the
rising population, and a maintaining of Chadwick's dictum of one
to 1,700.

The Borough police forces demonstrated a fantastic range of
strengths. Manchester and Liverpool were, in comparative terms,
gigantic, while Lancaster and Warrington were still very tiny
forces at the end of the period. Liverpool, in answer to the needs
of a cosmopolitan and crowded port, built up an enormous force
far exceeding even the county strength. The Watch Committee's
sub-committee on police continued to report on the 'operations of
the Constabulary force', having had its initial recommendations
implemented. Two Divisions, North and South, were formed,
which in turn were divided into eight sections. A sub-committee
of three met daily, and the Liverpool police was mounted to a
lively start. With a reserve of sixty or more, not counted in the
figures given, and with the early addition of 189 Dock Police to its
strength, the Liverpool Police had, by 1856, more than one
policeman to every 400 citizens. Manchester had had 328 police
under Sir Charles Shaw, and when the Corporation gained control,
they were augmented immediately by seventy. The Police Commissions of Ardwick, Chorlton and Hulme transferred their

L

powers in the early forties, and the ambit of jurisdiction became more rational. Despite protests at the expense and demands for a reduction, the force grew steadily, until, by 1857, it mustered 554. Once more the growth should be set against population increase. None the less, both cities were quick to sense a drastic problem and answer it in forthright fashion.

The other nine towns were very different propositions. Between 1824 and 1857 the Lancaster force moved painfully from nine to ten. Preston was reluctant to budge from around seven, but, in the last ten years of the period, the numbers abruptly sprang to forty. Wigan stuck at a bare half-dozen or so for many years, but managed to reach twenty-three by 1857. Bolton's strange police history continued after the Borough resumed control from the government commissioner. A decision to retain the government force of forty-two was quickly rescinded, and twenty unfortunates were given a fortnight's notice. The force was reduced to eighteen in 1847, and was no more than twenty-six in 1857. Salford, which had turned grudgingly to police reform, fluctuated between thirty-three and forty-four until, with another sudden spurt, eighty-one was achieved by 1856 and ninety-five by 1857. Warrington's force of eleven was reorganised in 1838 by the Improvement Commission and perpetuated by the new Corporation. Only one was added by the first state inspection. Of the late starters, Oldham remained at twenty-two, but Ashton and Blackburn had, by 1857, roughly doubled their numbers. By 1857 three Borough forces still failed to meet the ratio of one to 1,700 people. Bolton, Warrington, and especially Oldham were the offenders. Preston, Ashton and Blackburn only just managed to meet this particular criterion, with Lancaster, Wigan and Salford the only establishments well clear. It was apparent from the Manchester and Liverpool departments that conurbations required intensive policing, and, by their criteria, only Salford was adequately policed. A notable feature is the precipitate increase in the police of the nine smaller Boroughs in the years just before 1857, when grants based on central inspection were instituted by the 1856 Act. Between 1852 and 1857 their combined totals rose from 176 to 280. Apart from Salford, all these forces were criticised during their first inspection for insufficient numbers. If, therefore, the numbers were inadequate in 1857, despite a recent augmentation of 62 per cent, then for the greater part of the era, the police coverage must have been shoddy indeed. The 1856 Act offered authorities a subsidy for pay and clothing of

25 per cent, provided the department was functioning efficiently. Possibly this fillip caused the rapid appointments of the mid-fifties. In 1852 the ratio of police to people in the nine towns was one to 2,300, which, for urban conditions, was deplorable.

Thus by 1857 there were 2,447 police in Lancashire. 2,167, or 88 per cent, were in three forces, and only 280, or 12 per cent, were in the remaining nine. The fear of forces varying wastefully in strength and effectiveness is vividly emphasised by these figures. In fairness to the Lancashire police, their statistics should be placed against the figures for the nation as a whole. In 1846 there were 5,099 police in the United Kingdom, excluding London, of whom 1,783, or nearly one-third, were Lancastrian. In 1851 Lancashire had by far the largest county force. It had 509 of the country's 2,749 County policemen, with Staffordshire (254) and Gloucestershire (250) being the next highest. Yorkshire, at this juncture, had only nine County police, working in one Petty Sessional Division of the East Riding. In 1852, Lancashire's Boroughs employed 1,431 of the nations 4,181 Borough policemen, that is more than a quarter. Lancashire was certainly not the worst-policed area in the country, numerically speaking, and, before 1856, the county might even be described as a pioneer region for police-work, so numerous were its policemen in relation to the United Kingdom figures.

Arithmetic is, however, only one side of the medallion. Perhaps of more significance is the capability of these men, and the extent to which they met Chadwick's desire for a trained expert force. The County Constabulary was lucky in having John Woodford as the Chief Constable. He was an earnest and efficient soldier who, in September 1856, became one of the first three Inspectors of Constabulary. He had two ex-officers as his Assistant Chief Constables, and many of the Superintendents were ex-army officers. Woodford published a 55-page Rule Book for his underlings. P.C.s could have neither business interests nor political and religious affiliations, nor could they marry without permission. They were allowed one greatcoat, one cape, one dresscoat, dress and undress 'Trowsers', two pairs of boots, a hat, a stock and clasp, an armlet, a truncheon, a rattle, a belt and cape strap, and a button stick and brush. There is a military ring about the whole publication. This military character was sustained throughout some of the other forces. Manchester and Bolton had two years under direct military government, and on Shaw's retirement from the scene,

Captain Edward Willis, Assistant Chief Constable of Lancashire, became Manchester's first Chief Constable. Two of Liverpool's first four Superintendents—Lieutenants Jones and Heath—were ex-soldiers, and it seems that several retired officers and other ranks joined the various forces. The indirect influence of the Metropolitan Police, itself organised by Rowan on army lines, was maintained by appointments such as Superintendents Dowling and Thomas to the Liverpool and Manchester forces respectively. Foot-drill was an important part of what training was offered, and the Liverpool police was congratulated for its 'very competent knowledge of military movement'. The police-work in the County had a distinct paramilitary flavour, with uniforms and regulations and military officers and the ever present knowledge that the military were waiting in the background. This was, it appears, the extent of military quality in the police. The character of individuals in the various forces, however, conveys a totally different impression.

An examination of Lancashire's policemen in this era does reveal a notable lack of distinction between the bad old days and the golden dawn of sweet reason. A moment's thought should suggest to one what the records reveal; namely, that much of the recruitment for the new police must necessarily have come from the existing officers. It was an unpopular, dangerous and arduous job, and the incumbent constables were the only ones with the experience and probably the wish to join such bodies. The level of pay dictated their recruitment from the working classes, and it was precisely here that suspicion lay heaviest. The service and discipline accounts exhibit not only this kind of continuity, but also a most discouraging picture of the character of the purportedly new personnel. The rapid recruitment of 428 men for the County force within a year of its inauguration suggests a pool of personnel ready for adaptation. Similarly the access of these men to offices, accommodation and lock-ups suggests a corresponding pool of facilities. In 1857, Lancashire County police had 120 Station-houses. There were quarters for 326 men, and there were 211 cells, with as many as seven in some stations. Eleven had Petty Sessional court-rooms, and only the Ulverstone office had no residential quarters, despite its three cells. There were Divisional as well as County Headquarters. It will be recalled that only twenty-four schemes for facilities had been presented by 1856, and many of these could not have been completed. Again, adaptation rather than innovation seems likely.

Manchester made no bones about its recruitment. 'It is due to
the Chief Commissioner to state that he has selected a very liberal
proportion', so the Hackney Coach Committee were told, 'of the
men employed under this Committee for the new force.' When the
Borough force was formed, that is, the authorities drew largely on
the Watchmen whose inefficiency had been a reason for the Incorporation controversy. Liverpool tried to be more thorough. The
Watch Committee's Sub-committee wished 'to take such men
from the present establishment of police as may be deemed
eligible'. It was felt, however, that of the Watch of 166, forty-five
were ineligible and twenty-five had 'very doubtful' qualifications
and that of the day police, 'few of its members will be found
eligible for reappointment'. The Superintendent of the Nightly
Watch, M. J. Whitty, was, none the less, made Head Constable,
and fifty-three Watchmen were engaged. The Preston police were
the same seven men before and after the 1835 Act, and, in believing
that concentrated populations needed but few constables, they
completely reversed the argument used by the J.P.s in agrarian
areas. When in 1844, the Salford Police Force was established it
was merely a case of the thirty-one Watchmen and Day-Police
being renamed Constables. The Bolton Borough Police, finally
under way in 1842, was much the same as the Government force,
save that twenty of them were discharged. The Lancaster police
was the same before and after the 1835 Act. The Warrington
Borough force of five was exactly the same as the Township body
formed in 1838, while the Ashton Commissioners' force of thirteen
became the Borough Police force, with Robert Newton changing
his title from Deputy to Chief Constable. Oldham, which had
mustered a force of about ten since 1827, continued with a Borough
complement of a dozen, when threatened with a County establishment of nearly twice that number. The Blackburn force led by
Superintendent Thomas Marshall, late of the Liverpool Police,
mustered twelve and replaced the County men. A drop in the
County pay schedules for 1852 with no corresponding rise elsewhere in the County, suggests that the County policemen were
dismissed, and possibly some were employed by the new department. In Wigan six police were substituted for a Watch of sixteen.
The first major point to realise, therefore, is that the Lancashire
police were, more often than not, precisely the same men as in the
previous bodies, and, in two or three cases, there was an evident
weakening of the existing safeguards.

A few examples of indiscipline emphasise the pathetic quality of these men. Of the County Constabulary's first 200 recruits, fifty were discharged within six months, thirty of them for intoxication. There were no licensing hours then and no friendliness towards the 'blue-butchers'. One visualises a gloomy picture of constables hunched for long hours over their lonely tankards. Recruitment could not have been helped by the extensive violence, for many had to retire injured, usually with pensions of 1s. or 1s. 1d. a day. In December 1843, Woodford had to forbid the use of pistols, two men in Manchester Division having armed themselves. The Rochdale Improvement Commissioners sent a memorial to the Home Secretary about three county policemen—S. Fowler, T. Leary and G. Twist—who had abused and threatened Alice Roberts in the 'Three Crowns Inn', Rochdale, one of them going so far as to thrust his head up her petticoats. The Commission were very worried about the insufferable behaviour of the police, and they complained bitterly at 'this glaring act of oppression and tyranny'. No sooner was the Liverpool police force—possibly the most competent at this stage in the county—under way than disciplinary actions fell thickly and heavily. Some five or six weeks were all that elapsed before Inspector Bradford was dismissed, and, at weekly meetings of the Watch Committee, an average of six appeals for reinstatement after dismissal were heard over the next nine years. In 1838 there were 101 sackings out of a total of 175 leaving the force. In that year 876 cases of dismissal, fining or cautioning were recorded, including 282 for inebriation. In the report for 1842 there were self congratulations because the suspensions were down from the 1841 figure of 130 to 108. It was 123 in 1843 and 103 in 1844. Disciplinary reports against constables ran to 2,674 in 1842, 2,223 in 1843 and 1,952 in 1844, while four investigations were held into that state of the police between 1844 and 1857. The early years of the Bolton police were fraught with disciplinary troubles, for, between 1839 and 1842, although membership never dropped below twenty-nine, there were eighty-one dismissals and fifty-seven resignations.

Wigan provides an amusing final illustration of most of these features in a smaller establishment, and its early Watch Committee Minutes read like the scenario of a Will Hay comedy. Thomas, a Manchester police officer, advised the Watch Committee to have 'a body of preventive police', forty strong, but the Committee plumped for six only. Thirty-five applied for these posts, of whom the only one with experience appointed was John Whittle, the new Chief Constable. Hugh Fegan (there was a Richard Fegan on the Watch Committee) was the first appointment while William Lancaster was made Constable for the Scholes district. The other three formed a night patrol, and they were all Wigan men. Bradley, a confessed illiterate, Halliwell, a private watchman, and Bolton were the names of this trio. Duties were strenuous. The day patrol worked from 8 a.m. to 11 p.m. with overtime on Saturdays, while the night watch were on duty from 10 p.m. to 5 a.m. This left an unguarded three hours, but as the night watch had to present a report at 11 a.m. this was unavoidable. Over the eight years covered by these minutes, twenty-seven men shared these six posts, of whom twelve were discharged and four did not remain long enough for their appointments to be confirmed. Only three served over two years, and fourteen remained less than twelve months. Thirty-nine cases of grave indiscipline were judged by the Watch Committee over the period. Bradley and Halliwell were dismissed for drunkenness only two months after the force was organised, and Hugh Fegan was admonished by the mayor because his prisoners tended to become 'more intoxicated when put into prison'. P.C. Bolton who was 'in the habit of getting drunk', had, while inebriated, locked up Henry Ashworth and 'knocked down James Fairbrother and after abusing him took him up and locked him up'. The following month, despite a severe admonishment, he was discharged for claiming expenses illegally and because he 'had a woman with him . . . with the door fastened inside'. Lancaster was dismissed for drinking after several reprimands, and it was said of him that 'the liquor overcame him before he was aware of it'. Eventually Fegan was dismissed, the last of his many offences being false entries. Thus, in little over a year, all the Wigan police, save Whittle, had been sacked. Whittle's turn was to come. Martha Seddon accused him of drunkenness and misconduct when serving a warrant upon her. 'I thought', she said, 'it was not proper for him to put his hand on my bosom drunk.' After much testimony and a close vote, he was dismissed in September 1840.

The comic series was continued. P.C. Dobson was discharged for a catalogue of crimes. He cheated on prison expenses; he spent his duty in bed when disorder was such that the militia was called out; he refused to wear his uniform; he drank excessively; he slept in front of the police station fire when he should have been on his beat; and, when roused, he 'made water upon the floor and against the desk'. Thomas Latham, the new chief constable, did little to abate the criminal tendencies of his troop. P.C. Anton gave his comrade, P.C. Lancaster, a black eye. While drunk he called P.C. Heath 'a damned thief', and vicious fighting broke out between them. His estimate may not have been lacking in shrewdness. Heath, once considered for an Inspectorate in Manchester, was expelled from the force for raffling a watch he had stolen from a murdered man. The premises of the Wigan Brewing Company proved too much of a temptation for various members of the force, and the firm complained bitterly of policemen found drinking in its storerooms.

It might be argued that frequent dismissals proved the sincere wish of the authorities to maintain high standards, and that a constant purification of the police was essential to acquire a fine strain of men. The turn-over, however, in both large and small forces, appears to have been so rapid that solidity or continuity must have been all but impossible to obtain. Whatever the genuine wishes of the authorities to raise standards, their methods of selection were often deplorable, seemingly based on the proverbial thesis of poachers making the best gamekeepers. The Wigan cameo suggests that, in the tiny forces, standards were at an abysmal level. In brief, it may be concluded that Lancashire's policemen were not so wonderful. They fell far short of the immaculate level postulated by the reformers, and progress towards a high and effective standard took rather longer than a superficial inspection might suggest. The uniforms and regulations were new; but the faces seemed depressingly familiar.

Finances

The financial issue requires some investigation for two reasons. First, the basic motive for any legislation inspired by Chadwick and his supporters was economic. This has already been observed earlier with regard to the Poor Law and Public Health. Just as the problems of pauperdom or ill-health meant, to Chadwick, huge monetary waste, so did unbridled crime impinge heavily on the national economic maintenance. His report in 1839 argued the economic case stoutly, inferring that criminals enjoyed a higher standard of living than that of the honest worker. In 1834 alone two million pounds were spent on punishing and preventing crime, and Chadwick believed that a national force, costing as little as £450,000, would pay for itself and still save thousands of pounds. Second, local government agencies were notoriously tight-fisted. When police reforms were mooted, the financial issues were amongst the most eloquently discussed. The supporters of reform argued, after Edwin Chadwick, that investment in a police force would reimburse itself in terms of crimes avoided. Their opponents pointed to the large increase in the rates necessary to sustain police establishments. The fiscal aspect of the police was regarded with concern at both national and local levels, but the statistics are not easy to solve. It is relatively simple to present the accounts of the reformed police over the years but it is impossible to estimate the money saved in terms of crimes prevented or foiled. The result would be little better than comparing a hard fact with a wild hazard. The issue is, however, so important that certain hesitant steps must be made. A fair starting point might be Chadwick's own calculation included in the 1839 Report, that the cost per policeman should be roughly £56 per year, and it is proposed to examine the expenditure on Lancashire's police forces in terms of this costing.

The Rural Police cost £26,591 in the year ending March 1840. There was a sharp increase to £39,693 the following year, which led to an equally sharp decrease in personnel. There was, by 1842, a sharp drop to £20,574. The figure stayed between £25,000 and £30,000 for the next four years. By 1852 the annual sum had levelled out about £34,000. Over the same period, the force was augmented in strength until it had 614 members in 1855. Apart from the early forties, when the drastic slashing of members occurred, the cost of each employee remained over £70 per annum, and was sometimes as high as £80. The increase in expense kept pace with the increased population, at something a little under one shilling *per capita*. With each police officer costing some £80 per year, Lancashire overshot Chadwick's optimistic target, although in this the County was by no means alone.

Given such a large force and with many industrial areas exempt from the county's jurisdiction, one might have anticipated a more economical result. One obvious explanation for the high expense of the Rural Constabulary lies in the overheads caused by a large and diffuse area. Police-stations, section houses, and lock-ups had to be maintained at a large number of strategic points, and travelling and communication expenses must have been proportionately high. Nevertheless, police finances were mainly concerned with the equipping and paying of individual officers, and Chadwick's estimate allowed for 10 per cent overheads.

The Borough forces had very differing financial histories. The Manchester force cost an average of £23,622 in the period 1839–1842. On being organised by the Corporation once more in 1842, the average cost dropped slightly to £23,026 in the years 1842–44 and in 1852 it was £25,478. In terms of the rise in population and the extension of the Manchester Police area, the cost per head of population remained almost exactly at the rather exorbitant rate of two shillings, from 1841 to 1860. The Liverpool police, planned to cost £18,000 in its first year, cost £24,000, and by 1852, total costs were around £45,000. Again given increases in population, the cost per head stayed at a similar rate—about two shillings—to that of Manchester. Two examples of smaller establishments provide helpful information. Preston averaged an annual cost of £500 before 1840. By 1859 it was £3,199. Here the *per capita* rate rose abruptly over a twenty-year phase from 2¼d. to 9d. Bolton had began in 1839 with ambitious hopes of a rate raising £2,900. These hopes having been dashed by vigorous opposition, the Bolton Watch Committee, following the dismantling of the government force, thought in terms of £2,100. Eventually the cost of the force settled down at the even lower figure in 1850, of £1,220, an average rate of 5d. a head.

No Lancashire Borough approached the expensive upkeep of the County force. On the other hand in 1852 only five of the Borough forces approached Chadwick's estimate. Notably these were Manchester and Liverpool which were uncannily near the £56 calculation in 1852. Oldham was the least expensive, with a figure of £52 whilst Blackburn and Wigan ran relatively cheap departments. The two large towns, however, paid very heavy rates, with 2s. 6d. *per capita* in Liverpool looking most extravagant against Blackburn's 4d. or Oldham's 5d. None the less, the important place of Manchester and Liverpool can easily be demonstrated. 1,251 out of Lancashire's 1,427 municipal police officers were in these two forces, leaving only 176 outside. Given changing money values, their average cost—£57—is remarkably near the 1839 suggestion. The average for the other nine towns was a little over £62. Just as the city forces were becoming the most efficient, so do they appear to have been economically operated, despite having abnormally large complements and paying slightly higher rates of pay. Needless to say, their need was the greater, but the book-keeping of Manchester and Liverpool tends to throw the rather trivial nine small forces into an absurd light. It seems an administrative nonsense that, in the same county, three establishments should employ 1,776 men at a cost of £109,582, whereas ten other establishments should employ 1,776 men at a cost of £10,975 for a similar task. The three major departments employed 91 per cent of the personnel and spent 91 per cent of the money.

Expenditure on police-work was not the only money spent on combating crime. There was also the cost of prosecutions. The national statistics show that, in 1850, prosecutions cost £364,312. Nearly 28,000 were committed for trial, giving an average prosecution cost of £13 to £14. In 1851, 3,459 people were committed for trial in Lancashire, and, by applying the mean of £13, one can make a rough calculation that the tax and rate-payers had to find a further £45,000. Then there were the prisons. Lancashire's five main gaols reported 24,836 confinements during 1849. This cost £48,912. Receipts, however, amounted to £25,150, thus reimbursing over half the cost, leaving £23,761 for the rate-payers to find. It may be submitted as a rough yardstick, that, when all Lancashire's pre-1856 police forces were under way by the early eighteen-fifties, some £2,000,000 was being annually expended. A calculation based on the statistics provided by the 1839 Report shows that, taking police, prosecutions and prisons into account, the national crime costs in 1834 amounted to 2s. per head, although for Lancashire it might have been slightly higher. The national expenditure by 1850 approached £2,000,000, a *per capita* cost now a little over 2s. In Lancashire the outlay of, say, £200,000 represented a sum of 2s. a head. No concrete conclusion may be drawn, for this is, admittedly, a case of arithmetic in the dark. The inference remains, nevertheless, that Lancashire and, indeed, the country, was paying much the same price for crime as before 1835 although possibly the changing monetary values affected the issue marginally. Despite variations in money values, the pressure on the Lancastrian rate-payer remained fairly constant. Again, as with the Poor Law and with Public Health, the onus was in part a psychological one. The rate-payers were not acclimatised to a burdensome rate, and extended police establishments contributed largely to a high County and Borough rating.

The major items in police finances were wages, and a study of them has the incidental by-product of offering a guide to the real value of money. There was an obvious dichotomy between the salaried officer and the wage-earning other ranks. Superintendents' salaries rarely fell below £100 per year, and rose as high as £300, whereas Sergeants never earned more than £70 at the very outside. Inspectors lived in a kind of twilight zone; sometimes their pay is quoted as a weekly wage, sometimes as a yearly salary. £100 was a very high rate for an Inspector in 1860. Five Chief Constables and seven Superintendents were in command of the police forces, and, as might be anticipated, their salaries covered a vast range, from £500 and more in the three big departments down to little more than £100 in places like Wigan and Oldham. The wage structure is fairly uniform over the twenty years period, although with exchequer grants introduced in 1856, there was some noticeable rises in the later figures. A policeman's lot did not vary particularly. Wigan's 14s. for its night patrolmen was outstandingly low, although a rueful Watch Committee possibly felt this was overgenerous. 16s. to 18s. was the normal wage in the eighteen-forties, and, by 1856, many police constables were earning a pound or more. The Liverpool and Manchester police were relatively well-paid, but even in 1860, Lancaster, Preston and Warrington were paying some of their employees as little as 16s. a week. In order to view these incomes a little more realistically, one might compare them with the earnings of other working men in Lancashire in 1860. Pattern-makers and iron-founders earned over 30s. per week, and miners an average of 25s. Bricklayers varied from 18s. to 21s. A family of five, it was calculated, required some 30s. to live adequately. Most police Constables, therefore, would have needed additional income, such as children of working age, to maintain sufficient standards. Parity with the Victorian bricklayer suggests that policing was a depressed occupation, in spite of perquisites such as clothing. The hours were 'heavy and oppressive', up to fifteen-hour shifts being not uncommon, and there was always the threat of violence and little or no compensation, or superannuation.

The conditions of service for the lower ranks were, considering the responsibility accorded them and the high hopes surrounding them, gloomy and unprepossessing. The Victorian caution with regard to public money, local government's traditional care of the purse strings and the economic theories of men like Chadwick all combined to produce a zealous economy. Woodford told each Superintendent that 'he must pay the utmost regard to economy, and whenever he sees any means of reducing the expense', he must act. This might well have been a slogan for all the police authorities, and it was perhaps on the unlucky constables that austerity fell most heavily. Little wonder that, in 1853, one of Britain's first rare police wage disputes took place in Oldham, when the P.C.s paraded with placards urging fair dealings. The two chief conclusions to be drawn from this inspection of police finance are, firstly, that there were no great cuts in expenditure on crime, and, secondly, that the miserly wage structure suggests a sound reason for the feeble quality of the constabularies in Lancashire.

The Preventive aspect
The key to effective policing lay in the decline of crime figures. If the Utilitarian thesis was accurate, a Preventive Police should have caused a sharp decrease in the rate of crime. Herein lay the crux. However badly the departments were administered; whatever the character of their officers; notwithstanding financial difficulties; as long as crime was reduced precipitately then all would be well. Unfortunately, criminal statistics are possibly the most suspect category of a suspect breed. Until 1857 figures were not full, neither were they indisputably accurate. The many changes in both Common Law and local bye-laws seriously affect any readings of these figures and changes in social conditions in especial localities form another critical factor. The Blackburn magistrates, for instance, insisted on short terms of imprisonment for drunkards, whereas their colleagues elsewhere were not quite so severe. The meaning of an increase in reported offences and consequent commitments is confused. It could as well suggest improved law-enforcement, particularly in the short run, as a fall in such figures. Thus for one reason or another, a study of Lancashire's crime sheet in the mid-nineteenth century must be approached with due delicacy.

A straightforward survey of commitments for trial on indictable offences is the safest, most reliable, and yet perhaps the most negative test. The years 1825–31 had yielded an annual average of 2,226 commitments, or one to every 600 inhabitants. Police reform certainly led to increased commitments. The period 1840 to 1843 was especially disastrous, when the 3,000 mark was passed each year, and, in 1842, there were 4,497 cases. In that year one in every 360 Lancastrians was tried. During this period the population of Lancashire was about 11 per cent of that of the United Kingdom, and the county's fraction of national commitments never fell below 11 per cent and it was often 12 or 13 per cent. In 1841 it was 14 per cent and in 1842 it was 14½ per cent, but, after 1844, there was some improvment.

In 1849, 2,974 out of 3,290 commitments were for larcenies and related indictments, leaving only 316 other offences. Eighty-seven of these latter cases were for riot, indeed a large increase on the thirty-four of 1838. What is remarkable, however, is that fifty-one of these were acquitted, and a further twelve were discharged on sureties to reappear. The outstanding twenty-four were given short terms of prison or fines. There were thirty-five assaults on peace officers, but it is impossible to tell how many of these were connected with political agitation as compared to thieves or drunkards attacking policemen when resisting arrest. Of the 3,290, 749 were acquitted, 2,240 were fined or imprisoned locally, while 311 were transported, either for larcenies or severe assault. Again this does not align itself with the view of a county fearful of rebellion, and smashing it violently with the judicial machine. Briefly, the pattern is as before. Some two to three thousand committals led to approximately one-fifth acquittals, the number of men remained constantly higher than that of women, the punishments meted out seem much the same; and illiteracy remained a feature. Above all, the motive of profit was almost monopolistic. Murder, for instance, was not a frequent crime, given such high figures. Between 1842 and 1845 there were sixty-one homicides but many of them were newborn babies, including eighteen in Blackburn alone. Only twenty-four convictions for murder resulted. Violence for reasons other than gain was also infrequent.

Finally, the figures for 1856 show that Lancashire had 2,097 commitments, which, at a ratio of one to a thousand, seemed a considerable improvement. This was, however, the first year in which the Larceny Summary Jurisdiction Act of 1855 operated. Under this new law many larcenies were dealt with by the Magistrates, thus relieving the higher courts of some of their onerous tasks. It is not easy to estimate the effect of this Act. James Taylor, Chief Constable of Salford, reckoned that 99 tried under this dispensation would normally have accompanied Salford's 216 other miscreants to the Sessions or Assizes. If this figure is representative, a statistic comparable with the earlier ones, would be about 3,030. Of the 2,097, 617 were not convicted, and, of those remaining, five were executed (a relatively high number); 395 were transported or sentenced to penal servitude and 1,080 were given short imprisonments or were fined. Forty-four were charged with riot and 309 with miscellaneous offences. 1,080—87·5 per cent—were charged with crimes of gain, very similar, in fact, to 1838, when 89 per cent had been so accused. Major crimes had by no means declined rapidly, especially crimes of monetary advantage. It must be underlined that commitments refer only to cases serious enough to warrant proceedings at the Assizes or Sessions. Thousands of other less alarming cases were tried by the J.P.s. The proportion of committed to apprehended was, very approximately, one-tenth throughout this period, according to such pairs of figures as are available. Most of the rest were tried summarily.

Prison figures are another guide, and again, whatever reservations are made, they fail to indicate any considerable decline in crime. In 1830, 8,974 people were committed to Lancashire's prisons, while the years 1840 to 1849 saw an average of 17,201 commitments to Lancashire's prisons. The individual averages for those ten years were Lancaster: 508; Liverpool: 7,866; Salford: 10,650; Kirkdale: 1,862; and Preston: 1,671. Committals doubled, therefore, between 1830 and 1840, although the population rose only 23 per cent. During the forties it remained fairly constant.

The attested lists of convicts for the quarter ending 31 December 1849 form an interesting sample. Most of the convicts had been imprisoned since 1846, with the few outstanding all convicted since 1839. It has been possible to extract the data of those committed in Lancashire, and the total is 409. There were 74 in Portland Prison and 25 in Shorncliff Prison. The others were in Convict Hulks. 31 were in the 'Stirling Castle' at Plymouth; 37 in the 'York' and the 'Defence' at Gosport; 79 in the 'Justitia' and the 'Warwick' at Woolwich; 8 were on the 'Thames'; 73 were in the 'Dromedary', the 'Medway', the 'Coromandel' and the 'Penedos' Hospital Ship at Bermuda; and 82 in the 'Owen Glendower' and 'Euryalus' at Gibraltar. 220 were sentenced to 7 years; 154 to 10 years; 2 to 20 years; and 9 to life. By far the great majority of these prisoners had been convicted for larceny, with but a small number guilty of manslaughter, murder, rape, carnal knowledge of children, and arson. Of especially poignant note were John Jones, ten years at Portland for stealing a spade, and the seventeen-year-old Miles Beckett, imprisoned for ten years for stealing a waistcoat. The list covers the period during which Chartist and other rioters or agitators might have been cast into national prisons or hulks. Given a minimum seven-year term, the catalogue reaches well back into the early forties. Possibly a few had been transported within the old meaning of the act to New South Wales, while some Lancastrians may have been indicted in Cheshire. What is clear, however, is that none of these 409 convicts were, in any sense, political prisoners. It seems that, whatever society felt about mass agitation and its threat to undermine authority, stealing waistcoats and spades was still rated a more heinous offence. This random selection of statistics is not, of course, conclusive. It does not, however, indicate the mammoth decline in crime anticipated by many police reformers.

The issue of mass agitation already alluded to, must next be faced, particularly as it is usually regarded as the principal element in Victorian public order. The spectre of Chartism manifested itself on further major occasions, about 1841 to 1842, and again in 1848. In the earlier phase, there were demonstrations throughout Lancashire, most of them having their focus on Manchester. There was a close correlation with the indifferent economic conditions at that time, and the wage-cuts attendant upon them were the primary cause of the Plug-Plots and the General Strike of that winter. Troops were needed then, and again in 1844, during the St. Helens Colliers' Strike. Sometimes the fighting was hectic. The Plug Plot Riots of 1842 centred on Preston, where wage-cuts had reached a dreadful 10 per cent. A mob stoned the police in Lune Street, and the 72nd Highlanders shot and killed five of the rioters, of whom another twenty-six were arrested single-handed by the legendary Police Constable Sam Harris. The last fling of Chartism in the revolutionary year of 1848 saw action in Manchester, Bolton, Oldham and Ashton. This included a march of hands, armed with pikes and bludgeons, on Manchester where, alongside regular and yeomen troops, there waited almost 11,000 Special Constables. The 1848 riots, however, were more colourful than dangerous, and they fizzled out more swiftly than their predecessors. The tension between capital and labour hereafter slackened, for as conditions improved materially, the one became less oppressive and the other less militant. Respectable Trade Unionism and peaceful action became the rule and virtue reaped its rewards. None the less, when mass agitation flared into violence the army was invariably needed. By 1880, for example, Preston had thrice been the scene of military operations; during the Great Lock Out of 1853–54, in April 1863, when 250 soldiers were required to quieten a mob, and in 1878 during the cotton disorders.

The status of the police in all these proceedings is an ambiguous one. Only five forces were in operation to meet the first wave of Chartism and only nine to meet the second, so it is difficult to judge the actual influence of the police. Add to this that the Lancashire County Police indulged in its mammoth reductions just before the Plug Plot era, and judgement becomes even more cloudy. Right through the period, extensive tumult was met by military force in any case. There is little or no evidence to suggest that the police were able to handle mass action with any comfort; rather would it appear that they sometimes exacerbated the conflict. There is also, perhaps, an oversimple identification of Chartism with mob activity. The end of Chartism is thus seen as the beginning of social order, neatly corresponding to the arrival of the professional police. As the St. Helens Colliers and the Preston Spinners bear witness, there were other instances of ugly crowd action, and oftentimes the military were needed. The 1926 General Strike is a twentieth century illustration of the same tragic theme. The Police were not and are not fitted, in number or in equipment, to grapple with huge rioting which is organised and purposeful. When one recalls the quality of Lancastrian policemen in mid-century, one has no difficulty in realising this. Mass action, therefore, occurred before the establishment of the Provincial Police in Lancashire; it continued during the period when they were being founded; it was sustained after their foundation. In most cases, before, during and after, military reinforcement was essential. The major reason for a decline in such activities was, more probably, the permeation through to the lower social levels of the material proceeds of industrialism. In a sense, the very principle of a preventive policing demonstrated the point. The ostensible manifestation of riot meant, in effect, that the deterrent had failed to deter, and the cure had to be found elsewhere, namely at the War Office. The relation between Police Reform and Chartism is, therefore, of only marginal relevance, for the former did not much halt the latter, and the latter did not much advance the former.

Certainly the criminal statistics include few references to men arrested while indulging in mob-action. What must rather be stressed is the relative unimportance of political misdemeanours against the full perspective of crime. Indeed, all types of crime and

M

punishment fade into oblivion in comparison with the enormous
amount of economically motivated misdemeanours and the severe
treatment of the culprits. This may sound a truism; but even by
today's standards, there were, in mid-nineteenth century, few
crimes of malice, damage, violence, personal assault or sex.
Drunkenness was chief among the petty offences, which was
probably explicable, as the Public Health reformers opined, in
terms of a degraded social milieu. It was this, presumably, which
also drove men to steal. There was, in 1842, one in every four
hundred Lancastrians whose attempt at theft was serious enough
to warrant trial at the Assizes. In addition there were those whose
thefts and cheats were small enough to require but magisterial
reckoning, and, of course, an unaccountable number whose illegal
efforts were successful. There can be little doubt that, day by day,
the main preoccupation of the police was to defend property and
persons, not from arson, destruction and violence, but from
mundane theft.

   There was, indeed, a tacic admission that prevention did not
pay, for, early in modern police history, the principles of detection
began to supersede it. Reith has attacked this proclivity most
strongly stressing that a democratic police depends largely upon
police co-operation, and that, if its exemplary presence among the
populace is insufficient, the system has failed.[1] The Metropolitan
C.I.D. commenced its famous exploits in 1842 with a small group
of eight detectives, and Lancashire police forces soon followed suit.
In 1843 Woodford faithfully emulated the Metropolitan model
with a general order to divisional chiefs 'to employ constables in
particular duties in plain clothing'. Liverpool formed a detective
department in 1844 of a Superintendent, a Clerk and six constables, and, by 1860, it consisted of a Superintendent, four clerks,
two inspectors, one Beadle, and seventeen Constables, a total of
twenty-five. In the same year the Manchester detective office had
one Superintendent, two Inspectors and six Sergeants. In 1856 the
Salford Watch Committee reported that 'in consequence of the
increase of robberies within the Borough, your Committee, with
the sanction of the Council in August last, organised a detective
force, consisting of eight officers in plain clothes'. Detection is an
indirect form of deterrent, but its emphasis on action after the
commission of crime was not in keeping with the original preventive spirit. As with medicine, cure is more spectacular than pre-

[1] Reith, *A New Study*, op. cit., pp. 221–49 and 264–86.

vention, and detection began to oust prevention as the principal
feature of police work, as perhaps the increasing eagerness of
Chief Constables to record number of arrests and the value of
recovered stolen goods suggests. The original deterrent theory
tended to give way to the view that policemen, both in uniform
and in mufti, were chiefly concerned with solving crime and
arresting offenders. The focus of public interest in policemen was
and remains predominantly on their actions once an offence had
been committed. This very human appetite for the positive aspects
of crime was whetted by newspaper and broadsheet accounts of
the 'melancholy incident' (that favourite Victorian by-line) and
the subsequent hunt, capture and trial, and later mass media of
communication were to sustain it. A massive weight of fiction has
fostered this craving, with Wilkie Collins and Conan Doyle
setting an early pace for many a mystery writer, to say nothing of
the energy devoted to crime by the theatre, the cinema, the radio
and the television. In this romanticism and popular fascination lies
a meaningful difference between police-work, and Poor Law or
Public Health. Once these latter two were functioning, their work
could proceed in relative calm, with only a dramatic epidemic or a
Workhouse scandal to disturb the quiet laying of sewers or distribution of gruel. The police, first in their white 'trowsers' and
toppers and later in their blue tunics and cone-shaped helmets,
were from the beginning distinctive features on the social scene.
They were ever in the public eye, and their ceaseless warring with
the lawless excited sympathy or emnity according to one's tem-
perament and inclination. It is impossible to measure the psychological pressure on the police to act positively rather than neg-
atively, but it should not be overlooked. What cannot be denied is
that a symptom of the lack of success of the preventive principle
was that it was quickly replaced, in part, by other theories of
police management.

From all points of view it is difficult to see strong evidence for
a decline in the crime rate in mid-victorian Lancashire, even when
due allowance has been made for increased population and the
possibility that efficient policing might initially mean more
prisoners. Probably the 1856 obligatory Act was a recognition of
this at a national level. Throughout this era the police give the
impression of officials holding their own. One might submit a
tentative suggestion that, if crime was not fast disappearing,
neither was it growing alarmingly. The reform of the Lancashire

police forces appears to have righted the balance between law and
crime. The tide of crime was possibly stemmed, but it was not
turned back.

iii. Summary

A contemporary summary is obtainable from the 1857 report on
Lancashire by John Woodford when he became one of the first
Inspectors of Constabulary. He inspected the county force most
thoroughly over thirteen days, visiting every Divisional H.Q. and
many other stations. He found 'a most satisfactory state of order,
cleanliness and efficiency'. The rifle-green clothing and other
accoutrements were 'in conformity with the rules made by the
Secretary of State'. The Chief Constable's forty-two books, the
Divisional Superintendent's thirty books and the forty-four
periodical returns were 'well and regularly kept'. Woodford confessed to an endearing modesty about assessing the department he
had created, but candour forced him to admit his 'deliberate conviction' that the County force was as sound as any. Liverpool, with
its vast complement and relative strength, was 'unsurpassed' in
quality. The only criticism was a lack of station-houses. Manchester was policed by 'a remarkably fine and effective body',
with ten station-houses—including a new 'very commodious'
one—and thirty one cells—some of them 'very unsuitable'. It was
reported to be a 'well-organised force, in a highly satisfactory
state of discipline'.

Ashton's police were 'effective and respectable' and the twenty-
seven books were 'well-kept'. The force was 'not sufficient in
number' and it had no set of rules for the men. Blackburn's cells
were 'of unequally good description', but the force's number was
not sufficient. Bolton also had 'very clean' cells, but once more, the
force was 'far from being sufficient in number'. The Lancaster
authorities were persuaded by Woodford to enlist a further four
men. Those already employed were of good quality but their
equipment was insufficient. Oldham's books and offices were in a
'very regular and satisfactory condition', but, yet again, that 'smart
and active body of men', the Oldham police force, was in need of
reinforcement. Preston's lanterns, truncheons and capes were
criticised, and the establishment was faulted on the grounds of
number and age. Salford came in for heavy criticism. The men
were 'very slovenly' and lacking in 'vigilance', and discipline 'has

not been very firmly maintained'. The Warrington police had 'very inferior' clothing and equipment, and, felt Woodford, their number should be doubled. Woodford was received with 'courteous attention' in Wigan, where he found a force of twenty-three 'very respectable' men. Again the number needed augmenting. The clothing was in 'tolerable condition', whilst some of the accommodation was 'unfit'.

Woodford was obviously feeling his way a little in his first report, and he either avoided trenchant criticism or was moved by feelings of loyalty to his old stamping-ground. His second report was rather more vigorous. His major criticisms were general ones, and these he made the basis for a fairly swingeing attack. He was clearly angry that his previous recommendations about personnel had been ignored. He was most worried about the continued lack of superannuation schemes. He was anxious about the turn-over of staff, especially the prevalence of early resignations, before, as he commented, either usage or change had been wrought. There was in some Boroughs, he concluded, 'a determination to evade' the necessary duties and expenditure and, not unpredictably, he suggested the consolidation of all forces into one County establishment.

Woodford's reports, although polite and official in tone, noted many of the points which have become apparent in this study. Four questions have been posed, and four necessarily inconclusive answers have been returned. The inferences that may be drawn are largely negative. Police reform did not strike Lancashire in a dramatic moment of terror; rather did it come slowly, grudgingly and prosaically. The new Police Forces in Lancashire were not brand-new bodies of eagerly dedicated experts; rather were they reshapings of and additions to the old systems of policing, and progress towards reasonable efficiency was laborious and piecemeal. The reformed police did not halt the criminal in his tracks to any great extent; rather do they seem to have kept level in the race with crime. The new Police Forces did not bring vast savings to the County; rather did they draw on the rates in much the same way as their predecessors. If one matches inference with inference, then, as the crime rate was maintained and the expenditure remained constant, one must conclude that the situation was basically unaltered.

It is to Lancashire's credit, none the less, that its police system was reformed at all. The 1856 Act was necessary because only twenty-two Counties had adopted the permissive Act of 1839 and because, as the first Constabulary inspection confirmed, 120 County and Borough forces were insufficient. In one way or another Lancashire had, by 1856, police coverage of a purportedly modern brand, and just prior to that year, a remarkable spurt in establishment had prefaced the implementation of the 1856 Act. But the twenty-one years from the Municipal Reform Act to the obligatory Act of 1856 constitute no watershed. On the one side, administrative change is difficult to hurry for it immediately concerns personnel, finance, established customs and accepted mechanisms. On the other side, the industrial and social scene was not so reticent. It changed its character with frequency and fluidity, and, with it, the character of crime. So the story of Lancashire police takes on a greyer colour. It is not a tale of black suddenly becoming white. It is a tale of cautious, often ramshackle, adjustment to an ever-changing problem of crime and disorder. Lawlessness was not throttled, nor was it, particularly in the major field of larceny, very much reduced. Policemen and criminal seem to indulge in a kind of arms race, with first one and then the other forging slightly ahead. On this occasion, the reforms seem to have been sufficient to regain police parity with the law-breaker. The situation was perhaps marginally better; it could have been a good deal worse.

The Marxist accusation that the police is a bourgeois weapon to oppress the proletariat has possibly some slight justification, in that police reform was designed by governments representative of the middle and upper classes to protect property from theft and damage. There is little doubt that acute 'class-conflict' was present in Lancashire until the mid-forties, with the new police incorporation, fear of violence, the National Debt, the Poor Law, Chartism, Trades Unionism and Factory Reform all showing the lines of division between employer and employee. This clarity was marred by the Tories who, on certain of these issues, sided with the workers. By 1846, and as prosperity mounted, the hiatus between the two classes narrowed, and, for instance, the success of the Anti-Corn Law agitation was welcomed on both sides. Politically and administratively, however, the masters and landowners were securely in the saddle throughout the period and the police forces, born in an era of sharp class-conflict, were originally in the control of the middle and upper classes. The County forces were controlled by unelected Justices, and the magistracy, given the property qualification of £300, was in effect an organisation of the gentry, while, in the Boroughs, representation was still strictly limited to rate-payers of quality. The traditions of police administration were sustained, for the technical powers of the police, rooted in the Common law, and their localised supervision were both preserved. Effective power fell securely into the hands of the local County and Borough authorities, although the magistracy's powers have waned, especially since the 1888 County Councils Act.

What is sure is that localism thrived, and that this piece of constitutional pragmatism has become the basic principle of English police administration. Occasional inroads, like Home Office inspections, have been made by the central government since 1856, but attempts to nationalise the police forces have so far been doomed to failure. Whatever, therefore, the initial success of the Victorian police in practice, there is no gainsaying the theoretical precedent created by them. The local system has certain weaknesses. It has, indeed, been argued that the limitations of local government are almost the inverse of the needs of a police service, with disproportionate waste of equipment, training facilities and other amenities; grave difficulties of co-operation; varying chances of promotion; Watch Committees too close to the police for some administrative tastes; and, in general, an uneconomic functioning of so many tiny forces. Conversely, the very diversified nature of the police forces is a sound guarantee against their being used nationally as an instrument of tyranny. Despite arguments urged cogently and consistently, the traditional separation of town and country legislation remained unimpaired. A glance at the Lancashire scene in 1967 revealed an institutional picture not too different from the one of 1856. The Ashton and Lancaster forces had amalgamated with the County force, and Barrow, Bootle, Burnley, Rochdale, St. Helens and Southport had joined the other nine independent Boroughs. In 1856 there were eleven Borough forces dotted about the area covered by the County police. In 1967 there were sixteen Borough forces in exactly the same situation. An investigation of a provincial police in early Victorian times takes on an added meaning when it is realised how much help it offers to those attempting to understand the nature of police administration in the nineteen-sixties, especially now the Home Office has begun its difficult task of amalgamations in Lancashire and elsewhere.

V. Conclusion

A study such as this cannot pretend to be conclusive, but some light is thrown, perhaps, on the now fashionable problem of administrative history in the nineteenth century. Certain points emerge from the three themes to form a constant pattern.

Firstly, the Benthamite or Utilitarian solution was accepted and the other solutions ignored each time, and yet, when these issues were under discussion, countless other formulae were advanced. The Preventive ideal was the theoretical basis of action. The ring was, artificially, to be cleared of the obstacles of a shackled labour mart, an economically crippling health problem, and the inroads of crime into the national produce. The elective board principle, the use of expertise, a central agency and an inspectorate were usually established. Overall was the stringent wish to avoid economic waste and to keep a watchful eye on the rates; and this criterion of utility was operated at the lowest levels of administration. Even where 'administrative momentum' operates, it must take on some format, and this mould was frequently Benthamite. The 'Intolerability' theory—the belief that reforms came when the burdens became unbearable—is difficult to prove. Poverty, disease and crime came with a closeness which indicates a general policy rather than a random provision. This particular trio of social ills certainly formed an interlocking pattern with, in illustration, the Poor Law authorities concerned with health and crime as well as pauperdom. Perhaps one explanation of a relatively abrupt awareness of 'intolerability' is the pressure of events on the middle classes, at a time when political power was coming their way. The gargantuan nature of insanitary conditions and the threat of epidemics menaced alike the factory-owner and the labourer. Lawlessness, whether theft or riot, and labour difficulties also pressed hard on the well-to-do. It is interesting to note that the classic case of 'inherent momentum'—the emigration service—affected the middle classes but little.

Secondly, the so-called conflict of *laissez-faire* and state inter-

vention leaves local government in an anomalous position. Were
the Vestry and the Corporation the victims of governmental intervention, or were they themselves wreckers of the *laissez-faire* ideal?
Central authority was not the only type of interference with which
the individual had to fend. In Lancashire there was public provision for law enforcement, pauper welfare and even, occasionally, sanitary regulation, before 1830. The efficiency of these
agencies is, in this philosophic sense, immaterial—*laissez-faire* was
never a working proposition; it is often confused with local
autonomy and anti-centralisation. This leads to an important point.
The continuity between the old and the reformed services in
Lancashire is most marked, and it is frequently difficult to find any
qualitative change in the administration of social amenities before
the eighteen-sixties. For all manner of human and physical reasons,
these social reforms did not 'bite' as they were intended to do in
Lancashire in the 'Individualist' era. In 1860 Lancashire was
barely keeping pace with the crime-rate, its incidence of ill-health
and its pauperdom, while rates were growing heavier and heavier.
The significant time-lag between national legislation and local
implementation leads to the odd conclusion, that, in terms of
practical results in Lancashire, Dicey was right by accident. The
pre-1865 era looks a little like a pro-Diceyan phase of negligible
intervention. Indeed, one is even tempted to argue that the period
is more akin to the 'quiescence' which Dicey believed to be
characteristic of the first decades of the century. The blazing glow
of great parliamentary enactments tended rather to flatter to
deceive. It was only after 1865 that the on-rush of Collectivism
gathered critical force. It was only then that field administrative
techniques were sharp enough, not only to grapple with the
challenge of Gladstone's massive programme, but to make effective
the legislation of earlier years.

Thirdly, it is important to observe the origins of contemporary
social administration in these first responses of an industrial society.
A barnacle-like adherence to traditional techniques and boundaries
may be traced. The synthetic poor Law Unions have vanished, but
the County and Parochial divisions they tried to supersede remain.
A compound of indoor and outdoor relief is still, in effect, the
chief characteristic of present-day welfare amenities, despite a
temporary enthusiasm for the Workhouse Test. We still have the
County Police Forces, with Borough Forces dotted along the
country area, and suggestions for a national police have so far met

with failure. We still have local control of sewage disposal and
water supply, and no national undertaking has so far been possible.
The theoretical precedents created by Chadwick and his followers
were slowly grafted on to this enduring administrative body.
Although they took many years to become effectual and significant, the Benthamite techniques of local elective boards, trained
salaried officials, central advisory authorities and inspectorates are
now major planks in the typically bipartite structure of the modern
English state.

Much work needs to be done before the picture is clear. Here
only three items in one area have been under review, and the
evidence unearthed is no more than straws in the wind. There
appears, however, some possibility that Victorian social administration did not produce the crucial change in the everyday life of
the man-in-the-street which at first sight one might suppose. The
Relieving Officer, the Inspector of Nuisance, and the Constable
could scarcely have excited the mid-Victorian Lancastrian as
harbingers of startling innovations and wholesale social benefits.

Select Bibliography

I. Primary sources

Victorian administrative documentation is wellnigh inexhaustible, and this guide is by no means exclusive.

a. Public Record Office

i. Ministry of Health Papers

Correspondence of Poor Law Unions, 1834–1900. M.H. 12. (16,741 vols, arranged alphabetically under counties and unions)

Correspondence of Local Boards of Health, 1847–1871. M.H. 13. (272 vols, arranged alphabetically under Local Boards)

Papers of Assistant Poor Law Commissioners and Inspectors 1834–1964. M.H. 32. (arranged alphabetically under Officers' names)

ii. Home Office Papers

Convict Prisons: Attested Lists of Convicts, 1824–1876. H.O. 8. (quarterly returns arranged under prisons)

Criminal Registers, 1805–1892. H.O. 27. (annual registers of commitments, arranged alphabetically under counties)

Riots and Disturbances: Papers and Correspondence, 1812–1855. H.O. 40. (arranged chronologically under counties)

County Constabulary Correspondence, 1795–1907. H.O. 65. (running series of outletters to provincial police, especially H.O. 65/4 and H.O. 65/5 for 1839–1856 period)

Constabulary Commission Letters and Papers, 1836–1839. H.O. 73/2, 3 & 4. (random bundles of evidence submitted to Constabulary Commission)

b. Parliamentary Papers

1842, Grounds of Exemption for Liverpool from Poor Law Amendment Act, xxv (232)

1842, Distress in Rochdale, xxv (89)

1846, Reports relative to Macclesfield and Bolton Unions, xxxvi (661)
1850, Return of Towns which asked for inspection under 1848 Public Health Act, xxx (iii)
1850, Report of Select Committee on County Rates, xiii (468)
1857, Receipts of Water Companies in England and Wales, xlviii (137)
1857, Return of all Local Boards of Health, xli (328)
1862, Area and Population of Unions in England and Wales, xlix (485)
1867, Return of Districts where 1848 Public Health and 1858 Local Government Acts in force, lix (80)

c. Government Reports

Annual Returns of Criminal Offenders, 1830–1863
Annual Reports of Inspectors of Prisons, 1835–1860
Annual Reports of Poor Law Commission, later Board, 1835–1869
Annual Reports of Registrar General, 1839–1863
Annual Reports and Papers of General Board of Health, 1848–1858
Annual Constabulary Returns, 1839–1856
Annual Reports of Inspectors of Constabulary, 1857–1860
1834, Report of Commission into State of Poor Laws in England and Wales
1839, Report of Commission into best means of establishing an efficient Constabulary Force in England and Wales
1840, Report of Select Committee on Health of Towns
1842, Report on Sanitary Condition of Labouring Population of Great Britain
1844, First Report on state of Large Towns and Populous Districts
1845, Second Report on state of Large Towns and Populous Districts
1858, Papers relating to the Sanitary state of the people of England (E. H. Greenbrow)

d. Local Authority Minutes, Reports and Records

i. Poor Law

The Minutes of the following Boards of Guardians are held, with very few gaps, by the Lancashire County Record Office, Preston: Ashton-under-Lyne, Barton-upon-Irwell, Blackburn, Bolton, Burnley, Bury, Chorley, Clitheroe, Fylde, Garstang, Haslingden, Lancaster, Leigh, Lunesdale, Oldham, Ormskirk, Prescot, Preston, Rochdale, Warrington, Wigan and Ulverstone.

The statistical records and Workhouse returns of the Manchester and Prestwich Unions are held by the Manchester Central Reference Library (Local History Library) but the Guardians' Minutes were destroyed by bombing.

The papers of the Salford Union are held by the Salford Public Library.
Papers relating to the Liverpool, Toxteth Park, and West Derby Unions are held by the Local History Library of the Picton Reference Library, Liverpool.

ii. Public Health

The three major archives in Lancashire (Preston, Manchester, and Liverpool) have some records, but, as the present public health authorities are normally in direct descent from the Local Boards, public libraries and municipal offices often retain the relevant records. Enquiries should be made direct. The most useful documents are the General Board of Health Reports of Preliminary Enquiries and the Local Board Minutes, e.g. the Manchester Local History Library hold both reports and minutes for the Bradford (Manchester), Crumpsall, Moss Side, Newton Heath and Rusholme Boards of Health.
The large towns which had no Local Boards usually have a considerable amount of material available locally, e.g. the Liverpool Local History Library has the Liverpool Health Committee minutes and annual reports of the Medical Officer of Health from 1847, together with a wide variety of incidental reports on water, sewering, nuisance, etc.

iii. Police

The main sources are Watch Committee Minutes and Chief Constables' Annual Reports. With critical gaps these and other relevant papers may be found for the following Borough forces in the appropriate public libraries: Ashton-under-Lyne, Bolton, Blackburn, Lancaster, Liverpool, Manchester, Oldham, Preston, Salford, Warrington and Wigan.
Papers relating to the county force may be seen at the Lancashire Record Office, or, by appointment, at the Lancashire Constabulary Headquarters, Hutton, near Preston.

iv. Miscellaneous

Most of the libraries mentioned have a certain amount of private reports and commentaries. For example:
T. E. Ashworth, *An Account of the Todmorden Poor Law Riots of 1838* (Manchester)
J. Entwistle, *A Report upon the Sanitary Condition of Bolton, 1848* (Bolton)
W. Rathbone, *Local Taxation and Poor Law Administration in Great Cities 1869* (Liverpool)
T. Smith, *Results of the Central Administration of the Poor Laws in West Derby 1848* (Liverpool)
N

Many libraries also hold local newspaper files which may profitably be consulted.

II. Secondary sources

i. Standard works

T. S. Ashton, *Economic and Social Investigations in Manchester, 1833–1933* (1934). King

T. C. Barker and J. R. Harris, *A Merseyside Town in the Industrial Revolution; St Helens, 1750–1900* (1959). Cass

W. M. Bowman, *England in Ashton-under-Lyne* (1960). Sherratts

Asa Briggs, *Chartist Studies* (1959). Macmillan

Asa Briggs, *Victorian Cities* (1963). Odhams

C. F. Brockington, *Medical Officers of Health 1848–1855* (1957). Hodgetts

J. J. Clarke, *A History of the Local Government of the United Kingdom* (1955). Jenkins

C. Creighton, *A History of Epidemics in Britain* (1894). Cambridge University Press

A. V. Dicey, *Law and Public Opinion in England* (Second Edition 1934). Macmillan

F. Engels, *The Condition of the Working Class in England* (1845, trans. W. O. Henderson and W. H. Chaloner, 1958). Blackwell

W. Farr, *Vital Statistics* (1885). Sanitary Institute

W. Farrer and J. Brownbill, ed., *Victoria Country History of Lancashire* (1908). Constable (reprinted 1966) Dawson

H. Finer, *The Theory and Practice of Modern Government* (1950). Methuen

S. E. Finer, *The Life and Times of Sir Edwin Chadwick* (1952). Methuen

W. M. Frazer, *A History of English Public Health 1834–1939* (1950). Ballière, Tindall & Cox

A. L. Goodhart, *English Contributions to the Philosophy of Law* (1948). Oxford University Press

E. Halèvy, *The Growth of Philosophic Radicalism* (1924; Eng. Trans. 1928). Faber

J. Hart, *The British Police* (1951). Allen & Unwin

M. Hovell, *The Chartist Movement* (1918). Manchester University Press (Third Edition 1966)

B. L. Hutchins, *Public Health Agitation 1833–1848* (1909). Fifield

R. J. Lambert, *Sir John Simon* (1964). MacGibbon & Kee

H. Laski, et alia, *A Century of Municipal Progress* (1935). Allen & Unwin

R. A. Lewis, *Edwin Chadwick and the Public Health Movement, 1832–1854* (1952). Longmans

O. MacDonagh, *A Pattern of Government Growth* (1961). MacGibbon & Kee

S. Maccoby, *English Radicalism, 1832–1852* (1935). Allen & Unwin
J. D. Marshall, *Furness and the Industrial Revolution* (1958). Barrow Corporation
F. C. Mather, *Public Order in the Age of the Chartists* (1959). Manchester University Press
G. Newman, *The Rise of Preventive Medicine* (1932). Oxford University Press
K. Polyani, *Origins of Our Time; the Great Transformation* (1945). Gollancz
A. Redford, *The History of Local Government in Manchester*, Vol. 2 (1940). Longmans
C. Reith, *British Police and the Democratic Ideal* (1943). Oxford University Press
C. Reith, *The Blind Eye of History* (1952). Faber
C. Reith, *A New Study of Police History* (1956). Oliver and Boyd
D. Roberts, *Victorian Origins of the British Welfare State* (1960). New Haven
A. R. Schoyen, *The Chartist Challenge* (1958). Heinemann
J. Simon, *English Sanitary Institutions* (1890). Cassell
S. Simon, *A Century of City Government* (1938). Allen & Unwin
S. & B. Webb, *English Local Government*, Vols. iv, vi and viii (1929). Cass (reprinted 1963)
B. D. White, *A History of the Corporation of Liverpool* (1951). Liverpool University Press

ii. Articles

H. L. Beales, 'The New Poor Law', *History* (1931)
M. Blaug, 'The Myth of the Old Poor Law and the Making of the New', *Jour. of Econ. Hist.* xxiii (1963)
M. Blaug, 'The Poor Law Report Re-examined', *Jour. of Econ. Hist.* xxiv (1964)
R. Boyson, 'The New Poor Law in North-east Lancashire', *Trans. of Lancs. & Ches. Hist. Gaz.* 112 (1960)
R. M. Gutchen, 'Local Improvements and Centralisation in Nineteenth Century England', *Hist. Jour.* iv (1961)
J. Hart, 'Reform of the Borough Police 1835–1856', *Eng. Hist. Rev.* 70 (1955)
J. Hart, 'Nineteenth Century Social Reform; A Tory Interpretation of History', *Past and Present* xxxi (1965)
S. W. F. Holloway, 'Medical Education in England 1830–1858' *History* (1964)
R. J. Lambert, 'A Victorian National Health Service; State Vaccination, 1855–1871', *Hist. Jour.* v (1962)

O. MacDonagh, 'Delegated Legislative and Administrative Revolutions in the Eighteen-fifties', *Victorian Studies* ii (1955)

O. MacDonagh, 'Nineteenth Century Revolution in Government', *Hist. Jour.* ii (1958)

E. C. Midwinter, 'Local Boards of Health in Lancashire, 1848-1858', *Trans. of Lancs & Ches. Hist. Soc.* 117 (1965)

E. C. Midwinter, 'A Tory Interpretation of History; Some Comments', *Past and Present*, xxxiv (1966)

E. C. Midwinter, 'State Intervention at the Local Level; The New Poor Law in Lancashire', *Hist. Jour.* x (1967)

E. C. Midwinter, 'Central and Local Government in Mid-nineteenth Century Lancashire', *Northern History* iii (1968)

H. Parris, 'Nineteenth Century Revolution in Government; A reappraisal Reappraised', *Hist. Jour.* iii (1960)

D. Roberts, 'Jeremy Bentham and the Victorian Administrative State', *Victorian Studies* ii (1959)

D. Roberts, 'How Cruel was the Victorian Poor Law?' *Hist. Jour.* vi. (1963)

M. E. Rose, 'Anti-Poor Law Movement in the North of England', *Northern History* i (1966)

M. Whittaker, 'The Bury Improvement Commissioners', *Trans. of Lancs. & Ches. Hist. Soc.* (1933)

Index

The index falls into three parts. Firstly, there is an index of names. Lists of convicts' names and so on are not included, but officials and local worthies of various kinds are. As most of them have only a local significance, a brief description has normally been appended. Occasionally no initials were forthcoming from the records, and a plain 'Mr.' must suffice. The names of contemporary authors are italicised. Secondly, there is an index of places. All the place-names in Lancashire are indexed, and, to facilitate reference, a triple division, where necessary, has been used; namely, '. . . poor relief'; '. . . public health'; '. . . law and order'. Thirdly, there is a short general index.

Index of Names

Angelo, Lieut. Col (Bolton Police Commissioner), 143
Armitt, W. (Salford Relieving Officer), 43
Ashley, Lord, 81
Ashworth, E. (Bolton and Public Health), 72
Attlee, Earl, 63
Austin, H. (Secretary, General Board of Health), 54, 91, 107, 111

Babbage, B. H. (General Board Inspector), 99
Bachelor, J. (Liverpool Prison Governor), 131-2
Baines, Dr. (Poulton M.O.H.), 91
Bannister, S. (Chief Constable of Preston), 134-5
Bart, T. (Lancashire Salesman), 130-1
Bateman, F. (Manchester Water Superintendent), 95
Bell, J. (Poulton Board Inspector), 90
Bentham, Jeremy, 8, 65, 110, 124-5
Berry, J. (Crumpsall Board Inspector), 90
Billington, J. (Rusholme Board of Health), 88

Birley, E. (Kirkham Board of Health), 88
Blackhurst, Councillor (Preston), 135
Blaug, Mark, 15, 21
Booth, T. (Newton Health Board Inspector), 90
Boyd, J. (Superintendent Bolton Police), 143
Boyson, Rhodes, 30, 33, 46
Bradford, Inspector (Liverpool Police), 158
Brady, Mr. (Over Darwen Board Officer), 91, 105
Briggs, Asa, 110-11
Butterworth, J. (Rochdale Chief Constable), 137
Butterworth, T. (Rochdale Watch), 137

Campbell, Rev. A. (Chairman, Liverpool Select Vestry), 33
Carlyle, Thomas, 9
Catterall, Councillor (Preston), 135
Chadwick, Sir Edwin
and poor relief, 8, 9, 11, 12, 14, 15, 16, 18, 20, 21, 22, 23, 25, 29, 31, 36, 43, 44, 46-7, 49, 52, 59, 61
and public health, 65-70, 72,

Hoole, W. (Chairman Blackburn Improvement Commission), 149
Hope, John (Clerk to Salford Guardians), 32–3
Houghton, R. (Liverpool Select Vestryman), 33
Howard, Dr. B. (Manchester and Public Health), 73
Howard, John, 124

Ingham, W. C. (Todmorden Overseer), 24
Isherwood, J. (Manchester Contractor), 105, 120

Jebb, Major (Inspector of Prisons), 150
Johnson, C. (Chief Constable Rochdale), 137
Jones, J. (Warrington Constable), 137

Koch, R., 66, 69, 119

Lancashire, Mr. (Bury Relieving Officer,) 41
Latham, J. (Clerk to Chorlton Guardians), 49
Lefevre, C. S. (Poor Law and Police Commissioner), 124
Lewis, Sir G. C., 26
Lewis, Sir T. F., 9–10
Liebig, Dr., 67

MacDonagh, Oliver, 39
MacDonald, R. Captain (Lancashire Assistant Chief Constable), 153
Mackintosh, Sir J. (Law Reformer), 127
McKenzie, Col. (Military Law Reformer), 128
McKie, Mr. (Poulton Board Inspector), 90
McLansborough, Mr. (Clitheroe Civil Engineer), 100
Malthus, T., 8
Marshall, T., Supt. (Blackburn Police), 157
Martin, W. (Clitheroe and poor relief), 48
Mather, F. C., 136
Mayall, Betty (Oldham and poor relief), 23

Mellor, J. (Liverpool Select Vestryman), 33
Mill, James, 8
Milnes, S. (Rochdale Chief Constable), 137
Moore, Sir John, 128
Monk, Councillor (Preston), 148
Morpeth, Lord (President of Board of Health), 81
Mott, C. (Assistant Poor Law Commissioner), 18, 32, 47, 49–50, 54, 73

Napier, C. (Military historian), 128
Needham, J. (Newton Heath Board Officer), 90
Newlands, J. (Liverpool Borough Engineer), 95, 108, 114, 120
Newman, Sir G., 115
Newton, J. (Preston Water Engineer), 98
Newton, John (Ashton Relieving Officer), 42
Newton, R. (Ashton Chief Constable), 157
Normanby, Marquis of (Home Secretary), 141
Nuthall, C. (Haslingden Relieving Officer), 41

Orrell, R. (Lancashire Manufacturer), 130

Park, J., Councillor (Preston), 135
Park, P. (Clitheroe Water Engineer), 100
Pasteur, L., 66, 69, 119
Peel, Sir Robert, 25, 127–8
Pegge, Dr. J. (Newton Heath M.O.H.), 91
Pendlebury Mr. (Crumpsall Board of Health), 87
Place, Francis, 124
Platt, J. (Oldham Inspector), 147
Playfair, L. (Lancashire and Public Health), 75–6, 95
Power, Alfred (Assistant Poor Law Commissioner), 14, 16, 17, 18, 23, 31, 32, 36, 37, 38, 41, 47–9, 58

Ramsbottom. Mr. (Bury Relieving Officer), 41
Ramsden, S. (Oldham Relieving Officer), 42

Index of Places

Accrington,
  public health, 87, 99, 102, 116
Ardwick,
  public health, 67, 77
  law and order, 153–4
Ashton-under-Lyne,
  poor relief, 30, 31, 38, 42, 48, 55
  public health, 73–6, 85, 102–3,
    109, 115
  law and order, 140, 144, 148, 154,
    157, 168, 172, 175

Bacup,
  public health, 83
  law and order 24
Barrow,
  public health, 96, 115
  law and order, 175
Barton-upon-Irwell,
  poor relief, 18, 30, 32–3, 54
  public health, 83, 115
Blackburn,
  poor relief, 30, 34, 42, 48, 49, 56
  public health, 85, 95, 102–3, 109,
    116
  law and order, 24, 135, 140, 144,
    146, 148–9, 154–7, 162, 166,
    172
Blackpool,
  public health, 85, 93
Bolton,
  poor relief, 12, 16, 20, 30, 32,
    34, 38, 42, 49–50, 56
  public health, 71, 72, 73–6, 83,
    89, 98, 102–3, 105, 113
  law and order, 130, 135, 137,
    139–40, 142–3, 147, 149, 154,
    157, 158, 162, 168, 172
Bootle,
  law and order, 175
Bradford (Manchester),
  public health, 83, 115
Broughton,
  public health, 77, 83, 85
Burnley,
  poor relief, 28, 30, 34, 38, 48, 56
  public health, 85–6
  law and order, 24, 135, 145, 175
Bury,
  poor relief, 30, 34, 38, 41, 48, 53,
    56
  public health, 74, 79, 85, 95,
    102–3

  law and order, 129–30, 145, 151
Caton,
  poor relief, 15, 17
Chorley,
  poor relief, 30, 54, 56
  public health, 71, 102, 116
Chorlton,
  poor relief, 18–38, 49, 55, 56, 87
  public health, 74, 116
  law and order, 153–4
Clitheroe,
  poor relief, 30–1, 34, 39, 42, 53,
    54, 56
  public health, 83, 89, 90, 91, 100,
    102
  law and order, 145
Colne,
  poor relief, 23
  public health, 85–6, 102
Crumpsall,
  public health, 76–7, 83, 87, 90,
    92, 100, 112–13, 115

Denton,
  public health, 83

Everton,
  poor relief, 12

Fleetwood,
  public health, 79, 85, 95, 103
Fylde,
  poor relief, 30, 31, 50, 56
  law and order, 151

Garstang,
  poor relief, 12, 19, 20, 30, 50, 56
Garston,
  public health, 83, 90, 100

Haslingden,
  poor relief, 30, 34, 35–6, 41, 56
Heap,
  public health, 83

Kirkdale,
  law and order, 131, 133, 143,
    150, 167
Kirkham,
  public health, 83, 88, 92, 100,
    106–7, 113

General Index